BOONESBOROUGH
UNEARTHED

BOONESBOROUGH UNEARTHED

Frontier Archaeology at a Revolutionary Fort

Nancy O'Malley

 UNIVERSITY PRESS OF KENTUCKY

The Fort Boonesborough Foundation generously donated funds to support the publication of this book.

Copyright © 2019 by The University Press of Kentucky

Scholarly publisher for the Commonwealth,
serving Bellarmine University, Berea College, Centre
College of Kentucky, Eastern Kentucky University,
The Filson Historical Society, Georgetown College,
Kentucky Historical Society, Kentucky State University,
Morehead State University, Murray State University,
Northern Kentucky University, Transylvania University,
University of Kentucky, University of Louisville,
and Western Kentucky University.
All rights reserved.

Editorial and Sales Offices: The University Press of Kentucky
663 South Limestone Street, Lexington, Kentucky 40508-4008
www.kentuckypress.com

Unless otherwise noted, images are courtesy of the University of Kentucky.

Cataloging-in-Publication data is available from the Library of Congress.

ISBN 978-0-8131-7761-8 (paperback : alk. paper)
ISBN 978-0-8131-7763-2 (epub)
ISBN 978-0-8131-7762-5 (pdf)

This book is printed on acid-free paper meeting
the requirements of the American National Standard
for Permanence in Paper for Printed Library Materials.

Manufactured in the United States of America.

Member of the Association
of University Presses

For my readers, who keep the memory of Fort Boonesborough alive

CONTENTS

ILLUSTRATIONS

Figures

Table

PREFACE

Boonesborough was founded by Richard Henderson and his Transylvania Company partners in 1775 as the envisioned capital of a new colony more than two hundred miles west of the nearest settlements. The company's venture was an audacious attempt to create a colony governed under a proprietary model that circumvented a royal proclamation prohibiting settlement beyond the Appalachians. In claiming land obtained by an illegal purchase from the Cherokees, the company violated the terms of the Virginia charter. Moreover, the timing of the enterprise coincided with the American colonies' War of Independence (1775–1783). The convergence of the Transylvania Company's ambitions and the inception of a revolution created a unique situation that demanded a creative response. Out of that need, Fort Boonesborough was born. Wartime hostilities necessitated the construction of a defensible fort composed of log cabins and stockade cobbled together to house and protect settlers from attack. From this humble origin Fort Boonesborough became an important site in the intertwined stories of American beginnings: westward expansion and the War of Independence.[1]

Despite the fort's early importance in the unification of the American colonies into one independent country, it was abandoned after the end of the Revolutionary War and the town planned at the site did not flourish. The town lots were eventually bought up by a handful of landowners who converted them to large farms. A small resort retained the name as an attraction for guests who came to fish, swim, and be entertained.

Yet the memory of the fort and its significance in the history of Kentucky and the nation did not entirely fade. Since its establishment in the 1960s, Fort Boonesborough State Park has memorialized the site as one of the most important early settlement sites in Kentucky and a key point of defense on the western front during the American colonies' fight for independence from England. Park visitors can tour a replica of the fort to learn about the people who lived there and even visit the site of the fort itself, marked by a monument and a memorial wall erected by the Daughters of the American Revolution (DAR). But by the mid-twentieth century a persistent belief spread among many local residents that the monument marked the wrong site. Which story was true?

In 1987 I was asked to find the answer. The quest for the truth led me on a journey that extended over thirty years of archival and archaeological research. I began with the original question of the site's actual location and expanded to explore more questions about the site itself: How much of it was preserved, what archaeological evidence did it contain, and what could that archaeology tell us? When I began the Fort Boonesborough project, I already had researched the defensible residential "stations" established in Kentucky by late eighteenth-century Euro-American settlers and their slaves on land claimed under Virginia law. The large public fort at Boonesborough, another part of the early settlement story, had never been examined from an archaeological perspective. Archaeology offers a unique means to assess the cultural past, and historical archaeology focuses its attention on physical evidence such as artifacts and cultural features (e.g., structural foundations, storage pits, and other physical evidence in the ground) coupled with archival sources to reconstruct what a site looked like, who lived there, and how they lived. This book brings together all the archaeological data that have been gathered about the site of Fort Boonesborough, one of only a handful of large forts that were constructed in Kentucky during the Revolutionary War. The site is the only major colonial fort in Kentucky that still exists as an archaeological site.

The impetus for this archaeological project to confirm the exact location of Fort Boonesborough had unusual origins. In 1985 Jim Kurz, who worked in the economic development and regional planning field, was competing in the Bluegrass Triathlon. As Jim put it in an unpublished account, "The past is important to me. Sometimes when I least expect it, something from the past reaches out to me, captures my attention, and my mind turns back to days gone by." In the midst of completing the swimming portion of the triathlon, part of his mind was occupied by thoughts of Daniel Boone and his fellow settlers and the stories of their establishment of Fort Boonesborough. A graduate in American history at Eastern Kentucky University, Jim knew of the DAR monument that marked the traditional site of the fort at the state park in Madison County. He was also aware of the local belief that the actual site was elsewhere. He felt sure that an archaeological search for the fort site would be a worthwhile endeavor. But where to begin?[2]

A visit to Martin's Hundred, the site of an early plantation in Virginia, and an encouraging letter from Colonial Williamsburg's noted archaeologist Ivor Noel Hume helped him formulate a plan, and he began looking for funding. Jim Kurz is an energetic and enthusiastic person who throws himself wholeheartedly into worthwhile projects. He identified four possible sources for funding and support: the Madison County Historical Society, the Fort Boonesborough State Park Association, the Kentucky Heritage Council, and the State Department of Parks. He wrote letters, visited organizations and influential people, and pitched his idea tirelessly. Along the way he garnered support and made useful contacts. I was one of these contacts, and after listening to Jim, I enthusiastically offered my professional services to the project. Following a luncheon at which Jim emphasized the potential economic benefits and I stressed the positive aspects of a public archaeology project, all four of the sources Jim had identified boldly pledged the necessary funding. I am indebted to Jim for getting the ball rolling, and I am grateful to our initial four funding sources for seeing the value of the project and providing the funds that made it possible.

The project began in 1987 with archival research. This was followed by an archaeological survey of the bottomland portion of the park and of adjacent private property to the current mouth of Otter Creek. Archival research identified several sites associated with the former town of Boonesborough and uncovered promising clues relating to the location of the original fort site. Several documents located the fort at the traditional site where the DAR had erected the stone monument and wall in the early twentieth century. Fieldwork identified the archaeological remains of nine historic sites, including remains at the site marked by the DAR monument.[3]

The origin of the claim that the fort site was somewhere other than the spot marked by the DAR monument also came to light. Although the location never seemed to be in doubt during the nineteenth century, controversy arose in the twentieth century, mostly among a contingent of local residents. Invariably, when pressed to provide credible evidence that the fort site was elsewhere than its traditional location, informants could provide only vague details and simply stated that they had always been told the site was somewhere else. Finally, a chance encounter with a local landowner, Ote Lisle West (1923–2010), who owned a house within the old

This commemorative monument and wall were erected on the site of Fort Boonesborough in the early twentieth century by the Daughters of the American Revolution. Courtesy of the William S. Webb Museum of Anthropology at the University of Kentucky.

Boonesborough Town Claim, provided the key to the origin of the belief in an alternate location.

Mr. West's mother, Ethel Lisle West (1894–1980), had always insisted that the fort site was on her property, which lay closer to the current mouth of Otter Creek than the marked site. Her son said that she held that belief because of the number of projectile points (commonly referred to as arrowheads) that had been found in the bottomland near her house. She reasoned that the Indians shooting arrows into the fort during their attacks were responsible for the presence of the projectile points. Mrs. West was a respected local resident whose family genealogy extended back to the early days of Boonesborough. People were willing to believe her without questioning her logic or the accuracy of her claim. And she was correct that the bottomland between the mouth of Otter Creek and the state park contained many Indian projectile points. She was also correct that the fort site marked by the DAR monument was not known for Indian artifacts. She erred on two key points. First, the artifacts found near her house were all prehistoric, dating hundreds or thousands of years prior to the fort's late eighteenth-century occupation. Most of them were not arrow points at all but were dart and spear points used during earlier cultural periods. Her second error was her assumption that the tribes' principal weapon during the late eighteenth century was the bow and arrow. By that period the Native Americans who fought so hard against Euro-American incursions into their territory were armed with guns provided them by English and French traders. They still used their traditional bows in specific contexts (such as attempts to set fire to forts with flaming arrows), but guns were their weapon of choice during their raids and sieges. In addition, primary archival documents unequivocally pinpoint the fort site immediately southeast of Sycamore Hollow near its mouth, precisely where the DAR monument stands. Two key sources were surveys by John Crooke: one of the Log Lick Trace, which used the fort as one of its survey points; and a second map that figured in a suit between Nathaniel Hart's heirs and William Calk and Samuel South. The fort's proximity to Sycamore Hollow as described by several other sources also pointed to the traditional site. Finally, excavation carried out around the DAR monument confirmed the archival evidence and uncovered archaeological features and artifacts that date to the period during which Fort Boonesborough was built and used. The site of Fort Boonesborough was confirmed to be correctly marked by the DAR monument.[4]

A secondary goal of the 1987 project was to gather information on other sites that had been associated with the larger community and town called Boonesborough. Nine historic sites were recorded on the bottomland portion of the Boonesborough community, including seven residential sites, two tobacco inspection warehouses, and an improved spring.[5] The results of the archival and archaeological research were presented in 1989 in a comprehensive report entitled Searching for Boonesborough. The research results also made possible a successful National Register of Historic Places nomination for the Fort Boonesborough Townsite Historic District in 1994 and National Historic Landmark status for the fort site in 1996.

Along the lengthy course of my research on Fort Boonesborough, I benefitted from the knowledge, encouragement, and interest of many people. Archaeology is paradoxically both a solitary and a collective endeavor. Hours of deciphering eighteenth-century documents, reading other authors' interpretations, scrutinizing miles of microfilmed records, and analyzing hundreds of artifacts contrast with the bustle of an archaeological excavation. Although the final analyses and interpretations remain my sole responsibility, no archaeologist reaches the end of research without incurring many debts to all the people who helped bring a project to fruition and a successful conclusion.

Jim Kurz's fundraising efforts for the 1987 phase of work paid for my time and that of my crew chiefs, Bill Sharp and John Carter, as well as for the subsequent report production costs. But none of the archaeological field research conducted in 1987 would have been possible without the willing hands of many volunteers who cheerfully wielded shovels and trowels and pushed dirt through screens in a collective endeavor that clocked one thousand hours of labor.[6]

Despite our success in verifying Fort Boonesborough's precise location, a hiatus of nearly twenty-five years ensued before a second round of archaeological excavations was funded. In the intervening years, I continued my research on the early Euro-American settlement period of Kentucky. I compiled a large quantity of historical data and gained valuable insights that served me well upon my return in 2012 to investigate the site once again for an American Battlefields Protection Program (ABPP) project. Fort Boonesborough qualified for funding because it was besieged in 1778 by a coalition of several hundred Indians armed by the British. The grant paid for my technical staff, Donald Handshoe and Matthew Davidson, as well as for the talents of graphic designer Hayward Wilkirson. My fellow staff members, Christina Pappas and Philip Mink, also provided their time and expertise for excavation and geophysical surveying. Dr. George Crothers, director of the William S. Webb Museum of Anthropology, allowed me the release time I needed from my job as assistant museum director to undertake the project during this and subsequent phases of research. Once again, volunteers provided much of the excavation and artifact processing labor. The ABPP grant funded excavation that further clarified the archaeological footprint of the fort and identified key landmarks that were important elements of the siege.[7]

The final phase of archaeological investigations took place in 2013 and 2014, when we continued to explore internal features of the fort site that had been identified during earlier phases of excavation. To support these excavations, the Fort Boonesborough Foundation launched a fund-raising campaign by raffling off a beautifully crafted flintlock rifle made by noted gun maker Wayne Estes of Bourbon County. Wayne not only came up with the idea of the raffle and built the gun; he also donated all the parts and labor. His involvement in my professional research is no accident; we have been married for over thirty years. The raffle money paid for faunal and botanical analyses to be conducted by Bruce Manzano and Dr. Renee Bonzani, respectively, as well as for the graphic design talents of Hayward Wilkirson and other technical assistance.

Excavations in 2013 relied heavily on the labor of students from Transylvania University in Lexington who were part of an archaeological field school that Transylvania faculty member Dr. Chris Begley and I conducted during the spring. The field school completed excavation of a hearth first identified in 1987, expanded excavations in the central part of the fort, and identified more fire hearths associated with cabins that formed the walls of the fort enclosure. These excavations made much clearer the architectural footprint of the fort.[8]

Subsequent excavations in 2013 and 2014 finished fieldwork the field school had begun and helped clarify aspects of the fort's plan and the extent of its preservation. My trusty volunteer excavators were on the job again. Once the fieldwork was completed, artifacts had to be washed and catalogued before I could analyze them. Megan Baker, Tiffany Campbell, Matt Davidson, Hannah Estes, and Hannah Weigle handled this task. The project benefitted greatly from further financial support by the Fort Boonesborough

Foundation, which provided funds for additional faunal (animal bone) analysis by Bruce Manzano, botanical analysis by Dr. Renee Bonzani, and graphics by Hayward Wilkirson. Foundation officers Elizabeth and George Chalfant and other board members have been particularly supportive of the research efforts, as have the staff of the Fort Boonesborough State Park. I am also very grateful to Dr. Ellen Eslinger and Dr. Kim McBride for serving as a sounding board for my ideas and offering useful and insightful comments on historical matters. Dr. Eslinger commented extensively on manuscript drafts and was a source of continual encouragement. Clary Estes also read the manuscript and offered helpful comments. I consider myself extremely fortunate to have the support of so many people.[9]

KENTUCKY ON THE CUSP OF REVOLUTION

Fort Boonesborough was founded at a pivotal point in American history that coincided with four key factors. First, Britain's victory over the French during the French and Indian War (1754–1763) established it as the premier colonial power. Second, population in the colonies was increasing at an unprecedented rate. Third, reports by hunters and traders of the economic possibilities in the trans-Appalachian interior fueled rampant land speculation fever. Finally, a series of treaties with various Native American tribes had, in the view of speculators with their eyes on western lands, weakened their positions as claimants of the Kentucky territory.[1]

French land cessions to Britain at the end of the French and Indian War expanded the British colonial empire to include a vast area that posed tremendous administrative challenges. Among other land cessions, the Treaty of Paris (1763) gave Canada and the eastern half of French Louisiana—an area that ran from the Appalachians to the Mississippi River—to Britain. Based on its colonial charter, Virginia claimed the Ohio River valley; hence, the Treaty of Paris set Virginia's western boundary at the Mississippi River. With French claims to the Ohio River region extinguished, Virginia was poised to expand westward. But the British monarchy had other plans.

King George III and his ministers had several compelling reasons for putting a brake on westward expansion. Numerous Native American tribes were alarmed by increasing encroachments by white hunters and worried about the specter of white settlers moving in permanently. They put up a spirited resistance in the face of mounting interest in land speculation as population pressure pushed against the frontier of the Mid-Atlantic and southern colonies. The British had just concluded a long, expensive war and had no stomach for more bloodshed or additional drains on their exchequer. Manpower and resources were inadequate to properly administer the new territory. British officials were also worried about the potential for new western settlements to forge trading arrangements with the Spanish, who controlled New Orleans, thereby encouraging political allegiance to an imperial rival.[2]

The king responded by issuing the Royal Proclamation of 1763, which reserved land west of the Appalachian Mountains for Native American tribes and prohibited any white settlement there. The line was intended to stave off costly conflicts so that eventual expansion into the trans-Appalachian west could take place in a controlled manner. However, by 1763 settlers were already living in parts of the prohibited area, and the numbers continued to grow in defiance of the proclamation. By 1774 an estimated forty thousand white settlers were illegally living in the prohibited land.[3]

Another problematical clause of the proclamation directed colonial governors to grant land to selected French and Indian War veterans who had served in the regular British Army or Royal Navy in North America. This directive presented a problem because the only area large enough to contain all the veterans' grants was the land reserved for native peoples. Rather than restraining white settlement in the west, the provision for land grants spurred surveying expeditions that contributed to Indian unrest.[4]

The region of Kentucky—then regarded as part of Botetourt County, Virginia's westernmost county—not only lay within the prohibited area but was also claimed by several tribes and was a great attraction to commercial hunters, land speculators, and colonists seeking land. British resources were inadequate to stem the influx of opportunists who defied the Proclamation of 1763 and penetrated Native American country. Backcountry hunters such as Daniel Boone, who made his first trip into Kentucky in 1769, increased their efforts to commercially harvest Kentucky's teeming populations of game animals.[5]

The proclamation line was unsatisfactory to many parties. Among them were Col. John Stuart and Sir William Johnson, the two superintendents assigned to administer the territory for Britain. Land speculators and colonists opposed the line, as did colonial governors, who resented the assertion of imperial control over their authority. The colonists had by this time developed a strong sense of autonomy and considered themselves partners with rather than subordinates of their mother country. British leaders on the other side of the Atlantic wanted colonists to pay more taxes to support the costs of a continued military presence in America. Postwar British policy toward the colonies laid the groundwork for sentiments that led to the War of Independence.[6]

By the late 1760s British leaders began to implement their long-term plan for western expansion. In 1768 Superintendent Johnson bargained with the Iroquois Confederacy at Fort Stanwix, New York, for a huge land purchase that would establish a new Indian boundary along the Ohio River to the mouth of the Kanawha River. There it was to connect with a line negotiated by Stuart with the Cherokees in the Treaty of Hard Labor (1768). Johnson instead negotiated a line that extended all the way to the Tennessee River. Despite the outrage of Secretary of State Wills Hill, Earl of Hillsborough, who favored limited western expansion, the royal ministry approved, and the king signed the treaty in May 1769. The new line eliminated Iroquois claims to lands south of the Ohio River but completely shut out the claims of the Shawnees and other tribes who actually used the ceded territory.[7]

The Treaty of Hard Labor negotiated by Stuart established the Cherokees' eastern territorial boundary as a line from the Holston River northeastward to the Kanawha River and on to the Ohio River. In 1770 lobbying by Virginia speculators and then-governor Norborne Berkeley, Fourth Baron Botetourt, moved the Cherokees' eastern boundary slightly to the west under the terms of the Treaty of Lochaber. The establishment of the new boundary signaled the inevitability of western expansion, but the proclamation line remained in force. While governors were not expressly forbidden to award grants across the mountains, the proclamation, by banning settlement, made fulfilling the residence and improvement requirements of the grant process legally impossible. Many simply ignored the ban and illegally settled on the restricted land.[8]

John Murray, Fourth Earl of Dunmore, became the governor of Virginia in 1771 and quickly aligned himself with land speculators and others wishing to expand westward. When Dunmore took office, veterans were already applying for grants under a proclamation issued in 1754 by Gov. Robert Dinwiddie, as well as pursuing land grants under the 1763 proclamation. In 1772 Lord Hillsborough confirmed the privy council's policy by forbidding Governor Dunmore from issuing any land grants beyond the mountains. The order frustrated veterans whose petitions were lying unfulfilled in the governor's office and irked the governor himself, since he aspired to become a land speculator. Despite the privy council's directive, in 1773 Lord Dunmore authorized a survey to be made in northern Kentucky to establish "proclamation rights" for veterans of the French and Indian War. Capt. Thomas Bullitt led a party that summer to survey land for these potential claims. Fincastle County surveyor Col. William Preston refused to allow the surveys to be entered into record because his deputies had not been involved, and most of the surveys were located on land reserved for Native American tribes. Bullitt appealed directly to the governor and his council, who validated many of the surveys. Preston then registered Bullitt's claims, but he also deputized John Floyd to conduct surveys (which became known as the Fincastle Surveys) in early 1774.[9]

Despite Preston's efforts, unauthorized surveys were taking place in Kentucky, and John Floyd learned of one of them in April when he reached Point Pleasant on his journey to Kentucky. Pennsylvanian James Harrod, who had accompanied Bullitt the year before, led a party of nearly fifty men to Kentucky in early March to mark land and establish a fledging settlement called Harrodstown, or Harrodsburg. Neither Harrod nor anyone in his company was a trained surveyor. When he and his men found a piece of land they liked, they marked a few trees and built a crude cabin in the belief that these acts would meet requirements for a preemption claim. Laying out lots at their planned town was another matter, however, since this required someone who had the necessary surveying equipment and knowledge. One of Floyd's surveyors, Hancock Taylor, may have provided this expertise when he and his party reached Harrodsburg in June. Normally, towns were established by petitioning for a town charter. Harrod may have reasoned that having an official surveyor lay out the town would help obtain approval for a charter when the time came.[10]

Surveys beyond the proclamation line, squatter settlements, and Native American opposition to the Treaty of Fort Stanwix fostered a tense, adversarial relationship between settlers and Indians that exploded into conflict in 1774. In April Cherokees waylaid a group of traders traveling down the Ohio River with trade goods for the Shawnee towns on the Scioto; one trader was killed, and the group's goods were taken. Shortly after, Michael Cresap and a party of squatters killed two Indians accompanying a trading trip to the Shawnees. This was followed by another attack against some Shawnee leaders returning home from Pittsburgh. A gruesome incident known as the Yellow Creek Massacre took place on the upper Ohio River on April 28 when three members of a Mingo chief's family were brutally murdered by Daniel Greathouse and some other men. Chief Logan had been conciliatory toward whites, but after this incident he launched retaliatory raids that killed thirteen settlers, and he encouraged other Indians to follow suit.

As hostilities escalated between the Ohio tribes and settlers, frontier residents built defensive outposts while surveyors and explorers, many of them encouraged and approved by Governor Dunmore of Virginia, continued their forays into the Ohio valley region. Settlers built a new fort, called Fort Dunmore, at the confluence of the Monongahela and Allegheny Rivers at the former site of Fort Pitt and made other private preparations for war. Governor Dunmore concluded by midsummer that an offensive campaign against the Shawnees, who claimed the Kentucky region as their hunting ground and considered the Treaty of Fort Stanwix invalid, would aid Virginian settlement efforts. He raised a militia force that defeated the Shawnees and their allies at the Battle of Point Pleasant. This brief but significant conflict, known as Dunmore's War, resulted in the Shawnees being forced to accept the Ohio River boundary line established by the Treaty of Fort Stanwix, to restrict their hunting to the north side of the river, to return all prisoners and stolen property, and to offer hostages to be held until a permanent peace could be negotiated the following spring. The outbreak of the American Revolution in April 1775 prevented the conference from happening. Dunmore's War convinced settlers that neither the crown nor the colonial governors could control them, and this justified proceeding with settlement in the contested area on their own terms months ahead of the official declaration of independence.[11]

Watching these developments was Judge Richard Henderson of North Carolina, the man who was the principal architect of an ambitious plan to form a new colony in Kentucky. Aware of the Virginia Charter, which claimed the Kentucky land, and of the Shawnees' acceptance of the Treaty of Fort Stanwix, Henderson approached the Cherokees with an offer to purchase land south and west of the Kentucky River. Buying land from Native Americans was not a new strategy, but Henderson and his partners negotiated the purchase in defiance of the British policy that banned any sales that were not supervised by the Indian superintendents Johnson or Stuart.[12]

The Transylvania Company intended ultimately to form a new colony that would hopefully be sanctioned by the British government and governed by the company partners. The Transylvania purchase covered a huge tract of land that was attractive to many other parties.[13] Moreover, the company aggressively pushed forward with plans to establish a physical presence on the land, and it began surveying land tracts for immediate sale. Men such as James Harrod, who had conducted an earlier unauthorized Kentucky survey, came together with the Virginia General Assembly in a manner that might not have happened had Henderson and his partners not attempted their illegal land grab. In this regard, the Transylvania Company precipitated governmental actions against the company and set the stage for the land law that opened Kentucky to legal settlement. All of these maneuvers took place in the context of a war for independence and the establishment of a new sovereign country. But these proscriptive actions did not happen immediately. The early part of Boonesborough's history was dominated by the Transylvania Company's efforts to establish a capital and woo participants into supporting their ambitious enterprise.

2

RICHARD HENDERSON AND THE TRANSYLVANIA COMPANY

Richard Henderson's background seems tailor-made for producing a man audacious enough to envision a new colony run by a proprietorial government. His great-grandfather Samuel Henderson emigrated from Dumfries, Scotland, to Jamestown, Virginia, in the early seventeenth century. His father, Samuel Jr., became high sheriff of Hanover County, Virginia, and married Elizabeth Williams, whose father, John, was a wealthy emigrant from Wales. The couple had nine children, of whom Richard was the oldest.[1]

Richard Henderson demonstrated ambition and a drive to succeed at an early age. Born in Virginia on April 20, 1735, he moved with his family in 1742 to Granville County, North Carolina, where his father again served as high sheriff. Richard was educated by a tutor and his mother. He served as a constable and undersheriff for his father, studied law under his cousin, Judge John Williams, and practiced as an attorney for several years. As an attorney, he made a good living handling debt collection cases for local gentry. In 1768 he was awarded a judgeship at the relatively young age of thirty-three. His legal experiences, from enforcement to adjudication, positioned him squarely within the "court ring," a group of local lawyers, judges, clerks, sheriffs, and other officials who controlled tax collections, debt suits, and many other civil matters that greatly affected, often adversely, the livelihoods and prosperity of local farmers.[2]

Henderson's judgeship came at a high personal price during a popular uprising known as the Regulator Movement (c. 1765–1771). The Regulators were a group of men who held political grievances concerning ruthless debt collection, exorbitant courthouse fees, and other issues involving the lawyers, clerks, judges, and merchants who dominated the county court system in the 1760s. North Carolina's governor, William Tryon, intended to appease discontented countrymen with Henderson's appointment. His assumption that Henderson was held in esteem by men who had been defrauded by the unscrupulous tactics of debt collectors and land speculators was in error. Henderson had made his fortune as an attorney for wealthy clients in debt suits. As a judge, he was reluctant to try Regulator cases. On September 24, 1770, Henderson was presiding alone at the fall term of the superior court in Hillsborough when a large group of men armed with clubs, whips loaded with lead or iron, and other weapons descended on the court demanding justice. They assaulted three lawyers and threatened Henderson, who gave them no sympathy. He managed to escape injury that day, and the next day he refused to accede to their demand that he hold court without lawyers present. Arsonists burned Henderson's house and barns in Granville County not long after. He served on the court until his term expired in 1773, having presided over one of the most tempestuous periods in pre–Revolutionary War North Carolina.[3]

After his term expired, Henderson turned his attention to plans for a colony in Kentucky. He reasoned that the Cherokees' claim of sovereignty and the various treaties they had entered with the British government made them the only legitimate claimants to the lands south of the Kentucky River; thus, negotiating a purchase with them would be sufficient to establish a defensible claim. That he intended to launch an enterprise "directly counter to the expressed will of the royal government" seems at odds with his involvement in the judicial system, where he was expected to uphold the law. Perhaps he reasoned that many other speculators were pursuing extralegal means to claim land that was not yet legally available but would inevitably become so, and he saw a chance to get ahead of the competition.[4]

Henderson's plan required collaborators, so he set about persuading some of his kinsmen and friends who had both money and connections to partner with him. In 1774 Henderson, joined by Thomas Hart and John Williams, organized the Louisa Company with the express purpose of renting or buying land from the Native Americans who claimed the territory. On January 3, 1775, three new partners—David Hart (Thomas and Nathaniel's brother); Leonard Henley Bullock, a former Granville County sheriff; and James Hogg, a merchant and promoter—were added to the company, which was renamed the Transylvania Company. John Luttrell, Nathaniel Hart's nephew by marriage and a former clerk in Henderson's court, and

William Johnston, a prominent Scotch merchant with many useful contacts, expanded the partnership to nine members. The company hired Daniel Boone to assemble a crew and cut a road to a location on the Kentucky River where the colony's capital was to be established.[5]

On March 17, 1775, after weeks of preparation and days of orations, negotiations, protests, and counterarguments over boundaries, the Great Grant was signed at Sycamore Shoals on the Watauga River in what is now Tennessee. Representing the Cherokees were Chiefs Oconistoto, Attakullakulla, and Savanooko. The company paid "two thousand pounds of lawful money of Great Britain" in the form of trade goods that were distributed among twelve hundred Cherokees in return for a huge territory bounded on the north by the Kentucky River and on the south by the Cumberland River. The grant described the land as beginning at the mouth of the Kentucky River on the Ohio River (at present-day Carrollton), then following the Kentucky upstream to

> the most northwardly branch of the same to the head spring thereof, thence a southeast course to the top ridge of Powel's Mountain, thence westwardly along the ridge of said mountain unto a point from which a northwest course will hit or strike the head spring of the most southwardly branch of Cumberland River thence down the said River including all its waters to the Ohio River, thence up the said River as it meanders to the beginning.[6]

The purchase covered all or portions of seventy-seven current Kentucky counties (amounting to approximately 16 million acres) and extended slightly into present-day Tennessee for an additional 1.6 million acres. The description mentioned Powel's Mountain, which is in present-day West Virginia, but the company does not seem to have made any attempts to sell land in this area.[7]

Despite Henderson's rationale for considering the Cherokees to be the primary claimants for the land south of the Kentucky River, the tribe was not united on whether they had an exclusive claim to the land. Among the unconvinced were Dragging Canoe and Oconistoto, who warned that Henderson and his partners might encounter resistance from other Cherokees not party to the purchase. As Daniel Boone was leaving Sycamore Shoals, Oconistoto told him that "we have given you a fine land, but I believe

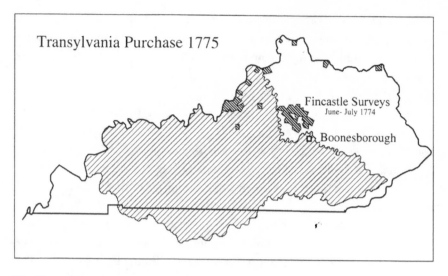

The Transylvania Company, organized by Richard Henderson in 1775, purchased land south of the Kentucky River from the Cherokees. The purchase, considered illegal by the British Crown and the Virginia General Assembly, covered all or portions of seventy-seven present-day Kentucky counties. Fort Boonesborough was built to serve as its headquarters. Map from *Virginia's Western War, 1775–1786* by Neal O. Hammon and Richard Taylor (Mechanicsburg, PA: Stackpole Books, 2002), 2.

you will have much trouble settling it." Moreover, the Shawnees continued to nurse grievances over being forced to give up their hunting rights south of the Ohio River. Shawnee and Cherokee opponents of the sale did not feel bound by the terms of the treaty, as Henderson was soon to learn.[8]

The official reaction to the purchase was swift and negative. Henderson's own governor, Josiah Martin of North Carolina, called him and his partners "land Pyrates" and issued a proclamation dated February 10, 1775, in advance of the actual land transfer between the Cherokees and the Transylvania Company. Governor Martin cited both the Royal Proclamation of 1763 and an act of the provincial assembly that prohibited white men from purchasing "any tract or parcel of land claimed or actually in possession of any Indian without liberty for so doing from the Governor and Council." He also expressed concerns over gunpowder being included with the goods given to the Cherokees as payment, stating that they might use it "as a means of annoying his Majesty's subjects in this and the neighboring colonies."

Finally, he cited his belief that Henderson had "invited many debtors, and other persons in desperate circumstances, to desert this province and become settlers on the said lands, to the great injury of creditors."[9]

The governor of Virginia also weighed in on the controversy. On March 21, just four days after the deed to the Transylvania Company was signed at Sycamore Shoals, Lord Dunmore issued a proclamation of protest. He cited the king's order for the survey of all land acquired under the Treaty of Lochaber into lots of one hundred to one thousand acres, to be sold at public auction to the highest bidder, who also would be subject to an annual quitrent of one and a half pennies sterling per acre. He then directed all "justices of peace, sheriffs, and other officers, civil and military to use their utmost endeavours to prevent the unwarrantable and illegal designs of the said Henderson and his abettors" and promised fines and imprisonment if his proclamation was breached. Dunmore's objections stemmed less from the position that Henderson and his partners were acting illegally and more from a desire to retain these lands for lucrative land speculation of his own.[10]

In response to Dunmore's proclamation, the Virginia Assembly appointed a committee consisting of Patrick Henry, Richard Bland, Thomas Jefferson, Robert Carter Nicholas, and Edmund Pendleton to determine if the British Crown had the right to advance such terms for granting land. The assembly advised people to refrain from accepting or purchasing land grants on Dunmore's terms. However, county surveyor William Preston wrote Lord Dunmore of the large numbers of settlers who would very shortly be inhabiting Kentucky and expressed his opinion that they could not be prevented from going.[11]

Despite the protests and threats of two governors, Henderson and his partners were already deeply committed to their enterprise and proceeded with their plans. Henderson envisioned Boonesborough becoming a center of government and commerce and anticipated profitable land sales, but his miscalculations ultimately doomed the enterprise. The Transylvania Company partners all had prominence and influence in the counties in and around Hillsborough, North Carolina, but they exercised little clout with members of the colonial assembly or with Governor Lord Dunmore and his council. Henderson underestimated the reaction of the Virginia Assembly, which did not look favorably on an interloper from North Carolina annexing so large an area of what they considered part of Virginia. Nor did he expect the opposition and countermeasures he encountered from other adventurers who were launching their own speculative land acquisition schemes. Finally, the onset of the Revolutionary War sabotaged the possibility of an imperial charter for the company and intensified an already fraught atmosphere as the British incited their Native American allies to carry out frequent, unpredictable raids against the Kentucky colonists. The Kentucky settlers were left largely to their own devices and could not rely on security or assistance from the Virginia Assembly. Fort Boonesborough was forced to assume a defensive role in holding at bay the British and Native American enemy.

The settlers' success in defending the trans-Appalachian frontier against British and Indian attacks was not a foregone conclusion, nor was the western theatre of war incidental or subordinate to events back east. According to Alan Taylor, "The British Empire displayed a fatal combination: threatening pretensions without sufficient power to enforce them. . . . The British failure in the West discredited imperial rulers at the same time that they tried to impose new taxes on coastal colonists." Taylor argues convincingly that subordination of western issues as "minor irritants less significant than the clash over taxes" is an unbalanced interpretation. Rather, western conflict and resistance to parliamentary taxes equally contributed to "a constitutional crisis that disrupted the British Empire in North America."[12]

3

ESTABLISHING FORT BOONESBOROUGH ON THE KENTUCKY RIVER

As Judge Richard Henderson was wrapping up negotiations with the Cherokees in the spring of 1775, Daniel Boone was dispatched with a party of about thirty-five people to clear a trail to the site of the future capital and to begin improvements (see the appendix). The party was mostly composed of white men, but Boone's daughter Susannah (the wife of William Hays), an enslaved woman named Dolly belonging to Richard Callaway, an enslaved man named Sam belonging to Capt. William Twetty, and perhaps other male slaves also came along. The group initially followed the Athiamiowee, or Warrior's Path, the same trail that Boone had taken in 1773 when he made an abortive attempt to settle in Kentucky that took the life of his eldest son, James, and several others. When they reached Flat Lick, near Stinking Creek, they left the Athiamiowee for another hunters' trail that led them to the Rockcastle River and its tributary, Far Fork. From there they blazed a trail toward their final destination on the Kentucky River. The journey took several weeks, and the party was further stalled when it was attacked by a group of Pict (Miami) warriors, who killed Captain Twetty and Sam and severely wounded a young man named Felix Walker. The slain were buried where they were killed, at a site that became known as "Twetty's Fort," although it was little more than a camp with crude shelters. Daniel Boone sent a letter to Henderson that described the attack and the chilling effect it had on his party, encouraging Henderson to make haste to join them. The party stayed at Twetty's Fort for twelve days, giving Walker time to stabilize enough to travel. He was strapped to a litter suspended between two horses and endured the twelve-mile trip to the site where Fort Boonesborough was to be built.[1]

Boone knew exactly where he was going; he had already visited the site on the (south) west side of the Kentucky River in 1774, and he probably suggested it to Henderson as a suitable place for the colony's capital. Among the favorable characteristics of the selected site were its location on a major navigable river, its proximity to both fresh and mineral springs, and its broad expanse of river terrace and adjacent uplands. The road-cutting party reached the fort site on April 1, 1775. Years later, Felix Walker wrote a memoir of his experiences in which he described his first view of the site. It was "situated in a plain . . . wherein was a lick with two sulphur springs strongly impregnated." As the party approached, "a number of buffaloes, of all sizes, supposed to be between two and three hundred, made off from the lick in every direction." The lick lay within a creek valley that became known as Sycamore Hollow. Judge Henderson described the terrace on which Fort Boonesborough was later built as "a beautiful plain surrounded by a turf of fine white clover forming a green . . . to which there is scarcely anything to be likened." Botanist Julian Campbell's research on the presettlement vegetation of Kentucky identifies this groundcover as running buffalo clover, a nutritious food source for wild and domestic herbivores. The openness of the setting, free of the deep forests that grew on the surrounding uplands, may have been created by late prehistoric Fort Ancient culture agriculturalists who lived in large villages and may have used fire to create open areas for cultivation. Unknown, of course, to the Boonesborough settlers, a Fort Ancient village occupied c. AD 1200–1400 once stood at a slightly higher elevation on the same terrace and about one-quarter of a mile from the fort site.[2]

Upon arrival at the site, Boone's party set up camp on the west side of the hollow and began improvements. The settlers initially occupied tents or lean-to shelters (often called half-faced camps). They staked out plots of two acres each, drew lots for them, and built a construction that Henderson called Fort Boone. Daniel Boone described it as a fort and Felix Walker called it a station. Although the terms "fort" and "station" suggest that the construction included defensive architectural features such as picketing, Elizabeth Poague Thomas observed no picketing when she visited Fort Boone in September 1775. She described the construction as "not more than half a dozen cabins built, on the river bank, perhaps a quarter [of a

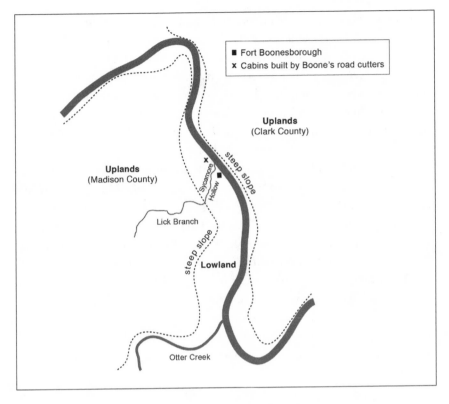

The location of Fort Boonesborough on the Kentucky River.

mile] below [downstream of] the Lick." Settler John Gass recalled years later that in 1776 Boone's cabin was located "right where the ferry is." The old ferry road ran along part of the current boundary between the park and the adjacent modern quarry. The old ferry landing is downstream approximately 900–950 feet from the current park boat dock. Boone's cabin and the others built as part of Fort Boone were probably on the terrace at a higher elevation, in what is now the older section of the park campground.[3]

Unbeknownst to Boone and his fellow settlers, as they constructed their new capital the battle at Concord and Lexington (April 19, 1775) set in motion the war for independence that was to have a momentous impact on the Transylvania enterprise. As the colonies moved toward armed resistance over the summer, the Boonesborough settlers labored on in ignorance for several weeks, surveying land and planting crops before the news and effects of war reached them. While the attack that killed Twetty and his slave alerted the settlers to the threat of Indian raids, they were, for the most part, not subjected to attacks for the rest of the year. As a result, the settlers deferred any real progress on building a defensible fort.

The arrival of Henderson's party on April 20 brought welcome reinforcements and supplies, but Henderson was not satisfied with what Boone and his men had accomplished. Henderson's journal provides the most detailed account of events from the early days of the settlement, from March 20 to July 25. Upon his arrival Henderson deemed inadequate the site where Boone had begun his small fort, and he selected another location on the east side of Sycamore Hollow. It was higher in elevation and located about three hundred yards from Boone's camp. Henderson, John Luttrell, and their "particular company" pitched their tents on the proposed fort site on Friday, April 21. Assisted by Daniel Boone and Richard Callaway, they began to lay off town lots and completed nineteen lots on the first day, including one around a fine spring; by April 22 they had plotted a total of fifty-four lots. The settlers drew a first round of lots on Sunday, but some were dissatisfied, and Henderson spent the next day arranging exchanges. There were more lots than men drawing for them, leaving thirteen yet unclaimed, so a second lottery was held on Tuesday, and after some exchanges everyone seemed satisfied.[4]

Henderson went to considerable trouble to accommodate the settlers in the drawing of lots, but he also made sure his own needs were met. He secured four lots for his fort and a garden. One of his lots contained a huge elm tree, its trunk four feet in diameter from the ground to the first branches nine feet above. The tree canopy was one hundred feet in diameter, and between 10 a.m. and 2 p.m. it cast a shade of four hundred feet. The original claimant of the lot hosting the elm "would have wished [the tree] in the Red Sea, at the devil, or anywhere, to have got clear of it," because it was too much labor to cut down or girdle. Henderson had no trouble convincing him to exchange the shady lot for another. Henderson called the tree the "Divine Elm" and intended to use it temporarily as a "church, state-house, council-chamber" until an appropriate building was erected.[5]

Henderson quickly found that organizing the settlers to work together for the collective benefit of all was challenging. Even one of his partners, Nathaniel Hart, refused to cooperate. Henderson was perplexed by Hart's remark to John Luttrell that "he would have nothing to say to the Fort, things were managed in such a manner"; Henderson could not "guess the reason of his discontent." Hart chose a tract adjacent to the town lands and established White Oak Station, named after the spring nearby. He refused to assist Henderson in building a powder magazine to protect the gunpowder stores from the rainy weather typical of a Kentucky spring. Nor would he cooperate on any other construction. Hart's attitude notwithstanding, Luttrell maintained a good relationship with Henderson, who described him as "exceedingly obliging and good-natured, and . . . desirous of promoting the company's interest." While Luttrell definitely looked after his own interests by claiming and improving two tracts nearby, he did not neglect his duties as a partner and helped Henderson in various ways. Once the town lots were surveyed, Henderson turned to showing lots to newcomers, planting a garden, and clearing the lot he had selected for the fort with the aid of his brothers Samuel and Nathaniel, and Luttrell. Because creating dry storage for gunpowder was a priority, Henderson first built a "little house" for a powder magazine on May 2–3. Cabins followed more slowly, and some settlers continued to live at the location Boone first settled west of Sycamore Hollow.[6]

Henderson's journal records a busy spring and summer of construction and improvements. Boone's party of road cutters and those who accompanied Henderson formed a complement of at least forty-five men who could be considered supportive of the Transylvania enterprise. But many men made the long trip to the Kentucky region in 1775 to investigate and survey land, and Henderson tried to win over hostile newcomers by enticing them with land. The company offered cheap land to attract settlers, but the partners viewed the enterprise very much as a private endeavor to enrich themselves. They reserved for themselves the rights to salt springs, and to lead, gold, silver, copper and sulfur deposits, should such sites be discovered. Their terms of sale also included the payment of a small quitrent to the company owners, a feature that harkened back to feudal times. By the late eighteenth century quitrents had been generally abandoned in the American colonies, not so much for economic reasons but rather because quitrents ran counter to republican ideals. Even where they were still legal, quitrents were no longer being collected. That Kentucky settlers would object to this type of land tax should have been foreseen: such requirements did not sit well with potential buyers.

Besides the Fort Boonesborough settlers, three other groups coalesced around three leaders. One of them was John Floyd (deputy surveyor for

Fincastle County surveyor William Preston), who visited Henderson on May 4. He represented a party of about thirty men from Virginia who wanted to know Henderson's terms for settling on his land. Floyd's party was camped at a locality called St. Asaph's (also known as Benjamin Logan's Station, at present-day Stanford). Henderson was nonplussed about Floyd's request since he represented Preston, who had a duty to prevent interlopers within his jurisdiction; Henderson recorded that Preston "did everything in his power or invention, as I am informed, to defeat our enterprise and bring it into contempt."[7]

Preston's opposition was definitely a matter of concern. County surveyors in eighteenth-century Virginia were powerful officials who, while lacking the aristocratic origins of the highest elite families, were "junior partners in the great land speculations of the age, men of influence and wealth in their own right whose assistance was requisite to the success of any land venture." A surveyorship was the path to economic influence, wealth, and social prestige. Preston assertively exercised his powers throughout his career by opposing the naming of special surveyors who might infringe on his jurisdiction and by promoting the land act of 1779, which confirmed the exclusive right of county surveyors and their assistants to measure public land in their jurisdictions. Henderson's enterprise was a threat to Preston's authority and designated powers and interfered with plans he had for the same land.[8]

Preston's deputy, on the other hand, seems to have taken another view and communicated his willingness to work out a mutually beneficial deal with Henderson. John Floyd impressed Henderson as a man with a "great share of modesty, an honest, open countenance, and no small share of good sense." He reasoned that gaining Floyd's support was preferable to his opposition but confided to his journal that he intended to keep "a very strict watch." Floyd left after making arrangements to acquire Transylvania lands, all located south of the Kentucky River, while retaining his lucrative position as surveyor for Preston on lands north of the river. He also promised to overcome Preston's opposition to the Transylvania purchase.[9]

James Harrod and Thomas Slaughter each led groups of settlers that claimed land in the Salt River drainage portion of the Transylvania purchase. Harrod hailed from the Monongahela region of Pennsylvania and had been part of Thomas Bullitt's surveying crew in 1773. He returned to Kentucky in 1774 to establish Harrodsburg and lay claim to land at the Boiling Spring in present-day Boyle County. Virginian Thomas Slaughter came to Kentucky with Henderson's party but did not remain at Fort Boonesborough, preferring to seek out land further west and taking up residence at Harrodsburg. Harrod and about fifty other men built improvement cabins on numerous tracts in the Salt River drainage, including Harrod's personal choice of land at Boiling Spring. This group was called the Boiling Spring settlement, even though they lived in Harrodsburg for security purposes. Harrod and Slaughter found themselves at odds over land and brought their dispute to Henderson to settle on May 7. Having acceded to the company's terms himself, Slaughter enlisted Henderson's help in countering Harrod's resistance to buying into the Transylvania scheme. Harrod, on the other hand, may have simply wanted to see for himself how much of a threat the Transylvania Company was to his earlier surveys. Slaughter complained that Harrod and his men had marked "every piece of land they thought proper," had built cabins that were no more than hog-pens, and had claimed every good spring. Since Harrod had the elder claim, Slaughter ceded first choice to Harrod and his men but urged him to leave some good prospects.

Henderson's explanation of the visit and the dispute clearly expressed a bias against Harrod and his group because they came from Monongahela, where "no law had ever extended or the right to the soil been determined." He sized up Harrod and his followers as "a body of lawless people, from habit and education," while he assessed Slaughter as "a sensible and experienced old gentleman—a man of good family and connections," whose men had industriously cleared land and planted corn. Henderson was loath to make a judgment on the matter because he did not think he could enforce a decree should Harrod and his men resist. He instead diverted the debate to persuading Harrod to join with him and the Transylvania Company in a compact that united the four distinct groups of settlers then claiming parts of Kentucky. The men agreed to call for an election of delegates to be held at Boonesborough on Tuesday, May 23. The agreement did not remove the threat Harrod represented, but Henderson hoped for some measure of cooperation and rapprochement. The incident underscores the weak authority that Henderson wielded and emphasizes his attempts to mitigate opposition by offering inducements. Even his call for a convention to discuss matters of mutual concern and to form a united compact suggests that he was willing to entertain the idea of popular governance rather than a top-down proprietary approach.[10]

The May 23 meeting was well attended by the settlers representing Boonesborough, Harrodsburg, Boiling Spring, and St. Asaph's (Logan's Station), and a spirit of cooperation seemed to prevail. Those attending convened under the Divine Elm at Boonesborough and elected delegates. Representing Boonesborough were Squire and Daniel Boone, Samuel Henderson, William Moore, and Richard Callaway. William Cocke was also a Boonesborough delegate but was absent. Thomas Slaughter, Rev. John Lythe, Valentine Harmon, and James Douglass represented Harrodsburg; Slaughter was elected to serve as chairman. Representing Boiling Spring were James Harrod, Nathan Hammond, Isaac Hite, and Azariah Davis. John Todd, Alexander Spotswood Dandridge, John Floyd, and Samuel Wood represented St. Asaph's. Matthew Jouett was chosen to serve as clerk. The meeting opened with a divine service performed by Reverend Lythe followed by a speech delivered by Richard Henderson.[11]

Henderson's speech was designed to promote unity and cooperation, and it emphasized the wisdom of banding together in the face of "one common danger, which threatens our common overthrow." He proposed that a plan of government by popular representation be formulated and suggested priorities such as establishing courts of justice to adjudicate laws, restraining vice and immorality, devising a system for the recovery of debts and settling disputes, establishing a militia, and controlling "wanton destruction of . . . game." Numerous bills were introduced and read over the next two days. The result was nine laws that established and regulated courts of jurisdiction and a militia, set up a system for punishing criminals, prohibited "profane swearing, and Sabbath breaking," regulated writs of attachment, ascertained clerks' and sheriffs' fees, preserved the range, improved horse breeds, and preserved wild game. Henderson must have been relieved that, in the very earliest days of establishing a foothold within the Transylvania lands, he had managed to enlist the cooperation of his principal competitors. With their support, Henderson and his partners hoped to prevail in what amounted to an illegal land grab opposed by colonial officials and the Virginia Assembly.[12]

In the meantime, his other concern was strengthening the company's physical presence on the landscape by cultivating crops and erecting a fort for safety. Limited food supplies meant securing adequate meat and raising crops were matters of great importance. One of Henderson's biggest complaints concerned the great waste of meat by hunters who killed as many as six buffalos at a time yet did not butcher more than half a horse load, leaving the rest to rot. They quickly drove away much of the larger game, necessitating travel of ever-increasing distances to procure meat. Exasperated, Henderson wrote, "These evils we endeavored to prevent, but found it not practical, many complaining that they were too poor to hire hunters; others loved it more than work; and some who knew little of the matter, but conceit, from having a hunting-shirt, tomahawk and gun, thought it was an insult to offer another to hunt for them, especially as pay was to be made." When the meat shortage began to cause a serious food problem, Henderson had to make "the strictest inquiry . . . into every hunter's conduct." Once the problem of wasteful hunting was publicly acknowledged and censured, Henderson thought that the practice decreased because of fear of discovery and that his edict "saved the lives of many buffaloes, elks, and deer." The fact that Henderson and his partners were initially kept in the dark suggests that the Transylvania enterprise garnered little social cohesion among its participants, many of whom were not amenable to bowing to the company's authority.[13]

In early May 1775 Henderson began organizing men to build the large fort on the east side of Sycamore Hollow. Once again he found it difficult to prevail upon the settlers to finish the fort. While visiting for several months, Elizabeth Poague Thomas observed that as of September 1775, besides the half-dozen cabins built by Boone and his road cutters on the west side of the lick, "other cabins were building—a pretty good sized one was being erected for Col. Callaway. . . . Nothing like forting [stockade]. . . . The cabins built were not in a row, but scattering." While Thomas did not discern any plan to the construction she observed, Henderson had a design in mind that he rendered as a sketch showing a rectangle formed by four blockhouses anchoring the corners, gates on the two longer walls, and cabins filling in the four sides. Stockade filled gaps between the blockhouses and adjacent cabins.[14]

While the fort was not completed until many months later, enough progress was made on building cabins, planting crops, and making other improvements that trips back east to fetch family and attend to pressing business were feasible. Daniel Boone took advantage of the peaceful conditions to travel in mid-June to North Carolina for his family, intending to return with them as soon as possible. Henderson and Luttrell needed to address mounting government opposition in the east. Nathaniel Hart had already preceded them, bearing a letter written by Henderson explaining conditions at the fort to the partners still residing in North Carolina. Henderson and Luttrell left Boonesborough in late August upon hearing that Boone and his family were well on their way to the Kentucky settlement, knowing they could rely on Boone's leadership to manage matters in their absence. Among other issues, Henderson and Luttrell meant to attend a meeting of the partners scheduled for September 25, where they would make plans to petition the Continental Congress to recognize Transylvania as a fourteenth colony.[15]

By this time colonial independence had been declared, and the Continental Congress was the only body that could recognize Transylvania as a separate colony. Its authority, however, was tenuous, especially given the opposition to the Transylvania land scheme from Virginia and North Carolina. James Hogg was selected to serve as delegate to plead the company's case. When he reached Philadelphia, where the congress was meeting, he consulted with many of the members, including Silas Deane of Connecticut. Deane advised him to sound out the Virginia delegates, who, as members of the largest and most prosperous American colony, had to be won over. This was a daunting and ultimately fruitless prospect. Deane was favorable toward the petition, but the Virginia delegates were not, largely because the proposed colony would annex land that Virginia claimed, and they disliked the principles under which the colony would be governed.[16]

Despite these disappointing developments, Henderson launched a broad advertising campaign urging would-be settlers to buy land from the Transylvania Company. He placed a notice in the Williamsburg, Virginia, newspaper on September 30, 1775, that was reprinted in several issues and appeared in other newspapers across the colonies. The ad promised that buyers who settled on and inhabited company lands before June 1, 1776, were entitled to take up and survey 500 acres at a price of fifty shillings sterling per hundred in addition to an annual quitrent of two shillings per acre, to begin in 1780. A grantee could also claim 250 acres for each tithable person in his family at the same price. The price per acre was a 150 percent increase over the original rate offered to settlers who accompanied Henderson to Kentucky earlier in the year.[17]

No doubt anticipating increased land sales as a result of these advertisements, the company set up a land office under the direction of Henderson's cousin and company partner, Col. John Williams. In late November, Henderson and Williams traveled to Fort Boonesborough with a party of about forty men. A scheduled meeting on December 21 failed to garner a majority of delegates because bad weather and their scattered distribution hindered travel, but those who came voted to make Capt. John Floyd surveyor, Nathaniel Henderson entry-taker, and Richard Harrison secretary. Williams quickly learned that the settlers, particularly those at Harrodsburg, were very dissatisfied with the increase in land prices. He responded to their grievances on January 1, 1776, with a document that justified the rate increase on the grounds that the company had secured the land at great expense, continued to incur costs, and could not offer land at the "inferior terms" offered in the spring. Williams's arguments did not sway the Harrodsburg settlers.[18]

Receiving no concession from Williams on the question of land prices, the dissatisfied Harrodsburg settlers took a different tack. In May 1776 they sent a petition directly to the Virginia Convention that laid out their opposition. Floyd, having thrown his support to the Transylvania Company, complained in a June 8 letter to William Preston that "no surveying of consequence goes on in Transylvania," and he predicted "that set about Harrodsburg" headed by John Gabriel "Jack" Jones would work against efforts to that effect. In fact, the Harrodsburg delegates prepared a petition dated June 20, 1776, on behalf of the "Committee of West Fincastle" to be submitted to the Virginia Convention, requesting that the Kentucky lands be declared formally as part of Virginia. The petition did not directly ask that a new county be established but referred to the long distance between Williamsburg and Kentucky and mentioned the need for representation of its settlers. Jones and George Rogers Clark were elected by Harrodsburg settlers as delegates to the Virginia legislature and in July 1776 left for Williamsburg, where they intended to make their case for their own surveys and speak against the Transylvania claims. The convention adjourned before the petition was submitted, but the delegates voted to accurately determine Virginia's claim to Kentucky and to inquire into the legality of land purchases from Native Americans.[19]

Henderson and his partners answered these ominous developments with a counterpetition asking for recognition of their claims, but the first session of the new Virginia legislature organized after the adoption of the Declaration of Independence passed an act on December 7 creating Kentucky County out of Fincastle County. The new county encompassed the Transylvania territory, and the act effectively rendered the company's purchase null and void. Thereafter, Henderson's only hope was to persuade the legislature to compensate the company in some fashion for the expenses and labor the partners incurred. Two years would go by before the general assembly passed an act during their October 1778 session that awarded Richard Henderson and his partners a large tract of land on the Green and Ohio Rivers.[20]

Although the Transylvania Company ultimately failed in its scheme to establish a fourteenth colony, the proprietors succeeded in one respect. Fort Boonesborough, established just a few days before the shots rang out that started the Revolutionary War, was positioned as a place of sanctuary for Kentucky settlers and became a critically important point of defense on the western war front. This role became increasingly crucial as the war spread throughout the colonies. Separated from the eastern seaboard by the Appalachian Mountains and threatened by the British and their Native American allies to the north and south, Fort Boonesborough, Fort Harrod, and St. Asaph's became the principal fortified sites in Kentucky during the first two years of the war.

The onset of the Revolutionary War led the British to enlist the assistance of Native American tribes by providing them with arms, ammunition, and trade goods in return for their attacks against the colonists on the western front. The tribes had their own reasons for fighting the colonists, the most significant being to halt the expansion of colonial settlement west of the Appalachians. Kentucky was the tip of the spear for Indian attacks that intensified from 1776 onward.[21]

The Revolutionary War was just one phase of a long war that Native Americans fought against colonial encroachment of their land. The relationship between the British and the Native American tribes during the war was complex. Some tribes sought peaceful solutions while others advocated armed opposition. Henderson's negotiations with the Cherokees for the Kentucky land exemplified these opposing attitudes: Dragging Canoe and Chief Oconistoto argued against the sale, while Chief Attakullakulla advocated for the treaty. Likewise, the Shawnees living north of the Ohio River still resented being forced to cede their Kentucky rights after their recent defeat in Dunmore's War. While most Shawnees initially advocated neutrality, the Chillicothe and Piqua divisions became increasingly militant. As the war progressed, more and more Shawnees shifted their allegiance to the militant contingent within the tribe and even joined other tribes, such as the Mingos, in raiding the American frontier. While the tribes were far from united in their reaction and response to colonial expansion, virtually all of the Kentucky settlers viewed all Indians as dangerous adversaries and made no distinctions between the militant factions and those who promoted peaceful coexistence. Retaliatory raids by the colonists destroyed Indian (particularly Shawnee) villages and crops, and settlers killed not just adult men but also women, the elderly, and children. Such aggression encouraged violent resistance and eroded any hope of "a good or lasting peace."[22]

The net effect on the Kentucky frontier was the acceleration of Native American attacks in 1776–1777. A famous incident in 1776 that presaged the increased Native American threat directly affected the people of Fort Boonesborough. Betsy and Frances Callaway and Jemima Boone went canoeing in the Kentucky River on July 14 and were taken captive by five Cherokee and Shawnee warriors. Headed by Jemima's father, Daniel Boone, and Richard Callaway, father of the other girls, men from Fort Boonesborough gave chase for over thirty miles and succeeded in rescuing the girls without loss of any of the settlers' lives. This event became one of the enduring tales of the Kentucky frontier, one that continues to be told. While the rescue party was gone, another party of Native Americans burned Nathaniel Hart's cabin at White Oak Spring and destroyed his young apple orchard.[23]

The year 1777 was one of the bloodiest and most violent times on the fledgling Kentucky frontier. Many settlers fled back east, and small settlements broke up. Attacks began at Fort Boonesborough on March 7 when a slave was killed and another wounded in a nearby field. On April 24 a party led by Simon Kenton, which was pursuing Indians who had killed Daniel Goodman, was attacked and had to flee for the fort. Daniel Boone, John Todd, Isaac Hite, and Michael Stoner were wounded. Kenton helped Boone make it to the fort, and William Bush came to Michael Stoner's aid. Everyone reached safety, but the raiding party harassed the fort until their own heavy casualties caused them to leave. On May 23 a large party of Indians, perhaps as many as two hundred, appeared on Hackberry Ridge west of the fort and fired on the fort for two days before they left.[24]

So many people abandoned the Kentucky frontier that when a census was taken on May 1, Fort Boonesborough had only twenty-two men along with an uncounted number of women, children, and slaves. St. Asaph's (Logan's Station) and Fort Harrod were the only other occupied sites in Kentucky that year. The severity and frequency of Indian attacks continued through the growing season and made cultivation of crops and hunting extremely dangerous. An attack on Fort Boonesborough in June killed some cattle, a grave loss since cows were the source of milk as well as meat. Militia support arrived on August 1 when Col. John Bowman reached Boonesborough with two companies of one hundred men before proceeding to Harrodsburg. September brought Capt. William Bailey Smith with a company of forty-eight fighters, and Capt. Charles Gwatkin brought fifty volunteers from Bedford County, Virginia. The added men were welcomed for the defenses they provided, but supplies were so scanty that everyone often went hungry. The year 1777 closed on a fort population exhausted by food deprivations, the constant threat of attack, and fear for what the future would bring.[25]

4

CAPTIVITY, ESCAPE, AND
THE GREAT SIEGE OF 1778

The year 1778 opened with the realization that Fort Boonesborough settlers had to remedy a particularly grievous shortage: salt. As well as being a critical component of a healthy diet, salt was essential to survival since it was necessary for the preservation of meat and other foodstuffs. To meet this need, in January 1778 Daniel Boone organized a party of thirty-four men to go to the Lower Blue Licks to process the salty mineral water at the spring there. The threat of Native American attacks made the trip perilous, but the need was great, and given that such raids tended to slack off in the winter, Boone took a calculated risk. What he could not have foreseen were the events unfolding in Shawnee country in the aftermath of the murders of the Shawnee peace chief, Cornstalk, his son, and two other noted men by soldiers at Point Pleasant on November 12, 1777. The Shawnee nation was outraged. With the encouragement of British leaders at Detroit, and abetted by two French Canadian men working for the British, Chief Black Fish assembled his warriors to take their revenge by attacking Fort Boonesborough. Their encounter with Boone and his men at the Lower Blue Licks altered the course of the plan.[1]

The salt makers had been at work for nearly a month when Boone, en route to camp with a load of buffalo meat on February 7, encountered four Shawnees to whom he was forced to surrender after a fruitless attempt to escape on foot. The warriors took him to a large Shawnee encampment nearby, where he found Chiefs Black Fish and Munseeka; French Canadians Peter Laramie and Jacques Baby; a black interpreter named Pompey, who had been adopted into the tribe as a child; colonial loyalists James and George Girty; and over one hundred warriors. It was an exceedingly large

27

force for a wintertime action. Black Fish, with Pompey interpreting, told Boone that he knew of the men at Lower Blue Licks and intended to kill them before continuing on to attack Fort Boonesborough.[2]

Boone was faced with a thorny dilemma. How could he save his men from slaughter and prevent Fort Boonesborough from being taken? As he described his actions later, Boone persuaded Black Fish to take him and his men back to the Shawnee towns north of the Ohio River, telling him that the fort was too strong to be taken (a falsehood, since the stockade was incomplete and there were only a few defenders). To save the lives of his men, he promised to deliver the people of Fort Boonesborough peaceably in the spring when the women and children could be safely transported. Boone and an estimated twenty-nine men were taken to Old Chillicothe, a major Shawnee village on the Little Miami River. Five men avoided capture because they either were carrying salt back to Fort Boonesborough (William Cradlebaugh, Jesse Hodges, and Stephen Hancock) or were out hunting for meat to feed the salt makers and went undetected. The hunters, Thomas Brooks and Flanders Callaway, found the empty camp and surmised what had happened; they returned to the fort and reported the incident. The loss of so many able men left Fort Boonesborough in a weak and vulnerable defensive position.[3]

Most of the captives survived, but only a few returned to Fort Boonesborough. Fourteen of them were sent to Detroit, where they were dispersed to various Native American groups with whom they remained until they escaped or were released. At least three were forced to run a gauntlet. A few were sent to Montreal or Quebec, where distance made escape attempts more difficult. Many remained in captivity for several years.[4]

Only two captives, Arabia Brown and Daniel Boone, escaped and made their way back to the fort in the spring or early summer of 1778, arriving in time to help prepare the fort for attack and defend it during the military engagement that came to be known as the Great Siege of Boonesborough. Little is known of Brown's escape, but Boone's return was a critical element in ensuring the fort's readiness. Boone, who was adopted by Chief Black Fish and received very favorable treatment, did not escape until mid-June when he learned of the Shawnees' plans to return to Fort Boonesborough with a party of several hundred warriors. He arrived back at Fort Boonesborough after a grueling 160-mile trip that he completed in four days.[5]

The topography of Fort Boonesborough presented both drawbacks and

28

advantages for the besiegers as well as the besieged. The fort's position on a large, open river terrace gave it a clear view of attackers approaching from the west, south, or north. However, its proximity to Sycamore Hollow less than two hundred feet to the west made it vulnerable to Native American snipers concealed by trees and brush along the edge of the clay bank that rimmed the creek valley. Likewise, the high, sheer cliffs on the opposite bank of the Kentucky River offered vantage points that would allow gunfire to be directed from above. This threat was mitigated, to some extent, by the long distance between the top of the ridge and the fort: the closest point was nearly 1,400 linear feet away. Even an excellent marksman with a good rifle would be thwarted by this distance, which is one and a half times longer than the normal range of a muzzle-loading rifle. Nonetheless, gunfire from the cliff was unnerving to the settlers, and snipers occasionally scored a hit. The river below the cliffs on the east side of the fort also was an effective barrier to an approach from that side. While Native Americans could conceal themselves at water's edge, shielded by a high, steep bank, they became visible and vulnerable to gunfire once they reached the top of the terrace.

The force attacking Fort Boonesborough in September 1778 was composed of several hundred Indians, who were accompanied by a small number of French Canadian militia officers and some interpreters in the employ of the British. Most of the Native Americans were Shawnees, but some of their allies, such as the Cherokees, were also involved. Shawnee chief Black Fish directed the Indian contingent, accompanied by two other Shawnee chiefs, Moluntha and Catahecassa (Black Hoof). Black Bird, a Chippewa chief, was also present. The principal white officer was Lt. Antoine Dagnieau DeQuindre, a French Canadian member of the British militia at Detroit. Pierre Drouillard, a well-known Detroit trader, served as one of the interpreters, as did Isidore DuChaine, Jacques Baby, and Pompey, the latter two men having been with the party that captured Boone and the salt makers in February. No British officers accompanied the group, possibly because the British did not have sufficient manpower to accompany every raid, or they did not think the expedition warranted their direct supervision.

In the late summer and early fall of 1778 the British were dealing with the aftermath of Col. George Rogers Clark's victory at Kaskaskia. Henry Hamilton, lieutenant governor of the Province of Quebec, enforced a policy of sending white men along on sanctioned Native American expeditions. As he explained in a letter to the British secretary of state, Lord Shelburne, he thought their presence necessary to "attend to the behavior of the Indians, protect defenceless persons and prevent any insult or barbarity being exercised on the Prisoners." The militia, for the most part, seems to have exerted little leadership during the siege.[6]

The Kentucky frontier was on the front lines of the western theatre of the war, and Fort Boonesborough was a prime target. There was much to be done to ready the fort for an attack, since it lacked stockade along one side and was generally in poor repair. After his escape from the Shawnees, Boone reached the fort in late June; at the time of his arrival he was expecting the attack to take place within days. However, a delay of several weeks allowed the men to repair the stockade, strengthen the gates, and build two additional bastions on the southwesterly and southeasterly corners.[7]

The lack of defenders was a worrisome concern as well. Estimates vary from as low as thirty to as many as eighty men who garrisoned the fort. Women, estimated to number seventeen, participated in the defense by making bullets, reloading guns, and providing other support. At least two male slaves also defended the settlement. Regardless of the exact number, the fort's occupants were greatly outnumbered by the approaching enemy. Boone sent a messenger to the Holston settlements to ask Col. Arthur Campbell, the commander there, for reinforcements. He next headed an expedition that crossed the Ohio River and scouted the vicinity of the village where he had been kept a captive, learning that the Indians had gathered in large numbers and were on the march to the fort. Boone's party hastily retreated to Fort Boonesborough.[8]

The event began on Monday, September 7, when a large party of Indians was observed descending from Hackberry Ridge, the upland ridgeline west of the river terrace on which the fort stood. They came from the north and crossed the Kentucky River at a shallow point afterward known as Blackfish Ford, about one and a half miles downstream of the fort. They encamped along the western border of the river terrace about three hundred yards from the fort, a position that placed them beyond the average range of muzzle-loading rifles. Their large numbers and the many horses they brought with them must have been a chilling sight.

The Indians entered the contest under the impression that Boone would live up to his promise to deliver the settlers to them without resistance. Pompey approached as an unarmed emissary, waving a white flag, within 150 yards of the fort and called to Boone, reminding him of his promise and telling him of letters Governor Hamilton had sent regarding the surrender. Boone came out alone to talk to Chief Black Fish and accept the letters. The chief expressed his disappointment that Boone had left his adoptive family and asked him what he thought of the governor's terms. Boone briefly perused the letters, then, stalling for time, said that other men had become leaders in his place during his long captivity and that he had to consult with them.[9]

A second meeting was held the same day and was attended by Boone, William Bailey Smith, Col. Richard Callaway, Chief Black Fish, Chief Moluntha, Lieutenant DeQuindre, and Pompey. The meeting began with seemingly friendly rituals like shaking hands and expressing friendship; the Indians laid out panther skins for the participants to sit on, shaded them with bushes held over their heads, and offered seven roasted buffalo tongues. The underlying threat emerged during Chief Black Fish's oration. The Shawnee chief reiterated his expectation for the fort's surrender and exhibited a wampum belt figured with three rows of beads in red, black, and white. He explained the red as the warpath they had followed to the fort, white as the path of peaceful surrender, and black as the promise of death if they resisted. Having by this ominous act made his intentions clear, Black Fish agreed to a two-day truce to allow the fort's occupants to consider the governor's terms of surrender. The settlers primarily wanted the truce in the hope that the delay would give reinforcements time to arrive.[10]

The fort leaders gained some valuable information during this parley that influenced their subsequent actions. To their relief, there was no sign that their adversaries brought artillery that would have been able to breach the log walls of the fort. This discovery gave the settlers hope that the fort's walls would provide adequate protection. A comment by Black Fish that he had forty horses to carry the women, elderly, and children back to the Shawnee villages signaled his ignorance of the small numbers of defenders. The settlers were determined to conceal their actual numbers for as long as possible.[11]

Black Fish honored the two-day truce and made no hostile movements toward the fort, allowing settlers valuable time to make preparations. Settlers took advantage of the delay to send women to the springs to stockpile water, herd their livestock inside the fort, strip the fort garden of its remaining vegetables, replenish their supply of bullets, and make sure that their guns were in good repair. The structural repairs already made to the fort ensured that the settlers could barricade themselves within stout log walls and defend themselves from a greater position of security.[12]

At the close of the truce on Tuesday evening, September 8, Black Fish and some of his warriors approached the fort expecting a surrender. When Boone announced that the fort intended to put up a defense, Black Fish asked him why the settlers thought they had claim to the land. When Boone told him of the purchase by the Transylvania Company, a Cherokee in attendance confirmed it. Black Fish and his French Canadian advisors deliberated briefly and offered a new plan through the interpreter DuChaine. Citing instructions from Governor Hamilton to avoid bloodshed and saying that the purchase gave the settlers an equal claim to the land, they suggested a meeting to discuss a peace treaty. This seems to have been a cautious tactic by Black Fish, since he probably did not think the Cherokee had any right to sell the land. Given their superior numbers, the Indians might have simply elected to overrun the fort. That they did not may have been due to their belief that the fort was better manned than it was and their native reluctance to expose themselves to the high casualties a frontal assault threatened.[13]

While the settlers were surprised that hostilities did not immediately commence, they were wary of the Indians' motives and insisted on certain conditions for the parley. First, they rejected meeting inside the fort and selected instead the Lick Spring, a location close enough to allow the fort's riflemen to cover the position from the bastion nearest to it. Second, no more than twenty Indians could attend the meeting. The first parley was attended by Boone, Richard Callaway, William Bailey Smith, and William Buchanan as ranking officers along with Squire Boone, Flanders Callaway, Stephen Hancock, and William Hancock. Chief Black Fish, Lieutenant DeQuindre, and other unnamed chiefs, interpreters, and older attendants represented the other side. Much of the day was spent on largely symbolic acts such as passing the pipe, drinking whiskey, and feasting, but an agreement was reached by the end of the day.

Under the terms of the treaty, Black Fish and his warriors agreed to return home without any captives while the settlers were obligated to adhere to Governor Hamilton's authority by taking a British oath of allegiance. Following ratification of the treaty by British and Virginian authorities, both the Indians and the settlers could hunt and trade with each other on both sides of the Ohio River. The articles of agreement were stipulated in writing and another meeting was scheduled for the following day (Wednesday, September 9) to sign the treaty.[14]

The meeting began ominously when the white negotiators noticed that the elder Indian representatives that had accompanied Black Fish previously had been replaced by young men. Black Fish denied that the participants were different, but the change put the settlers on guard. After the treaty was signed, Black Fish insisted on a handshake with two warriors for each white man. Grasping each settler's hands and forearms, the Indians attempted to drag them away from the protection of the fort's guns; other Indians hiding in the nearby underbrush began to emerge. The men managed to free themselves, waved their hats to signal the fort's riflemen to cover them, and ran for the fort under heavy gunfire. Miraculously, all of them reached the fort unhurt except Squire Boone, who was wounded in the left shoulder. Another man was pinned down behind a stump but reached the fort safely after nightfall.[15]

Thereafter the siege ensued. On Thursday, September 10, the Indians first pretended to leave the premises, a strategy that fooled no one in the fort. When their stratagem failed to lure the settlers outside the safety of the stockade, the Indians concealed themselves as close to the fort as they dared and rained gunfire on every porthole and crack they could discern. Heavy gunfire continued all day and into the night.

The next day, Friday, September 11, the settlers were alerted to a new tactic when they noticed a plume of muddy water flowing from the riverbank into the main channel. To ascertain the cause, they built a watchtower on top of Richard Henderson's old cabin at the northeast corner of the fort, which was nearest to the mysterious muddy water. Concluding that the enemy was digging a tunnel from the riverbank toward the rear wall of the fort, the settlers began digging a countermine that started in the floor of Henderson's former kitchen cabin and continued through several more cabins. The fort stood seventy or eighty yards from the river. A tunnel of that length would have required adequate reinforcing supports, which do not seem to have been employed.[16]

About halfway through the siege, rain began to fall intermittently, a development that proved to have important benefits for the settlers. Although a well had been started to replace one that had run dry, it remained unfinished. The fort's water supplies were running low, and the besieged settlers welcomed the rain to replenish them. Another benefit became apparent on Sunday night, September 13, when the Indians began hurling flaming torches against the fort walls and shooting flaming arrows into the cabin roofs, all the while keeping up steady gunfire to deter efforts to extinguish the blazes. The tactic might have been effective except that the construction of the inward-sloping shed roofs with boards held in place with rib poles made it easy to simply push any board that caught fire off the roof and to the ground where it could be extinguished. The rain also soaked the logs of the stockade and cabin walls making them difficult to ignite, and the blazes fizzled out.[17]

The settlers endured the next two days as they tried to discern the progress of the tunnel, dug their countermine, and fired at every combatant who exposed himself. Bullets were not the only things flying back and forth between the combatants. Both sides kept up a steady flow of insults and taunts, each side "blackguarding" the other. Several factors improved the settlers' ability to resist. The biggest advantage was the fort itself and the physical barrier it presented to the attackers. Simply barricading themselves within the fort afforded significant protection from gunfire. The enemy combatants outnumbered the settlers four to one and might have been able to overcome the fort with a frontal assault, but such a tactic was generally not used by Native Americans because of the high risk of casualties. The Indians had ample places of cover from which to fire at the fort, but they suffered many more casualties than the settlers nonetheless. Excellent marksmanship among the settlers probably played a role.[18]

By the evening of Tuesday, September 15, the excavators working in the countermine could hear the sounds of tunnel digging, and the mood among the settlers was apprehensive and fearful throughout the rainy night. Wednesday, September 16, opened to silence from the tunnel and the sounds of horses and men in retreat. By noon all of their adversaries were gone, and the fort gates were opened to release the hungry, thirsty livestock. The settlers saw the remnants of the tunnel, collapsed on itself by the weight of the saturated, silty soil of the river terrace.[19]

The siege of Fort Boonesborough was unusual because of its ten-day length and the use of a particular siege tactic that was a departure from typical Native American modes of warfare. Indian raids were usually short in duration and involved limited numbers of participants. The number of enemy combatants, estimated at 444 by Boone, was unusually high. The Indians employed familiar strategies such as flaming arrows aimed at the log cabins and firing from concealment, but they also attempted to tunnel into the fort from the riverbank. The settlers attributed the decision to dig a tunnel to the French Canadians with the party. None of the strategies worked, and Chief Black Fish and his cohorts gave up in the face of rising casualties and the settlers' sustained resistance.

The failure of the siege underscored the overextended military resources of the British along the Ohio River, a weakness emphasized by George Rogers Clark's seizure of Kaskaskia in the summer just before the siege. That defeat was a blow to the British, and letters about the engagement and its aftermath dominated much of Governor Hamilton's correspondence. Conspicuously absent in official British records was mention of the failure of the Fort Boonesborough attack. In a letter dated August 17, 1778, to Governor Haldimand, Hamilton did mention that "at least 400 Native Americans" were assembled to attack "the Fort of Kentucke where Boone was taken last year" (Boone was actually taken captive with his salt makers at Lower Blue Licks), but no formal report of the expedition's failure was found among the preserved correspondence.[20]

Daniel Boone's conduct—actions that spared the lives of the salt makers and saved the fort from certain defeat—was not forgiven or understood by everyone in spite of his leadership and heroism during the siege. He was subjected to a court-martial at St. Asaph's called by Richard Callaway and Benjamin Logan to answer charges of treason. They cited his surrender of the salt makers in February, his seeming friendliness toward his Native American captors and the British, his risky Paint Lick expedition to spy on Native American actions just before the siege, and his behavior during the peace negotiations that some thought favored capitulation. He defended himself by insisting that his actions were patriotic subterfuges designed to mislead the enemy and stave off an attack until the fort could be readied. The members of the court-martial acquitted Boone, much to Callaway's and Logan's dismay. Even one of the captured salt makers concluded that "Colonel Boone was not to be blamed but lauded for his good management. . . . The course he pursued was the only wise, safe and prudent course he could pursue. . . . This treaty was the means of saving the host." Exonerated, Boone left for North Carolina to reunite with his family shortly after the trial, feeling bruised and insulted by the ordeal.[21]

As news of Fort Boonesborough's survival became common knowledge on the Kentucky frontier, settlers throughout the territory understood that the victory did more than save the fort; it was a significant achievement with ramifications for the defense of the Kentucky country generally. The Fort Boonesborough siege demonstrated that the strategy of stockaded forts was an effective defense even against an aggressive and substantial enemy force. The fort's survival ensured that it would continue to function as yet another strategic point of resistance against a formidable foe. While the future was still far from certain in terms of threats yet to come, the settlers must have reflected on the difficulties of the past two years and felt more hopeful that they could prevail and persevere toward a more peaceful future.

5

ESTABLISHING A TOWN

Shortly after the Great Siege of Boonesborough concluded in the settlers' favor, the Virginia House of Delegates on November 4, 1778, passed the resolution that declared the Transylvania purchase null and void. This legislation paved the way for the residents at Fort Boonesborough to chart a new course. The Transylvania Company partners were awarded an extensive tract of land in the Green and Ohio River drainages of Kentucky as compensation for their loss, and they shifted attention to developing that area. However, some of the Transylvania Company partners did not completely abandon their interests in the Boonesborough area, and one tried to initiate the establishment of a town under conditions favorable to him and some of his friends. In response to an act passed by the Virginia General Assembly in May 1779 that allowed for the establishment of towns in the western lands, Nathaniel Hart "warmly recommended to the Inhabitants of this fort to lay off a Town," and he put forward the names of Richard Callaway, Nathaniel Hart, George Madin, James Estill, and Robert Cartright to serve as trustees. When the settlers were asked if there were any objections to these men acting as trustees, they said nothing, even though they privately disagreed. The fact that the settlers raised no vocal objections at the time while privately disagreeing strenuously speaks to the social gulf between them and Hart, who was perceived to be a gentleman. The settlers did not consider themselves to be in the same class, but they were not willing to concede control in deference to Hart's social position.[1]

The May 1779 act provided for families that had settled in villages or townships for security and had laid off lots and cultivated crops communally but did not have title. It further directed that 640 acres "whereon such villages and towns are situate, and to which no other person hath a previous legal claim, shall not be entered for or surveyed, but shall be reserved for the use and benefit of the said inhabitants until a true representation of their case can be made to the general assembly." This provision was particularly germane to the Boonesborough settlers and provided a means by which they could seek a town charter on terms that suited them.[2]

A group of thirty-two men, who described themselves as "the Distressed Inhabitants of Boonsfort," filed a petition for a 640-acre tract they wished to have designated as a town "for the reception of traders." The petitioners opened with a detailed explanation of how and by what methods the fort/township was first settled. They explained that in 1775 the Transylvania Company "agree'd to lay it off into two acre tending lotts which was to be given up the next year for the use of a Town and Town commons." In return for temporary custody of the lots, every man was entitled to a free town lot as well as five hundred acres of land, subject to a corn crop being grown. After Indian threats drove many of the settlers out of Kentucky, Richard Henderson "had the fence that was made by the people broke and took the rails and fenced in betwixt twenty and thirty acres of the most convenient ground next the fort which has been held under sd [said] Henderson ever since except the value of one or two acres that was taken for gardians [gardens] for people in sd fort." The settlers were upset that they had to improve land at a greater distance from the fort, which put them at greater risk to their lives. They included a list of "the names of every person kill'd and taken belonging to this sd fort since the time of its being first settled" as further proof of their worthiness.[3]

The petition further outlined additional complaints about the trustees, the proposed town boundaries, and the terms for claiming land. The petitioners complained that three of the trustees proposed by Hart (George Madin, Robert Cartwright, and probably James Estill) were "intire strangers to us" and "not even settlers in the country." Moreover, the petitioners disagreed with Hart's proposal to reserve two hundred acres on the south side of the Kentucky River and three hundred acres on the north side for a town and town commons. A large, steep hill bounded the land on the north side of the river (in present-day Clark County), making it extremely difficult to transport timber down from anyplace on that side. The settlers suspected that Hart had encouraged this plan in order to obtain a large tract upstream of the proposed town site where he had in 1775 established a station for himself. John Luttrell, another Transylvania partner, claimed land within the proposed township on its southwest side.[4]

The terms under which settlers could claim town lots were deemed unfair because no distinction was made between people who had arrived early (or widows of such) and those who had just arrived. In the petitioners' view, early arrivals, who had settled at great personal risk, and widows deserved special consideration in town lot selection. The requirement that every lot holder build a hewed-log or frame house with a shingled or clapboard roof and a brick, stone, or mud chimney by February 1780 also rankled, since several of the petitioners had no horses to haul timber.[5]

The petitioners described how they asked Richard Callaway that a fair election of trustees be held, promising him that he could still be a trustee, but he refused to serve under any conditions other than those set forth by Hart. They may have gone to Callaway because he had a reputation of leadership, courage, and resolve that situated him favorably with many settlers. When he refused to cooperate, the petitioners asked that 640 acres be established as the Town of "Boonsborough" and that James Estill, David Gass, John Holder, John South, Pemberton Rawlings (also spelled "Rollins"), Stephen Hancock, and John Martin be named as trustees. None of these men were former partners in the Transylvania Company, and only James Estill had been named as a potential trustee previously. The petition also asked that each settler be entitled to draw one free lot and have three years to build a house on the land. The petitioners made special mention of single men who lived at the fort and helped to protect the inhabitants and asked that they also be entitled to a town lot under the same terms. This inclusion is significant; it may have been done as an incentive to retain single men valued for their role as defenders. Finally, they requested that the town lands be laid "upon the south side of the Kentucky river" rather than on both sides.

The petition was submitted by Richard Callaway to the Virginia Assembly on October 16, 1779. Callaway was a delegate and was duty-bound to submit the petition even though he had initially resisted the settlers' desire to name trustees of their choosing and seemed to have sided with Nathaniel Hart in his attempt to establish a town on terms more similar to the original plan of the Transylvania Company. He agreed to submit the petition in the form the settlers stipulated, perhaps in anticipation of future benefits.[6]

While Callaway was presenting the town petition to the General Assembly, he also requested that he be granted the right to establish a public ferry across the Kentucky River. This lucrative business was granted to him, his heirs, and his assignees as long as they complied with the directions of the enabling act. The act stipulated standard rates for various types of traffic, from a single individual and horse to wheeled conveyances of all sorts, hogsheads of tobacco, and livestock. The Kentucky River at Boonesborough could be crossed on foot during the dry summer season, but for the remainder of the year, crossing required a boat. A ferry concession not only rewarded the owner; it was a boon to the town by providing a means of crossing a major waterway during times of high water.[7]

The Virginia Assembly passed "An Act for Establishing the Town of Boonsborough in the County of Kentuckey" during the session that commenced on October 4, 1779. The act authorized the establishment of a town on twenty acres that had already been laid out in forty lots; another fifty acres were set aside for additional lots and streets. A tract of 640 acres was designated for a town commons, which usually served as communal grazing and haying land for inhabitants who did not own property. Community events such as festivals or other gatherings were also generally held on the commons. The act appointed Richard Callaway, Charles Mimms Thruston, Levin Powell, Edmund Taylor, James Estill, Edward Bradley, John Kennedy, David Gass, Pemberton Rawlings, and Daniel Boone as trustees. The assembly's choice of trustees differed significantly from the recommendations that the petitioners had put forward: only three men out of the seven recommended by the petitioners were named. Most of the trustees appointed had not signed the original petition, and some of them did not actually live in Boonesborough at the time. Significantly, Richard Callaway was named a trustee, even though he had initially refused to serve. Daniel Boone was not politically well connected, and his lack of elite status would have excluded him from consideration under normal circumstances, but he was admired as a leader and had been involved with Boonesborough from its inception. His selection thus fulfilled the settlers' desire to have familiar men serving as trustees. Boone was still in North Carolina, where he had gone to rejoin his family after the siege in 1778, and he was not involved in the discussions for the town. He may not have known his name was put forward as a trustee. Moreover, the inclusion of Callaway as a trustee threatened a potential conflict since Callaway had been a principal accuser in Boone's court-martial and feelings still ran high over the incident.[8]

The selection of trustees who were not the petitioners' choices is puzzling because some of those named could not have had much if any personal commitment to the proposed town. Thruston, Taylor, and Powell were not in Kentucky at the time. All three were land speculators who obtained thousands of acres of Kentucky land in the mid-1780s. Their selection was undoubtedly politically motivated, perhaps intended to further their land investments in some way or to repay political favors. Boone returned to Fort Boonesborough briefly in the fall of 1779, then moved to what is now Fayette County to establish his station near the present-day village of Athens. He never lived at Boonesborough again. James Estill had been in Kentucky in 1775 to mark and improve a claim he later received from the land court. He came back sometime after the siege of 1778 and lived at Fort Boonesborough until around 1780, when he moved away to establish his own station. David Gass, John Kennedy, and Edward Bradley had all been members of Daniel Boone's road cutting party. David Gass and his family joined Estill at his station in spring of 1780. John Kennedy was the brother of Gen. Thomas Kennedy, who in 1780 had commanded a company during the Battle of King's Mountain in present-day South Carolina. John Kennedy settled a station in present-day Garrard County in 1780 and was killed in the Cumberland Gap on December 27 of that year, just a few months after marrying Mary Anderson at Fort Boonesborough in April. Edward Bradley had raised corn in 1775, which entitled him to a settlement and preemption on Jessamine Creek in present-day Jessamine County; he applied to the land court during its session at Fort Boonesborough in 1779. Whether by death, distance, or disinclination, the appointed trustees were not likely to be effective, as events over the next few years attested.[9]

Boonesborough's development during this time was hampered by the trustees' desultory attention to their duties. The provisions allowed for the replacement of trustees who refused to act or who died or moved away by empowering the freeholders of the town to elect replacements. The process required the other trustees to notify the sheriff of the need for a replacement; the sheriff then notified the freeholders, who chose and voted on new trustees. However, a town inhabitant could only enjoy all the rights and privileges of being a freeholder after he built a house or otherwise improved his lot. In the first few years of the town's existence, this provision seems to have been an impediment. No deeds of early lot sales were filed in the county clerk's office, and the trustees were not replaced until 1787, even though the men appointed in 1779 accomplished very little.[10]

The first task required of the trustees was to create a town plan showing the lots and streets already laid out on the initial twenty acres as well as the additional fifty acres. Once the town plan was surveyed and filed with the Kentucky County court, the trustees were empowered to convey lots to purchasers. Lot sales required the purchaser to build "a dwelling-house sixteen feet square at least, with a brick, stone, or dirt chimney, to be finished fit for habitation" within three years, at which time a deed was issued. The Boonesborough trustees should have filed the town plan and the deeds for lots at the county seat of Harrodsburg. Problems, some of which are outlined above, arose immediately and resulted in the trustees failing to properly file a town plan or any of the early deeds for town lot purchases.[11]

Although a plan was not filed at the time Boonesborough was established, two plats were surveyed by William Calk, an early settler and surveyor who first came to Kentucky in 1775. The plats include one showing a seven-hundred-acre tract on the south and west side of the Kentucky River where the town was located and another showing sixty-six numbered half-acre in-lots plus an unnumbered lot called the Spring Lot. Calk kept a journal in 1775 that made reference to the fifty-four lots that Henderson surveyed on April 21–22. Calk family tradition claims that he helped Henderson conduct the survey, but his journal does not refer to his direct involvement, stating simply that "they [referring to Henderson and others] begin laying out lots in the town" on April 21 and "they finish laying out lots" on April 22. He was one of the men who drew for a lot on April 24, but on April 26 he and his companions began "building us a house & a plaise of Defence to keep the indians off" on land at the mouth of Otter Creek upstream from Boonesborough. Between 1775 and 1778 Calk made several trips between his home on the Potomac River, where his wife and children lived, and Kentucky. In 1778 he moved his family to Kentucky to live permanently, and he remained in the Boonesborough area working as a surveyor until 1799, when he and his family moved to Montgomery County.[12]

The documents found among Calk's papers do not originate from Henderson's survey of lots in 1775; rather, they are related to the establishment of the town of Boonesborough in 1779. The large plat of seven hundred acres is similar, but not identical, to the plat that was eventually filed with the county clerk in December 1809 and formally recorded in July 1810. The southern boundary of the Calk plat extended to the mouth of Otter Creek. The 1809 plat shifted the southern boundary northward. This change is probably due to the town claim covering 640 acres in accordance with

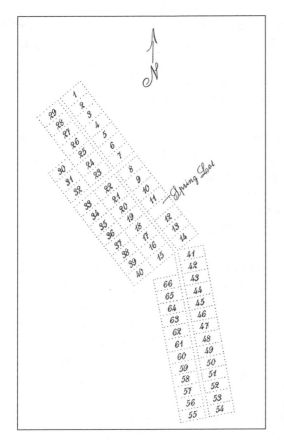

William Calk surveyed lots
for the proposed town of
Boonesborough c. 1779.

Virginia law. The 60 acres excluded from the 1809 plat corresponds to a 60-acre land grant awarded to William Calk. Calk's 60 acres were surveyed in 1783 and granted in 1786; the 700-acre plat he surveyed for the town trustees probably was an earlier survey that was replaced later with another plat that conformed to the 640 acres designated by the town charter and allowed for Calk's 60 acres.[13] The separate plat showing sixty-six half-acre in-lots and the list of lot owners for lots one through forty also conform to stipulations in the town charter. The lots numbered one through forty are arranged in three rows oriented north 45 degrees east. The plat is accompanied by a list of lot owners for the first forty lots (see table 1). These lots are referenced in the petition for the town charter as having already been laid out. Two more rows of lots numbered 41 through 66 are shown running north-south at the south end of the three rows. This section of lots was surveyed on thirty-three of the fifty acres designated for additional lots that had not yet been laid out when the petition was filed. The orientation of the sixty-six lots more or less mirrors the angle of the bend of the Kentucky River where the fort site is located. Five of the trustees named by the town charter are on the list, as are seven of the men who signed the original petition sent to the Virginia Assembly.[14]

Although neither of the two plats is dated, the list of lot owners for the first forty lots provides the key to the date of the documents. Most of the signatories were men who had been at Fort Boonesborough or in the area for several years. Other names on the list include Nicholas Anderson and Edward Williams, who did not come to Kentucky until 1779, and the sole woman, Elizabeth Horn, who was a widow. (Her husband, Aaron, was killed in the fall of 1778.) These clues suggest that the map was created in late 1779 or early 1780 in response to the stipulations set out by the Virginia General Assembly when that body approved the town charter. Names excluded from the list include the four trustees who had no connection to Boonesborough at all: Charles Mimms Thruston, Levin Powell, Edmund Taylor, and Edward Bradley. Interestingly, Daniel Boone, one of the trustees, did not appear on the list either. He had moved to his station near present-day Athens in 1779 and does not seem to have actively engaged as a trustee in the town's development.[15]

The approval of a town charter should have been a catalyst for serious development, and the plats and list of lot owners in Calk's papers indicate that development was initiated. The 1779 town charter gave purchasers three years to build on their town lots, but frontier conditions may have made this stipulation difficult to meet, and some of the early claimants appear to have allowed their claims to lapse. Lapsed claims may explain why twenty-one of the forty in-lots on the list in Calk's papers were resold by the town trustees in 1795, 1809, 1817, and 1825, first to John Halley and then to other purchasers after the trustees repossessed Halley's lots. In any case, the plats in the Calk papers reflect the earliest years of the town before all of the town in-lots and out-lots had been laid out and the final boundaries of the town claim were established.

Fort Boonesborough continued to serve as an important point of contact and communication for the large numbers of settlers who streamed into Kentucky in 1779–1780. Part of the motivation for this increased emigration was the passage of a land law by the Virginia General Assembly in May 1779

Table 1. Lot Owners in Boonesborough, c. 1779

Lot Number	Owner
1	Richard Callaway (trustee)
2	J. Duncan
3	P. Madden
4	Samuel Estill (petitioner)
5	Bartlett Searcy
6	Bland Ballard
7	Robert Cartwright
8	Thomas Doyl
9	Hart & Hankin
10	Charles Tate
11	John South, Ensign
12	John Kennedy (trustee)
13	Ambrose Coffee (petitioner)
14	John Webber
15	John South, Sr. (petitioner)
16	Nathaniel Hart
17	James Estill (trustee)
18	Edward Nelson
19	David Gass (trustee)
20	William Johnson
21	Jesse Oldham
22	John Bullock (petitioner)
23	John Constant
24	Pemberton Rawlings (trustee)
25	Jesse Peak
26	(illegible) Watkin
27	Edward Williams
28	Nicholas Anderson
29	Nicholas Proctor (petitioner)
30	Thomas South
31	John Bost
32	J. Bennett
33	P. Sterns
34	V. Sterns
35	F. Leeper
36	Elizabeth Horn
37	Jacob Sterns (petitioner)
38	Stephen Hancock
39	Henry Smucker
40	Ruben Searcy

that articulated the conditions by which land could be claimed in unpatented territory and, not incidentally, which raised money to continue the war for independence. The increased emigration swelled the population of the major areas of settlement: Boonesborough, St. Asaph's (Logan's Station), Lexington, and the Harrodsburg area. Settlers were focused on claiming and improving their own land and, for the most part, spent relatively short periods of time in the large forts before moving out to their land claims to grow corn and build cabins.

Since the Revolutionary War was still raging and Native American raids and attacks continued to plague the Kentucky frontier, settler families often congregated in defensible residential sites called stations. Several families would join forces to build cabins close to one another on private land, and these groupings were sometimes further protected by stockade. The families often were related, had traveled to Kentucky together, or had past associations. Compared to the earliest years of the revolution, the central Kentucky area saw a fourfold increase in the number of stations established between 1778 and 1782. Forts like the one at Boonesborough were critical sanctuaries during times of threat and major nodes of a network of defensible sites developed as emigrants radiated out to establish stations.[16]

Fort Boonesborough was one of five locations in the Kentucky district where commissioners held court to grant and resolve land claims made under the new act. The land commissioners held court December 17–31, 1779, at Fort Boonesborough, and many settlers traveled to the fort to file their claims, including Richard Henderson, who appeared before the court on December 29. He filed a claim for 1,400 acres near Boonesborough for John Luttrell, presenting evidence that Luttrell had grown a corn crop in 1775. Henderson also presented a claim on behalf of John Luttrell as heir to Thomas Luttrell for 1,400 acres on Boons Fork of Silver Creek adjoining William Hays's land. On December 23 Richard Callaway filed a claim for Richard Henderson for 1,400 acres on Otter Creek, presenting evidence that Henderson had raised corn in 1775, 1776, 1778, and 1779.[17]

Fort Boonesborough was not directly attacked for the remainder of the war; however, attacks and threats in the Kentucky district occurred often enough to keep settlers on their guard. In mid-May 1780 two men, Abraham Chaplin and one Hendricks, escaped captivity with the Wyandots and arrived at the fort to warn of an impending attack by a force of British troops, Canadians, and Indians who were coming to Kentucky with cannon.

The force arrived in June, but Fort Boonesborough was spared. Instead, the expedition attacked and captured Martin's and Ruddell's Stations, less than forty miles from Fort Boonesborough. Nearly four hundred settlers were captured. While Fort Boonesborough remained unscathed on that occasion, the incident was a jarring reminder of the threats it and other settlements on the frontier faced. Several of the fort's inhabitants were killed while they were away from the settlement. Richard Callaway and Pemberton Rawlings were building a boat for the ferry operation Callaway was starting when they were attacked on March 8, 1780. Callaway was scalped, mutilated, stripped, and rolled in the mud, while Rawlings received mortal injuries from which he died later. Nathaniel Hart Sr. was killed while traveling on July 22, 1782. All three men had been prominent in Fort Boonesborough affairs since the Transylvania Company days. Hart was a former Transylvania Company partner. Callaway and Rawlings were serving as town trustees at the time of their deaths. All three men served in the militia, and Callaway was a member of the Virginia legislature and a justice on Kentucky's first court. Both Hart and Callaway had large families with underage children, and Rawlings was engaged to Callaway's daughter. Their deaths left widows and fatherless children and robbed the town of influential leaders.[18]

Preliminary articles of peace signed on November 30, 1782, followed by the finalization of the Treaty of Paris on September 3, 1783, ended the colonists' War of Independence and extinguished the need for a defensive fort at Boonesborough. Even though Indian raids and attacks continued along the Ohio River and at a few isolated settlements until 1794, when the Battle of Fallen Timbers finally brought peace, Fort Boonesborough remained undisturbed. Within a year of the war's end, the fort began losing its defensive architectural character. John Rankin, who spent the summer of 1784 at Boonesborough, told the Rev. John Dabney Shane that the picketing was all gone by the time he arrived, but the cabins were occupied and the "bastends" still stood. As the threat of hostilities diminished, efforts were renewed to develop Boonesborough as a viable, prosperous town. In 1785 Lincoln County was subdivided into Madison, Bourbon, and Mercer Counties. Boonesborough became part of Madison County and unsuccessfully vied with the community of Paint Lick for the county seat; both places lost to a new location that was named Milford.[19]

In 1787, when the Virginia Assembly learned that the acting trustees were developing property elsewhere and ceased to maintain an interest in

Boonesborough's welfare, it passed another act to amend the 1779 act that created the town. The amendment named as new trustees Gen. Thomas Kennedy, Aaron Lewis, Robert Rhodes, Green Clay, Archibald Woods, Benjamin Bedford, John Sappinton, William Irvine, David Crews, and Higgerson Grubbs. Most if not all of these men resided in Madison County, and several held influential positions on the county court. However, few of them lived in Boonesborough proper or owned property there. The trustees appointed in 1787 performed no better than the previous trustees, and they were replaced by 1792.[20]

Boonesborough also missed out when Kentucky became a state in 1792. A group of thirty-five men offered £2,630 and 18,550 acres of land to the new state government to locate the capital at Boonesborough. Among the men were some familiar names: Green Clay, a Boonesborough trustee who settled in Madison County and built a large farm named Clermont; John Holder, who settled on the Kentucky River in Clark County not far from Boonesborough; William Calk, who settled on Otter Creek; James French, who lived at Boonesborough until he moved to Montgomery County; and others who lived in or near Boonesborough and the surrounding counties. A capital at Boonesborough would have benefitted the economic interests of all these men. However, their offer was rejected in favor of Frankfort, which was more centrally located, and Boonesborough lost its chance to develop into a major center of government.[21]

The decade of the 1790s was a period of town building and development in Kentucky, and the legislature was often involved in passing acts to facilitate the process and aid town trustees in their responsibilities. In 1793 the state legislature passed an act that stipulated restrictions and assigned penalties for such activities as causing obstructions in the streets, racing horses within city limits, and showing stud horses. In a clause unique to Boonesborough, the legislature authorized the town trustees to sell an acre of land that was most suitable for erecting a saltworks. The strongest salt springs at Boonesborough were in Sycamore Hollow. The act seems to have been intended to create a lucrative business opportunity that would ultimately benefit the town. Although no deed has been found to indicate that the trustees sold the acre lot, one of the springs in Sycamore Hollow was enclosed sometime before 1797 when it needed repair. William Calk was involved in the "Plan for reparing the Lick in Boonesborough," which specified that the wall [is] to be cleared as low as it was before; the wall to be made good with stone and mortar two feet above the floor, a post and rail fence 12 feet square round the well, posts of black locust and rails of locust or walnut, posts to be eight inches square set three inches in the ground, first rail to set in the posts under the floor. A trough 40 feet long, eight inches wide & 12 inches wide in the clear. Bottom & sides 3 inches thick to be set level on the ground and let through the wall so as to receive the water and convey it from the well. The posts & rails to be four feet above the floor. Inside between the wall and fence to be filled with dirt and well rammed nearly as high as the top of the wall. Rails to 4 inches thick let through the posts by a tenant [tenon] 4 by 3 inches. The two top rails all round pined [pinned] through the posts with an Inch black locust pinn. The floor to be laid 2 feet thick with stone.[22]

In 1795 the trustees held a public auction to sell town lots. The main purchaser was John Halley, who bought at least sixty-nine in-lots and seventy-nine out-lots, but a deed was never filed by the trustees. Halley had moved to Boonesborough before 1778, and he ran a water-powered mill on Otter Creek, farmed, raised livestock, and took shipments of tobacco and other products by boat to New Orleans. Many years later, in 1821, an act naming new trustees made reference to Halley's 1795 purchase. The act stated that he purchased forty-three lots, but, "owing to the distant residence of the trustees of said town, and the little interest they had therein," he was unable to persuade them to finalize his deeds even though he had offered the purchase money repeatedly. The trustees put off filing the deeds for reasons not stated in the act. In an 1805 list of property holdings, Halley listed only three Boonesborough lots (in-lots 27, 28, and 29) among many other, larger, rural tracts. The 1821 act seems to have mentioned Halley's purchase to document the lack of effective trustees, but it did not direct that a deed be filed for him nor was a deed ever found reflecting the 1795 purchase.[23]

Halley's purchase of a majority of the town's in-lots and out-lots and the inaction of the trustees strongly suggest that the town of Boonesborough remained underdeveloped. The Kentucky legislature passed an act in 1795 that gave lot owners who had begun building on their lots twelve additional months to complete the construction without the threat of forfeiture. This act extended to four years the amount of time lot owners had to build in compliance with the town charter. Efforts to grow the town were stymied as trustees continued to cycle on and off the roster with little to show for their efforts. The lack of deeds filed in the county clerk's office makes an assessment of lot sales difficult. William Calk bought five lots (12, 97, 81, 118, and 62) on December 25, 1797, for five pounds twelve shillings and kept a receipt among his papers, but no deed was found in the county deed books for this purchase. Other purchases may have been made and not formally filed, precluding a true assessment of town development.

In December 1809 the trustees then in place finally filed a town plat with the Madison County clerk, and it was ordered to be recorded at the July court of 1810. The plat covered 640 acres and showed 119 half-acre in-lots, 118 two-acre out-lots, and streets on the west side of the Kentucky River north of the mouth of Otter Creek. The in-lots were concentrated on the lower elevation of the broad terrace inside the bend of the Kentucky River, while most of the out-lots were on the uplands known as Hackberry Ridge. The plat also showed a "buring [burying] ground" and a "Lick commons" (present-day Sycamore Hollow). The cemetery lot contained the former fort and was bordered by the lick commons and the Kentucky River. Boons Road more or less bisected the town and terminated at the ferry. Spring Road ran from Boons Road to an unnumbered in-lot containing a spring that is still partially visible near the park's maintenance building. These roads remained in use and even today are preserved with some modifications as part of the park's road system.[24]

Lot sales continued to be sluggish and sporadic. Green Clay bought twenty-two in-lots for $500 on December 11, 1809 (Madison County Deed Book G:350). The low price suggests that the lots were vacant, and it is unlikely that Clay was expected to improve them before a deed was formally conveyed to him. This sale was the only one filed that year or in the years that followed until February 5, 1817, when Margaret Branaham paid $400 for in-lot 30 (Madison County Deed Book M:64). This lot's location on the old Boons Road (now State Road 388) was less prone to flooding. Its price suggests that it had a house on it.[25]

The Kentucky Legislature passed an act in November 1821 that acknowledged the lack of "regular" trustees and, "owing to few inhabitants residing therein," directed that the town commons be divided and sold off. Green Clay, Thomas Lindsay, John Halley, Sam Buckley, Hiram Feamster, Dan Bentley, and Richard Oldham were appointed trustees to serve until

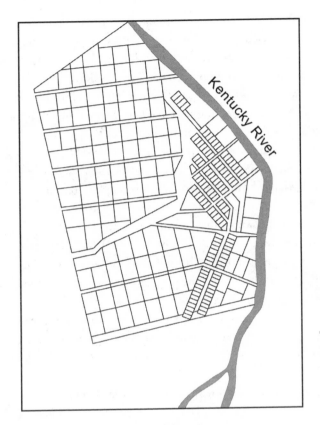

This expanded
Boonesborough town
plat was filed with
the county clerk in
December 1809.

January 1, 1823; thereafter, the county court was to appoint seven trustees annually to convey deeds. Few lots were sold until 1825, when sixty-nine in-lots and seventy-nine out-lots were conveyed to six men in eight deeds. Jesse Hedges, Elkanah Bush, Tilmon Bush, Thomas Lindsay, Green Clay, and Daniel Breck bought a total of 144 in- and out-lots. These deeds were filed with the Madison County clerk's office, and no further actions were recorded for town trustees conducting any official business for Boonesborough afterward, even though trustees were appointed by the county until 1831. Thereafter, all sales were between private individuals.[26]

Although the town plan for Boonesborough hints at ambitious plans for a large town, the community was never more than a very modest size. Gauging the number of inhabitants over time is complicated. The archival record contains clues at various points during the site's history but rarely offers hard numbers. Not only did the actual number of residents shift widely over time, the number of short-term visitors complicates an already complex, rapidly changing picture in which white men are accounted for—but rarely their wives and children—and slaves are only mentioned when they were involved in incidents remembered for other reasons. Town building attempts were launched by men who had a wide variety of vested interests but did not always live there. Boonesborough's population waxed and waned, sometimes within a matter of months. This had been true from the very start. Boone's road cutters and Henderson's party brought an estimated forty to fifty settlers in early spring 1775, and more came later in the spring, but many left within a few weeks or months. Richard Henderson chronicled in his journal that by June 6, 1775, an "abundance of people going away—Selling their lots etc.," and the losses continued into July. Population dipped substantially in 1776–1777 when emigration to Kentucky was hindered by heightened Native American resistance. By 1778 the fort housed families, single men serving in the local militia, and slaves, and the population possibly exceeded one hundred people. Passage of the Virginia land law in 1779 brought many new settlers into Kentucky, and many visited Fort Boonesborough. Some stayed on to help build a town, but most stopped only briefly before moving on to occupy their land claims. The town building efforts were stymied by indifferent trustees and an ever-shifting cast of characters.[27]

Adding to the confusion over the town's population is a document in the archives of the Canada entitled "No. 11—Observations upon the Colony of Kentucky," written by Lord Guy Carleton Dorchester to Thomas Townshend, Lord Sydney, in 1789. Dorchester reported that "Boonsburg" had "upwards of one hundred and twenty houses." The report did not indicate where or how its information was obtained; Dorchester was serving as governor of the Province of Quebec at the time, and Lord Sydney was home secretary to the English prime minister William Pitt. Dorchester obviously relied on reports by others. The Canadian report may have included upland regions of the 640-acre town claim in its estimate, but even allowing for the larger area, the reported density and, by inference, population, seems very high. All other evidence points to a much smaller population.[28]

The 1810 census was the only federal census to enumerate Boonesborough as a separate town. In that year only sixty-eight people inhabiting eight households were listed, hardly a thriving metropolis. William, Elisha, and Smith Estes each headed their own household and accounted for fourteen people. William Estes lived with his wife. Elisha

52

Estes and his wife had six children in their household. Smith Estes and his wife lived with two children. Other households were headed by Edmund Freeman, who lived with his wife and two slaves; John Gore, who had a wife and three children in his home; Thomas Stephens (a trustee), who lived with his wife, ten children, and nine slaves; Presly Wilkerson, who lived with his wife, seven children, and two slaves; and Thomas Taylor, who lived in a house adjacent to the tobacco warehouses with his wife, nine children, and two slaves.[29]

The establishment of Boonesborough as a tobacco inspection point boosted the town's economic vitality to some extent, but the seasonal nature of the inspections did not encourage long-term, consistent investment in urban development and growth. Tobacco inspections were intended to regulate and standardize the quality of tobacco offered to market. Tobacco producers took their product in hogsheads to the warehouses primarily in the fall. A licensed and bonded inspector opened and inspected the contents of each hogshead, assessed the class and grade, marked and repacked the hogshead, and issued a negotiable receipt to the owner. The receipts could then be sold by auction, and the buyer presented them to the inspector and picked up the purchase. The hogsheads were stored in warehouses until the buyers picked them up. Over many years, the hogshead inspection system gradually gave way to the loose-leaf auction system in the larger towns and cities.[30]

The Virginia General Assembly passed an act on December 24, 1787, that established numerous tobacco inspection points, many of them in Kentucky. That same year the assembly allowed tobacco to be used to pay taxes. The acts were intended to encourage production, but Kentucky producers were hampered by the Spanish authorities who controlled the Mississippi River trade and levied prohibitive export duties. The Pinckney Treaty guaranteed free American navigation of the river and repealed the requirement for export duties in 1795. The Louisiana Purchase in 1803 removed all fear of restrictions on river navigation and ushered in a period of profitable tobacco production that lasted twelve years.[31]

Numerous places in Kentucky began constructing tobacco warehouses after the act was passed in 1787. The facility built at Boonesborough was named Boon's Warehouse, but its operator was John Halley, who appears to have proceeded slowly. In 1788 Halley was summoned to court to answer whether he intended to build a public warehouse at Boonesborough. He does not appear to have moved forward on the project, and in 1791 Jacob Starnes was appointed to build a warehouse. Periodic warehouse inspection reports described architectural details of the warehouses, mentioned their storage capacity, and stated how many hogsheads of tobacco were accepted annually. Reports were usually filed in the fall after the cured tobacco crop had been turned in and processed for shipment to markets. The first warehouse was built on a stone pillar foundation, framed, weatherboarded, and shingled. The structure measured one hundred by forty feet and had a storage capacity of 130 hogsheads. In 1796 the inspectors stated that they inspected only two hogsheads from Boon's Warehouse that year and that repairs of the locks and hinges were needed. Matters had improved by 1799, when sixty hogsheads were inspected and shipped, and the warehouse was deemed "in good Order for [receiving] Tobacco." The same conditions prevailed the next year when fifty-nine hogsheads were inspected.[32]

The tobacco market experienced rapid growth after 1795, but the Napoleonic wars and governmental decrees in Europe that followed made American exports of tobacco practically impossible by 1807 and demand lessened dramatically. The War of 1812 also damaged the foreign market severely and greatly curtailed American exports. Nevertheless, Kentucky farmers continued to profitably grow tobacco for market even as crops such as hemp and increased livestock production grew in market share. An October 5, 1807, report stated that Boon's Warehouse took in 170 hogsheads of tobacco. Samuel South reported on the condition of the weights and scales on November 2, stating that there was "a good scale house and one good pair of scales with an iron beam 24 fifty sixes, 1 twenty-eight & ditto fourteen one ditto seven lb. [weight] all of which have been adjusted by the Lexington standard as I am told and marked TL Town of Lexington."[33]

In 1809 local planter and trustee Green Clay purchased in-lots 33 and 34, where the earlier warehouse stood, and probably built the second tobacco warehouse adjacent to it. An 1810 inspection report described this new construction as a "stone body warehouse well shingled with joint shingles" on a stone pillar foundation that measured one hundred feet in length and thirty-three and a half feet in width. A thirty-foot section was open. The rest of the building was accessed by a door hung on iron hooks. The new building housed the weighing scales. The two warehouses took in 237 hogsheads of tobacco that year.[34]

The War of 1812 seems to have curtailed tobacco inspections at

Boonesborough, although the weights and scales were regularly inspected, perhaps in anticipation of a resumption of trade. However, reports of the amounts of tobacco inspected yearly are sporadic, suggesting a sluggish market and the possibility that there were years in which no inspections took place at all. An exception was 1817, when a report stated that 726 hogsheads of tobacco had been received and 605 delivered, leaving 121 hogsheads on hand. By 1821 the amount inspected was only 240 hogsheads, increasing slightly the following year to 254. Thereafter, reports referred only to inspection of the weights and scales up through 1836. By the 1830s tobacco production was moving out of the Bluegrass region to the western part of the state. In 1837 Cassius M. and Mary Jane Clay, heirs of Green Clay, sold the two inspection warehouses to Samuel Halley, who was buying up Boonesborough lots and consolidating the land into a large farm. No reports of inspections of the weights and scales or of hogsheads of tobacco were filed after this date, and it is likely that the warehouses were used as barns thereafter.[35]

The story of Boonesborough, from the construction of its famous fort to persistent but largely fruitless attempts to build a prosperous town, is largely a tale of high-stakes gambles, ambitious plans, disappointments, and eventual erasure. Over time the area covered by the town claim was consolidated within a few families, deeds ceased to include town lot numbers, and the land was converted largely to agricultural use. The ineffective urban development attempts are graphically shown on an undated map drawn by Thomas Hinde for Lyman Draper. The map was based on Hinde's familiarity with the area, most likely dating from the early nineteenth century. Snaking through the center of the map is the Kentucky River and its recognizable broad bend that delineated the eastern boundary of Boonesborough. Twenty landmarks identify the "old fort," houses, ferry buildings, a tavern, a wool factory, a barn, mills, and Otter Creek, most appearing on the Madison County side but including a few landmarks on the Clark County side. An archaeological survey of the Boonesborough bottomland in 1987, which encompassed an area from the northern park boundary (the current limestone quarry) to the mouth of Otter Creek to the south, identified many of these dispersed sites.[36]

The first landmark listed is labelled merely "old fort" and does not specify that it was Fort Boonesborough. Considering Hinde's almost reverent description of Fort Boonesborough's important role in the settling of Kentucky, his omission of the name is curious but is probably because the

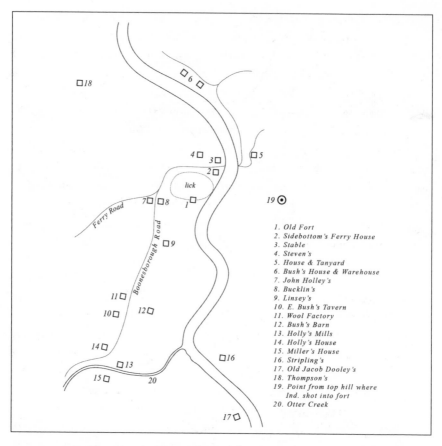

1. Old Fort
2. Sidebottom's Ferry House
3. Stable
4. Steven's
5. House & Tanyard
6. Bush's House & Warehouse
7. John Holley's
8. Bucklin's
9. Linsey's
10. E. Bush's Tavern
11. Wool Factory
12. Bush's Barn
13. Holly's Mills
14. Holly's House
15. Miller's House
16. Stripling's
17. Old Jacob Dooley's
18. Thompson's
19. Point from top hill where
    Ind. shot into fort
20. Otter Creek

The Thomas Hinde map of the Boonesborough environs was most likely drawn for historian Lyman Draper in the early nineteenth century, many years after the fort's active years.

fort was no longer a visible construction when he drew the map. The other buildings he indicated were still standing and in use at the time of the map's creation.

Hinde's map shows John Sidebottom's ferry house and stable on the terrace of the Kentucky River where the ferry was located. The ferry rights were granted to Richard Callaway in 1779, but Callaway was killed by Native Americans in 1780 while he was building a boat. His right was inherited by his heirs, but they did not move forward in establishing a ferry and the project languished. The delays induced other men to jump in the breach. In December 1787 the Fayette County court granted William T. Bush the ferry rights and land on the present Clark County side, while John Sidebottom (or Sydebottom) acquired the ferry rights on the Madison County side from Caleb Callaway and William Bush. Some of the Callaway heirs sold their interest to Robert Clarke Jr. Given that the ferry rights seem to have been extinguished for the Callaway heirs by these transfers, it is surprising that in 1788 the Madison County court vested the ferry rights to Richard Callaway's heirs (Caleb Callaway, Fanny Holder, Lydia Irvine, Doshia Callaway, Cuzza French, Richard Callaway Jr., and John Callaway) as tenants in common and acknowledged receipt of a security bond from Matthew Walton, James French, and William Irvine to keep the ferry in repair. The tenancy was confirmed again by the court in 1791. The Callaway heirs seem to have intended to block the ferry operation by Bush and Sidebottom, which was already in business. Clarke and Sidebottom sued to appeal the decision by the Lexington district court, and it was overturned. Elizabeth Patrick, Richard Callaway's granddaughter by his son George, filed several lawsuits (in conjunction with her husband, John Patrick) in connection with the ferry rights. George Callaway had not been one of the heirs who inherited ferry rights, but his daughter and son-in-law apparently secured the interests of the other heirs and thus gained legal standing. They sued Clarke and Sidebottom, seeking an ejectment against Sidebottom, who was operating the ferry. Eventually, William T. Bush gained the ferry rights, Sidebottom moved to upper Howard's Creek in Clark County, and the Callaways' rights were extinguished. Bush owned the ferry until 1824, when he sold it to James Stephens (incorrectly spelled Stevens). The ferry operated until 1931 when the Boonesborough Memorial Bridge was built.[37]

Houses shown on the Hinde map within the town claims were distributed along the road that ran from the ferry to Richmond (part of present-day State Road 388) and were labelled with familiar names. Just up the ferry road to the west was the Stephens house, a brick structure that still stood in ruins on the boundary line between the park and neighboring rock quarry in 1987. The Stephens family were longtime inhabitants of Boonesborough. P. Stephens, his wife, four sons, and six daughters were enumerated in the 1810 census; he owned nine slaves.

Another familiar name was John Halley (spelled "Holley" on the map), who was granted a license by Madison County in 1788 to "retail all kind of goods wares and merchandise in the Town of Boonesborough" and used the locale as a starting point for flatboat trips to New Orleans in 1789 and

1791. His house was stone and was dismantled in the twentieth century by Professor Jonathan T. Dorris, a local historian. The foundations of the house were documented during the 1987 survey, in addition to foundations for a later house built on the same lot by John Halley's nephew, Samuel. Its construction date is uncertain. Samuel Halley acquired the property from Samuel Bentley on March 2, 1832, and built a house in front of his uncle's house. Bentley had purchased John Halley's interest in the property at a sheriff's sale in April 1829. The sale was the result of a lawsuit against Bentley and Halley that they lost.[38]

Another house attributed to the Halley family is identified on the Hinde map as number 14 and was located near Otter Creek on the west side of the road. The map legend does not identify which member of the Halley family lived here. This house may have been the stone foundation with chimney recorded as the Monkey Covington House in the 1987 survey, or another stone foundation located nearby. This Halley house was near Halley's Mills on Otter Creek, also shown on the Hinde map but not documented as an archaeological site because it was outside the boundaries of the 1987 survey. The miller's house was located on the opposite (south) side of Otter Creek on Hinde's map.[39]

Located across the road from the John Halley house, on what is now park property, was a house that was identified as Bucklin's (number 8) by Hinde. He probably meant to indicate Samuel Buckley, who owned property in Boonesborough in the 1820s. The house was occupied by a Taylor in 1811 when surveyor John Crooke used it as a landmark for a survey he conducted for a lawsuit between Henry Banta and Green Clay. Thomas Taylor was head of one of the eight households listed for Boonesborough in the 1810 federal census. He was at the time a mature adult between twenty-six and forty-five years of age, living with his wife, three sons, three daughters, and two slaves. Local resident Dorothy Richards, now deceased, recalled seeing this house as a child and described it as being built into a slope on the east side of State Road 388. The 1987 survey confirmed its location and collected artifacts that dated from as early as the late eighteenth century to the early to mid-twentieth century.[40]

The house labelled as "Linsey's" (number 9) was occupied by the Lindsay family, who owned Boonesborough property in the early nineteenth century. Thomas Lindsay served as town trustee several times. His house was the former log house that was commonly referred to as Nathaniel Hart's house, located near where Hart first built his White Oak Station in 1775. A thorough architectural analysis of the structure was unfortunately never done before the house burned to the ground in 1989. However, it was built in several phases: the main block was a hewn and V-notched log, double-pen plan with two front doors; a rear ell that may have originally been built as a detached kitchen was later attached to the main block by a frame breezeway, and another section was added to the ell at some point. By 1987 the rearmost section was gone, leaving exposed a rear stone chimney with a hearth opening.

The White Oak Station was burned by Indians not long after it was built, and Hart did not attempt to rebuild until 1779. In 1781 he offered sanctuary to several "Low Dutch" (German) families. His son, Nathaniel Hart Jr., claimed that the station at one time had a population of one hundred people, but that number had dwindled to only three fighting men by August 1782. Nathaniel Hart Sr. was killed by Indians on July 22, 1782, leaving his wife, Sally, and nine children, all of them under the age of majority and seven of whom ranged from less than a year to fourteen years old. His will stipulated that each child was to receive, when they came of age or married, a "good likely young Negro, a good Horse and Saddle, a good feather bed & furniture and a good tract of land not to exceed one thousand acres." At the time of his death, only his oldest child, Keziah, was married (to Lawrence Thompson). His wife remained at Fort Boonesborough with her children until she died in March 1785. At the time of her death, another daughter, Susannah, was married to Isaac Shelby (who would become Kentucky's first governor in 1792) and may have been living at their farm, Travelers' Rest, in Lincoln County. Keziah and Lawrence Thompson were still in the Boonesborough area but were living in another house in an upland setting that was labelled No. 18 on the Hinde map. The demise of both Hart parents necessitated fostering the underage children into different households; Nathaniel Hart Jr., the second eldest, told Lyman Draper that he was sent to Harrod's Station in Boyle County. Susannah Hart Shelby and her husband took in the younger siblings.[41]

Nathaniel Hart Sr. is generally considered to have built the house named after him, or some part of it, but a precise construction date cannot be determined through deed records, and the architectural and archaeological evidence is also ambiguous. While Hart's White Oak Station must have included some log cabins to house its occupants, they are unlikely to have been fully hewn log houses showing the chinking between the logs and the shingled roofs that would distinguish them by the quality of construction. The chain of title after the death of Mrs. Nathaniel Hart is complicated. However, it seems to have been part of a large number of lots sold to John Halley by the town trustees. Halley defaulted on the purchase, and the town trustees repossessed the house in 1795, when Thomas Lindsay bought it and lived there until 1842, when he sold it to William D. McCord. McCord sold it in 1846 to William Bentley and Andrew J. Batterton. In 1853 Henry Lisle, who was married to Susan Shelby Thompson, Keziah and Lawrence Thompson's daughter, bought the property. It remained in the Lisle family for many years, and the Lisles were probably responsible for some of the additions to the house. T. K. Lisle sold it in 1881 to A. J. Lackey, who willed it to his heirs in 1904. The Lackey heirs sold it to David J. Williams in 1909, and it remains in the Williams family today.[42]

The Hinde map shows three structures located close to one another in the southern end of the town claims that either held businesses or were used in agriculture. Two of the structures, a wool factory and Elkanah Bush's tavern, were on the west side of the road. The other structure was Bush's barn on the east side of the road. The wool factory was probably a small-scale facility for carding cleaned, raw wool. Elkanah Bush bought the land from the trustees of Boonesborough in 1825, when they sold off the lots they had repossessed from John Halley. A structure that later became the home of Henry and Susan Shelby Thompson Lisle and their descendants still stands in the area and may be where either the wool factory or Bush's tavern operated. It is a clapboarded log structure, built originally on a dogtrot plan, that features interior brick chimneys at each end and a one-story frame ell in the rear. It is little altered from its appearance in the nineteenth century.[43]

Curiously missing from the Hinde map are the tobacco warehouses that once stood at the current entrance to the bottomland section of the park. The warehouses were still standing in 1837, when Cassius Marcellus and Mary Jane Clay sold them to Samuel Halley. The buildings were no longer standing by 1873, but the foundations were still visible. Their omission on the Hinde map is a mystery.[44]

The failure of Boonesborough to thrive and grow as a town had multiple causes. Its early establishment in 1779, its broad expanse of terrace that offered the town center room to expand, and its proximity to the Kentucky River should have been advantageous as Kentucky emerged from wartime and began to develop a mercantile network, public institutions, and its own government. Its bids to become first the county seat and then the state capital were unsuccessful, and its trustees failed to promote the town and were often replaced. Increased flooding along the Kentucky in the early nineteenth century inundated the bottomland along the river often enough to discourage building and to thwart urban development. Tobacco inspection facilities and the establishment of a post office at Boonesborough were encouraging developments, but neither function brought a sustained investment of people and capital, and few other businesses were based there. Although the town failed to reach its potential, the name lived on, to be remembered in near-heroic terms by the late nineteenth century, when widespread public interest in history prompted the creation of historical societies, genealogical associations, and national organizations with local chapters that celebrated the nation's founding. The internal strife in Kentucky during and following the Civil War led Kentuckians to focus on the frontier era as a time when people were united in a common goal. Boonesborough held a prominent place in that nostalgically remembered past.[45]

6

EVIDENCE IN THE EARTH

Reuben T. Durrett began his preface to George Washington Ranck's 1901 history of Fort Boonesborough with these words:

> Boonesborough, like a mist of the morning, has vanished, and the place which knew it once will know it no more forever. Not a cabin of the thirty that formed the parallelogram of the fort; not a picket of the bullet-battered lines that encompassed the station, and not a pale of the stockades between the cabins is left. Not even a chimney, the last of a human habitation to perish, is left standing or shows the little mound of debris at its base as survivor of its fall. . . . So thoroughly has the station disappeared that it affords no perch for the owl and no hiding-place for the fox.[1]

Writing in 1901, Durrett had little knowledge of or experience with historical archaeology. Like others of his day, he probably knew of archaeological excavations of such sites as the Egyptian pyramids or the temples of Greece. Perhaps he knew of Constantine Rafinesque's maps of prehistoric Indian sites in Kentucky or of Thomas Jefferson's investigation of an Indian burial mound in Virginia. But historical archaeology as it is known today did not exist then. When Reuben Durrett stood on the flat, broad terrace of the Kentucky River where Fort Boonesborough had once stood, he was unaware that archaeological remains of one of Kentucky's most famous historic sites lay beneath his feet.

Archaeological sites are like jigsaw puzzles that are missing some of their pieces. Assembly of the remaining puzzle pieces gradually reveals a picture, but the missing pieces leave holes that obscure the details and may even make the puzzle incomprehensible. When an archaeologist talks about site preservation, he or she means the physical evidence that survives the complex processes of decomposition, purposeful or accidental removal, and selective deposition that create an archaeological site. Some locations where humans conducted activities leave no archaeological evidence at all, or evidence that is too ephemeral to persist. A party of explorers who stop to create a camp for a night or two may leave the remains of a campfire identified by a concentration of charred wood, ash, and perhaps burned animal bone. Recognizing that hearth many years later as the remains of an eighteenth-century explorers' camp may be impossible. Generally speaking, the longer people occupy a particular spot on the landscape, the more likely an archaeological site will be the result.

Human activities often leave physical evidence, but some do not. A built structure leaves evidence of the foundation, the nonperishable materials with which the structure was crafted (e.g., brick or stone), the presence of certain features such as windows (glass panes), doors (e.g., hinges, doorknobs, key escutcheons), chimneys/fireplaces (e.g., brick or stone), or other remains that formed part of the actual fabric of the building. Some construction activities may leave very limited physical evidence. For example, early historic surveyors often established survey camps with log or brush shelters for temporary occupation. These structures, once decomposed, leave little or no recognizable archaeological footprint if enough time passes. Artifacts are the first physical evidence that comes to mind when considering archaeological sites. Ceramic sherds, glass fragments, nails or other metal, bone refuse from meals, lost buttons, and a myriad of other objects often survive in the archaeological physical record. Yet many other types of artifacts typically do not survive in the most common site-preservation environments. Textiles are a good example of a type of common artifact that normally does not survive in the typical archaeological site. Another is food stuffs that were not carbonized or were entirely consumed and digested within the human digestive tract. However, food refuse that decomposes and adds organic matter to the soil helps to form the archaeological soil known as midden that develops in residential and other types of archaeological sites.

Because archaeological evidence is so heavily influenced by natural and cultural processes, "the workings of these processes define . . . the nature of knowable history of human land use and cultural development." This idea of "knowable" history as it relates to archaeology is important because it colors all interpretations of what archaeological evidence means. A common reaction that people have when examining artifacts such as a button or a bead or some other item that once belonged to an individual is to ask if it is possible to identify the specific person who once owned it. While it is not out of the realm of possibility that specific artifacts could be associated with specific people, it usually is not possible. Thus when an archaeologist finds a gunflint or a breeches button, the former owner cannot be identified with any certainty. Gunflints made of a particular material and manufactured in a particular place indicate that fort inhabitants had access to and used gunflints (themselves indicative of firearms with flintlocks) that were made and traded from French, English, or other sources. Details observed among clothing-related artifacts support conclusions about how the settlers dressed. An obvious exception is an artifact that has some identifying characteristic, such as a monogram, that associates it with a particular person. But such artifacts are rare.[2]

Also important is the presence or absence of certain types of artifacts or artifacts that can be dated. If all of the artifacts in an assemblage date to a particular period, and the assemblage lacks either later or earlier artifacts, this information helps to pinpoint or confirm when a site was first occupied and when it was abandoned. Artifacts cannot usually be tightly dated to a particular year or short period of years because they may be used for long periods before they are discarded or lost. A good example is a coin minted in a particular year. Obviously, it cannot date earlier than the year it was minted, but it could be deposited in a site many years later, since coins often remain in circulation for decades. Other examples of artifacts with long use periods are ceramics that may have been used for several decades or preserved as heirlooms.

Some artifact types may have been scarce during some time periods only to become more common later. Glass bottles and containers are a good example. Mass-produced glass bottles for processed foods, toiletries, medicines, and other manufactured products did not become numerous and common until the mid- to late nineteenth century when glass factories developed manufacturing techniques that allowed them to produce bottles and containers very cheaply. Prior to mass production, glass containers were expensive and occur less often or in very small quantities in archaeological sites.

While artifacts are the most familiar aspect of archaeological sites, evidence observable in the soil such as storage pits, hearths, foundations, and the remains of posts or other features are equally important. The discovery, excavation, and mapping of cultural features are essential components of archaeological analysis and interpretation. One of the biggest threats to the preservation of archaeological features is physical impact to the site because of various land uses and modifications. Destructive land uses include activities like plowing, later building construction, and other forms of land modification that disturb soil.

Archaeological information derived from excavation and artifacts is what most people think of when they think of archaeology, but written documents are another key component of historical archaeology. Like artifacts, written documents such as letters, maps, journals and diaries, deeds, and other sources have to be interpreted with care. Some documents are more reliable than others. The reason that a written document was created contributes to the information that may be gleaned from it. For example, an interview conducted in the 1840s by the Rev. John Dabney Shane with someone who lived at Boonesborough in the 1780s is documenting memories that are more than sixty years old. Was the interviewee a child or an adult when he or she lived in Boonesborough? Did the interviewee actually live through the event being reported, or is it a secondhand account? Can the memory be corroborated by other independent evidence?

Because Fort Boonesborough had a transient population during the time it was occupied, anyone interpreting archaeological evidence has to take into account the fact that the actions of many people produced the artifacts and features preserved in the ground. Moreover, the inhabitants of the fort generally were not affluent, nor did they bring much baggage with them. In light of the relatively brief periods most people stayed at the fort and the length of time the fort was used, the archaeological footprint of the site is somewhat ephemeral, increasing the challenges of archaeological discovery and interpretation. Because Fort Boonesborough was built as a defensive structure designed to protect its occupants from the enemy, its primary purpose disappeared once the war was over and the need for defense was gone. The stockade sections were dismantled shortly after the war ended, but the cabins remained standing for a period of time. How does the site archaeology help to identify and explain the structural features that composed the fort, the lifestyles of the people who occupied it, and the timing of its ultimate disappearance? These are the questions this book seeks to answer.

7

DESIGNING A FORT FOR DEFENSE AND RESIDENCE

W hen the Transylvania Company's first settlers set out for Kentucky in 1775, their journey was marked by danger and violence. Daniel Boone's road cutters experienced this firsthand when they were attacked two weeks into the trip, and Henderson's party met panic-stricken adventurers who had turned back and abandoned their settlement attempts in the face of Native American attacks. Some of Henderson's party abandoned the enterprise as well. Many of the travelers had experienced border warfare during the French and Indian War and were familiar with defensive measures practiced in the backcountry of Virginia and North Carolina, where Indian attacks were frequent. The Kentucky-bound settlers knew that the land they sought to settle was contested ground, despite its purchase from the Cherokees. They held no illusions about the likelihood of violent altercations with well-armed enemies who had their own reasons for keeping settlers out of their treasured hunting territories. The need for a defensible fort that could house all of the settlers together was acute.

The architectural plan of Fort Boonesborough combined residential and defensive elements that incorporated log cabins to house settler families with borrowed aspects of European military components such as stockade (also of logs) and bastions. This hybrid design differed from forts built primarily for short-term emergency occupancy by militia companies, exemplified by Fort Arbuckle, a diamond-shaped, two-bastioned fort with an internal blockhouse built in the Greenbrier River valley in what is now West Virginia. From the outset Fort Boonesborough was designed to house numerous settlers. The structures were generally built for family units, but quarters for young, single men who served as scouts, spies, and protectors were also included. Log cabins provided the necessary residential components, while corner bastions and stockade met defensive needs. These architectural elements were combined in a rectangular plan in which a bastioned structure anchored each corner and the cabins were built in a line to form the walls of the enclosure. Spaces between the cabins were filled in with vertical stockade. Two gates provided entry into the fort but could be barred against hostile intrusions. The log walls of the cabins and stockade were not sturdy enough to withstand heavy artillery but were effective barriers to gunfire. Settlers familiar with Native American military tactics knew that the use of heavy artillery such as cannon was rare and that most raids and attacks were of short duration. Thus, a barricadable enclosure equipped with blockhouses and portholes built into the cabin walls offered sufficient protection to withstand most strikes.[1]

Determining the details of the architecture and construction of Fort Boonesborough began with extensive archival research to gain a better idea of what structures could be expected to leave archaeological evidence in the ground. Sources that documented the memories and experiences of settlers who lived in or visited Fort Boonesborough and that described what the fort looked like were essential resources. Students of Kentucky pioneer history are fortunate in the wide variety of archival sources available to them, ranging from land grant records to court depositions to petitions to personal recollections gathered from interviews, letters, and memoirs. Chief among these diverse sources, and most germane to understanding the architecture of Fort Boonesborough, are the settler interviews in the Lyman C. Draper manuscripts in the collections of the Wisconsin Historical Society.

Rev. John Dabney Shane and Lyman Copeland Draper loom large among the nineteenth-century chroniclers of Kentucky's colonial past. Shane was a Presbyterian minister by profession, but he spent a great deal of time and effort interviewing surviving pioneers in the 1840s. Draper was the secretary of the Wisconsin Historical Society. He spent decades collecting documents, conducting interviews, writing and receiving letters, and gathering even the most trivial bits of information. The books he intended to write never materialized in print, but the corpus of his work and the interviews he acquired from Shane's estate provide a rich trove of information.

Shane's and Draper's interests often overlapped, and they even interviewed some of the same subjects and asked them similar questions. Fort Boonesborough was the subject of many of their interviews, and Draper in particular went to great lengths to solicit information from former occupants of the fort or their descendants. Details in the interviews provide information not only on the fort construction itself but also on its placement on the local landscape. Location influenced defensive capabilities and provided ready access to resources such as potable or therapeutic springs, navigable water, and wood from nearby forests.

Geography of the Fort Setting

Tasked with selecting a location for the future capital of the Transylvania Colony, Boone chose a site on the Kentucky River that enjoyed several environmental and strategic advantages. The site selection was influenced more by perceived advantages for a future urban center rather than by factors that focused primarily on defensive considerations. While a fort was deemed necessary at that time for defense against Indian attacks, longer-term plans for a town privileged some factors that, in other circumstances, would have been disadvantageous for a fort. The site was positioned on a broad terrace inside a large bend of the Kentucky River. The winding river flows slightly northwest nearest the fort site and bends to the west about 1.3 miles north, then flows slightly southwest. Nearby fording places were located both upstream and downstream of the site. The broad expanse of the river terrace, a rarity along the typically engorged Kentucky River channel, offered ample space for lots to be laid off for a future town.

A prominent feature of the site's geography was the Lick Branch valley, commonly called Sycamore Hollow, which featured both fresh and mineral water springs. The 1809 town plat labelled this valley "Lick Commons," indicating that it was left open for communal use. The Lick Branch valley angles northeast and is on the northwest side of the fort site. Nearly all of the town's half-acre in-lots were laid out south of the Lick Branch valley and took advantage of the broadest dimension of the terrace between the river and adjacent uplands. Wood resources were readily available in the Lick Branch valley and from the forested uplands nearby.

Boone's choice of a broad riverine terrace raises the question of flooding potential from the Kentucky River. Initially flooding was not perceived as a serious threat, possibly because the elevation of the second terrace, where the fort was built and the town's in-lots were laid out, was some thirty feet above the river. Henderson implies in his journal that part of the reason he built his fort on higher ground was because there was insufficient room closer to the cluster of cabins that Boone and his road cutters had built further downstream. However, the threat of flooding may have factored into his decision. Flooding did threaten Boone's cabins in 1776; Elizabeth Poague Thomas describes floodwaters rising but not inundating the cabins.[2]

Opposite the fort site, across the Kentucky River, looms the high limestone cliffs that characterize much of the engorged valley cut by the river. The cliffs impede access to the river from the uplands, making breaks (formed by tributaries that cut their valleys down to the river level) particularly important places for crossings and fords. The presence of the cliffs became a point of contention in 1779 when the location of the 640-acre town claim was debated. The difficult access they posed and the large bend that the river created were the key factors in locating the town claim on the south and west side of the river. The river itself became a boundary later as smaller counties were formed out of the original counties of Lincoln and Fayette, illustrating the significant impact a natural waterway can have on the process of creating a cultural landscape.

The Fort's Architectural Plan as Described by Settlers

The architectural plan of Fort Boonesborough was obviously on the minds of Reverend Shane and Lyman Draper, both of whom elicited descriptions of it from their informants. Five interviews with sketches by five men who either lived at the fort or visited it in the 1770s offer clues about its architectural plan. Moses Boone and John Gass provided information for the most detailed plans of the fort as they remembered it during the siege of 1778. Moses Boone was the son of Squire Boone, Daniel Boone's brother. John Gass was the son of David Gass, who had visited Kentucky frequently before emigrating permanently in 1777. Both sketches were based on childhood recollections recorded well over sixty years after the event. Their plans did not agree completely, but they supplied some critical information that others did not. The other three plans were elicited from men who were adults when they were at Fort Boonesborough (Richard Henderson, Bland Ballard, and Josiah Collins). Henderson headed the Transylvania Company, who built the fort, while Collins and Ballard were settlers who visited or lived there briefly. Comparison of the five plans reveals important features as well as points of disagreement. Comments accompanying the sketches provide additional

70

details but ambiguities remain, and the evidence is as interesting for what it does not reveal as for what it does.[3]

The accuracy and detail of the five sketches reflect how familiar the settlers were with the fort and underscores their ability for recall decades later. In his correspondence with Draper, Gass commented several times about the difficulty of answering his questions, citing the passage of time and the effects of age on his memory. Not surprisingly, Gass and Boone provided many more details than the other men, even though they had been children when they lived at the fort. Their memories were informed by personal experience and observation as well as by years of hearing stories from other settlers and family members. Information obtained from the interviews was also influenced by the questions that Shane and Draper asked, many of which have to be inferred from the answers. The result is a series of interviews and letters that vary in detail and are occasionally contradictory. Nevertheless, the settlers provided a treasure trove of details that proved to be useful in interpreting the fort archaeology.[4]

The men were asked to estimate the amount of space the fort enclosed. While their answers varied, the estimates offer some idea of the size of the fort's architectural footprint. Moses Boone and Gass estimated that the fort enclosed about an acre. Boone was more specific about proportions, saying that the length was one third larger than the width. Another settler, George Michael Bedinger, who visited the fort as an adult in 1779, stated the dimensions were 125 by 250 feet, or just under three-quarters of an acre. Based on Richard Henderson's sketch plan, which omitted specific dimensions, James Hall allowed an average of twenty feet for each cabin and adjacent space and estimated that the fort measured 180 by 260 feet, slightly more than an acre. Bland Ballard estimated the enclosure at half an acre.[5]

Four of the five plans represented the appearance of the fort in either 1778 or 1779, while Richard Henderson's undated plan may be a blueprint for the fort he envisioned in 1775 rather than a plan already realized. Henderson's plan is known only from a secondhand source. James Hall borrowed documents relating to the Transylvania Company from James Alves, a descendant of proprietors James Hogg and William Johnson. Hall published his version from an original plan in the handwriting of Richard Henderson. Alves asked that Hall give the papers to the Kentucky Historical Society, but he failed to do so, and the original sketch and notes are since lost.

Hall's version therefore cannot be checked for accuracy against the original penned by Henderson, although some of the details can be corroborated from other sources.[6]

Henderson's plan represented a fort that consisted of a rectangular arrangement of four two-story, log bastioned corner structures and twenty-six one- or one-and-a-half-story log cabins connected by short sections of log stockade. His plan was the only one that explicitly indicated the total number of cabins. The fort had a large front gate and a smaller rear gate on the long sides. Hall's version included a north arrow and depicted the Kentucky River near the southeast corner. The orientation of the long axis of the fort is ten degrees west of north. Of the five plans, cardinal directions were only labelled on three, and two of these were obviously wrong. Determining the correct orientation of the fort was only possible with archaeological evidence.[7]

The rectangular plan was anchored at each corner with structures variously called houses, bastions, or bastends by the five informants. Although the corner structures are labelled as "houses" in the Henderson plan, an explanation by Hall clarifies that they were "larger than the others, and projecting so as to form bastions." Daniel Trabue describes the upper story of such structures as designed "to be much biger than the lower story and to Jut over so that you may be up on the upper floor and shot [shoot] down if the indeans was to come up to the walls and they cannot climb up the walls of these houses." All of the plans drew the corner structures with larger square footage than the cabins along the walls. Their key defensive features were the projecting upper stories on the two outside walls that prevented assailants from scaling the walls and the portholes through which settlers could deliver raking gunfire at close and long range.[8]

While less specific than Henderson's plan, the other plans also show a quadrilinear enclosure with bastioned buildings at the corners and cabins along the wall. Josiah Collins was an adult when he visited the fort in March 1778, just months before the siege. His sketch is the least detailed and contains several inaccuracies. He said there was only one gate on the south (west, if map is reoriented correctly) and omitted the smaller gate on the riverside wall that others mentioned. He drew the fort at an "enlarged scale" that showed the plan as a square rather than a rectangle and placed structures at all four corners. Like other informants, he used the terms "bastion" and "bast-end" to describe structures with protruding second

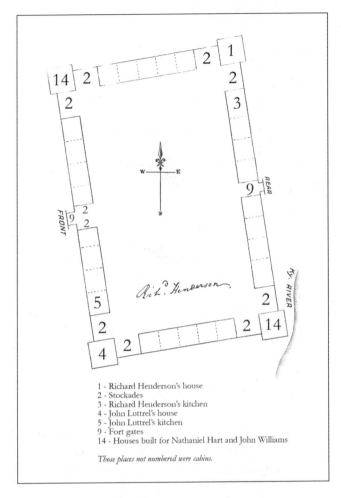

1 - Richard Henderson's house
2 - Stockades
3 - Richard Henderson's kitchen
4 - John Luttrel's house
5 - John Luttrel's kitchen
9 - Fort gates
14 - Houses built for Nathaniel Hart and John Williams

Those places not numbered were cabins.

Richard Henderson's plan of Fort Boonesborough.

stories. He specifically labelled the northwesterly and southeasterly corners as bast-end and bastion, respectively. He had lodged in one of the cabins on the easterly wall, noting "all cabins on this side." Moses Boone identified the northwest and southwest corners as "new bastions" and placed "Phelp's house" on the southeast corner on his plan but contradicted himself in his interview, where he said the new blockhouses were on the southeast and southwest corners.[9*]

Bland Ballard's sketch represents the fort as it appeared in the spring of 1779. Ballard came to Fort Boonesborough as a member of Capt. John

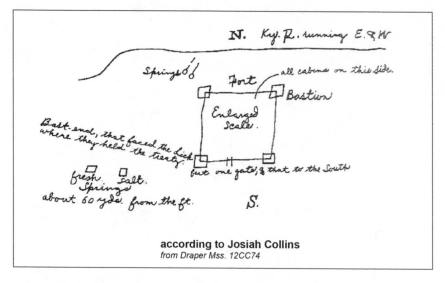

according to Josiah Collins
from Draper Mss. 12CC74

Josiah Collins's plan of Fort Boonesborough, drawn from memory, represented the fort as it appeared in 1778 or 1779. It lacks detail and contains several inaccuracies, including the cardinal directions indicated and the notation "but one gate, & that to the South." Collins's handwritten notations read (*from the top, left to right*): Ky R. running E. & W; springs; Fort; all cabins on this side; Bastion; Enlarged scale; Bast-end, that faced the Lick where they held the treaty; but one gate, & that to the South; fresh/salt springs about 60 yds. from the ft.

Holder's company during Col. John Bowman's expedition to the Ohio country to subdue the Shawnees in late May 1779. Later that same year, he was assigned lot 6 of the newly chartered town of Boonesborough. Ballard noted "bastions" on three corners and wrote that a "large house jutted over" was on the northeast corner where Richard Henderson had formerly lived. Ballard confirmed that the fort had a big gate on its front wall and a small gate on its rear (riverside) wall and placed them in the same location as Henderson's plan.[10]

The builders took advantage of the abundant wood resources of the surrounding forests, so the fort was largely constructed of logs. The cabins themselves were built of mostly unbarked logs, notched at the ends so that they could be stacked to form a wall. The gaps between the logs were chinked with small stones and plastered over with clay mud in the same way that gaps between stockade pickets were plugged. The cabins had shed roofs that sloped inward. Except for the shingled roof on Henderson's domicile, the

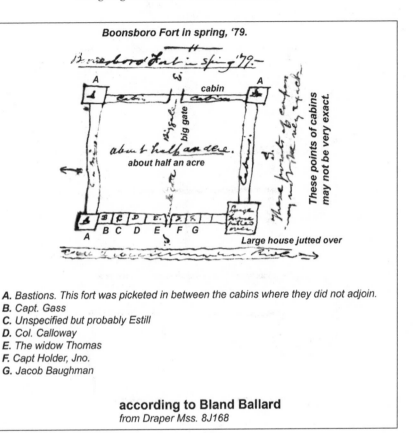

Boonsboro Fort in spring, '79.

cabin

big gate

about half an acre

These points of cabins may not be very exact.

A   B C D E F G   Large house jutted over

A. Bastions. This fort was picketed in between the cabins where they did not adjoin.
B. Capt. Gass
C. Unspecified but probably Estill
D. Col. Calloway
E. The widow Thomas
F. Capt Holder, Jno.
G. Jacob Baughman

according to Bland Ballard
from Draper Mss. 8J168

Bland Ballard's plan of Fort Boonesborough as it appeared in 1778–1779, drawn from memory many years after his time there.

cabins were roofed using rib poles to hold covering boards in place. Early chimneys are generally described as having dry-laid stone foundations built to a height of approximately four feet, while the remainder of the chimney was built to height with sticks and mud daub.

Later historians concluded that the cabins stood as separate structures, each with its own chimney, but settler accounts suggest more architectural variation. Three of the five fort plans draw the cabins as a series of connected squares. Henderson's plan very curiously shows four sets of four and two sets of five cabins that seem to share common walls with their neighbors. He does not indicate where the chimneys were, but if some of the cabins were connected, forming double cabins, then the chimneys could have been

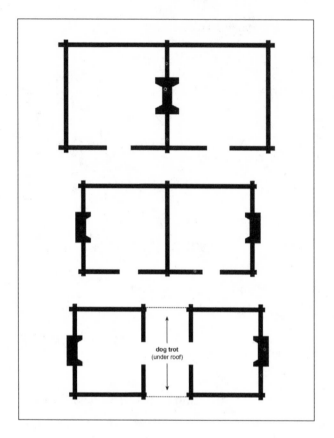

Plans for double cabins. The center cabin at Fort
Boonesborough were built on the dogtrot plan. Squire
Boone kept a gunsmith shop in the covered passageway
between the cabins.

built between each pair with hearths on each side that opened to the rooms,
an arrangement known as a saddlebag plan. This possible configuration
suggests a stone chimney base in the shape of an uppercase "I." Another
possible configuration places chimneys at each end of a pair of connected
cabins, a plan known as the double pen. A third configuration, known as a
dogtrot plan, consists of two single pens separated by a central, open hall
with all components under one roof.

Bland Ballard and Isaiah Boone both mentioned adjoining cabins.
Ballard's plan of the fort stated that the "fort was picketed in between the
cabins where they did not adjoin," a statement that could be interpreted to

mean that some of the cabins did adjoin. Isaiah Boone said in an interview that the settlers "cut doors from cabin to cabin as they adjoined—and thus could go around the fort without being exposed."[11]

The stockade was another feature that was borrowed from military architectural design, but its use was limited. By filling in the gaps between the log cabins with short sections of stockade, far less stockade had to be built since the cabin walls formed part of the enclosure and did not stand independently. Henderson's plan showed short sections of stockade on two sides of each corner blockhouse and on either side of the front gate on the westerly wall. Stockade usually reached a height of ten to twelve feet and typically was built with logs about a foot in diameter split lengthwise and placed upright in a shallow trench. They were held in place by horizontally placed split logs that were pinned at intervals to keep the individual pickets from shifting. Building stockade in this way could be accomplished quickly, but the resulting wall fell into disrepair easily. Such was the state of the stockade when Daniel Boone returned from his captivity in 1778 to warn the settlers of the impending siege.[12]

Construction quality of the stockade sections was not high, but it was good enough to present an imposing barrier against gunfire. The upright pickets, or puncheons, butted up against one another or overlapped slightly to make a solid wall, but where gaps did occur, clay mud was used to fill in the void. This mud sometimes dried out, cracked, and fell off, opening a gap for a sharpshooter to aim a lucky shot that might hit a human target. Portholes cut within the cabin or stockade walls and plugged with stone when not in use similarly drew concentrated fire in the hopes that a bullet would penetrate. While such an occurrence took some very careful aim and a generous helping of luck, occasionally someone was injured or killed by just such a lucky shot. While stationed at a porthole, David Bundrin was shot in his forehead on the third day of the Great Siege of 1778 and died three days later.[13]

Richard Henderson, John Gass, and Moses Boone provided information on various facilities in the open space inside the fort enclosure. None of the plans depict a powder magazine, but Henderson mentioned the log one he began on April 29 and finished on May 3, 1775. Henderson intended to make gunpowder at Boonesborough and brought saltpeter and sulfur for the purpose, but he had to leave most of these supplies behind when he discovered his wagons could not traverse the trail into Kentucky. He did,

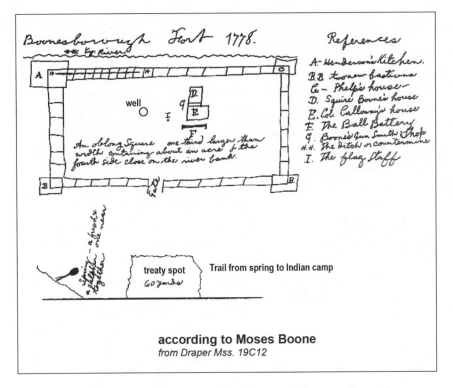

according to Moses Boone
from Draper Mss. 19C12

Moses Boone's plan of Fort Boonesborough as he recalled it years later. The handwritten notations read (*top, left to right*): Boonesborough Fort 1778; Ky. River; well; An oblong Square, one third longer than width containing about an acre & the fourth side close on the river bank; gate; spring—a fresh and a sulphur one near together; treaty spot 60 yards.

The letter keys read: A. Henderson's kitchen; B. two new bastions; C. Phelps' house; D. Squire Boone's house; E. Col. Callaway's house; F. The Ball Battery; G. Boone's Gun Smith shop; H. The ditch or countermine; I. The flag staff.

however, bring supplies of finished gunpowder. A key feature of the facility was to provide a damp-proof storage space. The powder magazine may have been semisubterranean to reduce the damage an accidental explosion might cause, or it could have been built above ground. It could even have been housed within one of the perimeter cabins. Gass mentioned the magazine, saying that it was well stocked during the 1778 siege and the settlers had access to it, implying that it was located within the fort enclosure.[14]

Both Gass's and Boone's plans show a structural complex located in the approximate center of the fort interior. Both men reported this structure as a

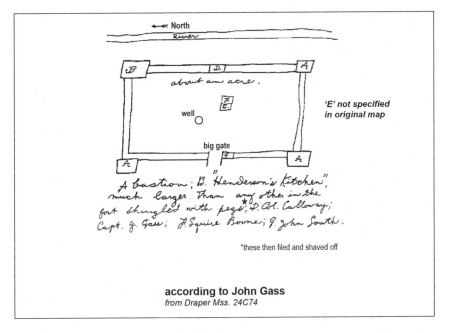

John Gass's plan of Fort Boonesborough c. 1778. The handwritten notations read (*top to bottom*): River; about an acre; A. Bastion; B. "Henderson's kitchen," much larger than any other in the fort[,] shingled with pegs* [these then filed and shaved off]; D. Col. Callaway; [E.] Capt. D. Gass; F. Squire Boone; G. John South.

double cabin, and Boone included a breezeway or narrow passage between the two rooms, suggesting a dogtrot plan. The structure was important to both men because each of them said that their family lived in one of the cabins. Boone said his father, Squire Boone, had a gunsmith shop in the breezeway. The central cabins also provided protection for the women and children of the fort during the siege. Inclusion of the structure on the plans was critical to interpreting some of the archaeological features uncovered by excavation.[15]

Both Boone and Gass also located a well in the central area. There were two wells within the fort. One was older and was not flowing adequately at the time of the 1778 siege. The second well, begun during the siege but never finished, figured prominently in the amusing story of Matthias "Tice" Prock, a German settler who was averse to fighting and refused to participate in the fort's defense during the siege. According to Moses Boone, who approximated Prock's German-accented English, the German explained,

"Sure, I was not made to fight. I ish a potter." Mrs. Richard Callaway resorted to a switch to roust him out when he hid under the bellows in Squire Boone's gunsmith shop. Col. Richard Callaway set him to work digging the well when he refused to fight. He made some progress but balked at the work after a while. Callaway threatened him with a tomahawk and he jumped back in the hole and stayed there.[16]

Moses Boone's sketch also included a flagstaff and a "ball battery." He mentioned the flagstaff because of an incident in which the top of the staff was targeted by gunfire and broken, causing the flag to tumble. The settlers restored the flag and the Indians abandoned any further attempts to shoot it down. Boone's use of the term "ball battery" is curious since a battery in military parlance refers to a line of artillery or cannon pointed in the same direction. He may have been referring to the two black gum logs his father Squire Boone had hollowed out and bound with iron bands to approximate small cannon or swivels. John Gass referred to Squire's contraption as a swivel, which is a smaller caliber piece of artillery usually used against personnel rather than walls. Gass and Boone both employed the military terms that best approximated the makeshift defenses the settlers fashioned.[17]

Occupants of the Fort Cabins

Incidental to construction details, Henderson, Gass, Boone, and Ballard all mentioned who lived in some of the cabins at various times. All four corner structures in Henderson's plan, which was probably drawn around 1775, were intended to be occupied by proprietors of the Transylvania Company. The larger size of the corner structures and the separate kitchens that were built for at least two of them speak to the class differences between the company partners and the settlers who threw in their lot with them.

Besides the bastioned house on the northeasterly corner, Henderson also used a separate cabin next to his dwelling as a kitchen, and he had carried in provisions and supplies to trade or sell that had to be stored. Henderson's brother, Samuel, brought at least one slave, London, who lived in the kitchen. Both Moses Boone and Gass stated that Henderson's kitchen was in the northeast corner bastion. This placement disagrees with the Henderson plan, which places the kitchen in a separate cabin south of the corner structure and separated by a short section of stockade.

Henderson's plan placed John Luttrell in the southwest corner cabin, which also had an adjacent cabin he used as a kitchen. Luttrell was a company partner and a member of Henderson's party who arrived in April 1775. He stayed at Fort Boonesborough until September, when he returned to North Carolina for a company meeting. Thereafter, he entered military service as a lieutenant colonel and was killed in 1781. His short tenure at Fort Boonesborough meant that his two cabins were vacated early in the fort's occupation but subsequent occupants are unknown.[18]

The other two corners were occupied by Nathaniel Hart and John Williams, according to Henderson's plan. Hart initially declined to settle at the fort and built a cabin on land nearby that he intended to claim. His cabin was burned down by Native American raiders in 1776, and he was forced to move to the fort. From 1775 to 1779 he made fourteen trips between his home in Caswell County, North Carolina, and Fort Boonesborough; in 1779 he brought his family to the fort. His son, Nathaniel Hart Jr., said that the family was living here when his father was killed in 1782. Hart's widow, Sarah Simpson Hart, continued living in the fort with her underage children until she died two years after her husband.[19]

John Williams did not come to the fort until after the September 25, 1775, meeting of the Transylvania proprietors in North Carolina, and his stay was short. He intended to remain at Fort Boonesborough until April 1776 to transact the company's business as its agent. In 1779 Williams filed a claim with the land court in which he offered sufficient proof that he settled in Kentucky in 1775 and lived there for twelve months prior to 1778. He was not present at the siege and probably returned to North Carolina in 1776 or 1777.[20]

Bland Ballard named occupants for nearly every cabin on the easterly wall but simply indicated cabins on the other walls. Of the families he named, most of them did not remain at the fort very long. David Gass and James Estill moved out of the fort in 1780, and Richard Callaway lived there until his death in 1782. John Holder moved out in 1782 to settle his station in Clark County. Jacob Baughman (also known as Boofman or Boffman) died in 1779. The widow Thomas's sojourn at Fort Boonesborough is unknown. Aside from Henderson's locating John Luttrell's cabin and John Gass's locating John South's cabin on the westerly wall in 1775, no one specified occupants on any other wall. One possible explanation for the omission is the use of cabins for slaves, single men, and transients. Although the number of slaves at the fort is not known, the slaveholdings of Richard Callaway and Nathaniel Hart

Sr. accounted for twenty-three individuals at the time of their deaths in 1780 and 1782, respectively. While Callaway and Hart owned more slaves than most people, other settlers brought them in fewer numbers. For example, Margaret Drake had a slave named Aggy when she lived at the fort.[21]

The population of single men varied, depending on who was stationed there for brief tours of duty, and transients cycled in and out of the fort frequently. On July 25, 1777, forty-five North Carolina riflemen arrived at the fort, and some of them no doubt stayed within. Col. John Bowman arrived a week later with one hundred Virginia militia. A smaller detachment headed by Capt. John Montgomery replaced Bowman's men. Some of the salt boilers who were captured with Daniel Boone were militia members and single men.[22]

Archaeological Evidence of the Fort

Archival information provided many details on the construction and appearance of Fort Boonesborough that informed expectations for the kinds of archaeological evidence that might be preserved on the site. Potential archaeological evidence specific to a residential fort site such as Fort Boonesborough includes late eighteenth-century artifacts, cabin hearths, stockade trenches, storage pits, post holes (such as the hole that held the flag staff), deep holes representing the wells, and midden.

Since the archaeological investigations at the fort site took place over several phases of fieldwork, the physical evidence unfolded gradually, and each field season built on the findings of the previous one. The initial survey in 1987 identified and mapped the archaeological midden and the distribution of fort-related artifacts that defined the total spatial area of the site. Archaeological features were discovered within this defined space. The features discovered in 1987 included part of a dry-laid stone foundation and one of the hearths associated with a cabin. The evidence collected in 1987 confirmed the precise location of the fort site and indicated the types of artifacts and features that might be encountered with additional excavation.

The fieldwork also identified some significant past land uses that had a direct impact on the preservation of the archaeological deposits at the fort site. Understanding how and where these land uses affected the site was an important component of devising a strategy for excavation and subsequent interpretations. The principal impacts to the site's preservation dated to three time periods: the nineteenth century, when periodic flooding and erosional episodes capped the central and southern portions of the site with layers of silt and eroded much of the north end; the early twentieth century, when the DAR monument and enclosing stone wall were installed and vacation cabins were built as part of a local resort; and the 1960s and 1970s, when Fort Boonesborough State Park was developed.

As mentioned in the preface, the Boonesborough chapter of the DAR marked the site of Fort Boonesborough with a stone monument in 1907. In the 1930s the chapter purchased a small parcel of land on which the monument stood and marked its boundaries with a stone wall. The construction of the stone wall, particularly, required the excavation of footer trench that may have extended into and destroyed underlying fort deposits.

In 1909 pharmacist David Williams built small vacation cabins on elevated post foundations as part of a modest resort that capitalized on the mineral water springs in Sycamore Hollow. The holes for the posts of one of the cabins extended several feet into the older archaeological deposits, and decades of trash disposal created a layer of early to mid-twentieth-century artifacts in the top 12–15 in. (20–25 cm) of soil. Luckily, this layer developed on top of the earlier fort occupation layer and did not cause any significant disturbance.

Conversion of the land into a state park in the 1960s and 1970s brought further construction modifications that had impacts on the preservation of the fort site. Construction of the road leading to the boat dock and a small parking area disturbed archaeological deposits of the fort site to an unknown extent beneath the asphalt surfaces. Similarly, a restroom was installed just south of the fort site and DAR monument. Water and sewer lines running to this restroom were laid through the fort site, a construction decision that unintentionally destroyed the archaeological deposits that the utility trenches cut through.

Understanding the prior impacts to the site informed later decisions on where to locate additional excavations by identifying the most promising areas. Subsequent excavations from 2012 to 2014 uncovered additional cabin hearths, a curious bone-filled pit, and other cultural evidence that identified where the fort walls ran, showed how much of the site was preserved archaeologically, and produced more artifacts.[23]

One of the first questions to be answered concerned the orientation of the fort. The orientation according to the cardinal directions was a point of disagreement between various settlers queried by Shane and Draper. The location of cabin hearths and other features found during excavation coupled with the distribution of late eighteenth-century artifacts suggest that the long axis of the fort ran twenty degrees west of north. This orientation disagrees with Hall's rendition of Judge Henderson's fort plan by ten degrees but confirms the northwest orientation. Allowing for a margin of error inherent in estimating structural footprints in absence of archaeologically identified wall lines, the archaeological footprint and the Henderson sketch are close. The distribution of features within the excavated areas of the fort site shows the footprint of the fort based on archaeological data. The orientation of the fort suggests that Henderson laid out the enclosure closer to a north-south alignment rather than strictly parallel to the Kentucky River. The orientation of twenty degrees west of north agrees with Henderson's sketch, which shows the river running closer to the southeasterly blockhouse. The orientation probably also accounted for the change in elevation from the first to the second river terrace. The fort was built near the edge of the second terrace where it descends to the first terrace above the river.

Discovery of stockade features at other late eighteenth-century forts suggested that similar evidence might be found at Fort Boonesborough. Archaeological excavations in other forts, such as Fort Donnelly and Fort Arbuckle in West Virginia (where stockade was built in much longer sections), identified long linear trench lines about 18 in. (50 cm) wide and 12–18 in. (30–50 cm) deep. A stockade section approximately 12 feet (4 m) long was identified at Daniel Boone's Station in Fayette County, Kentucky, with the same characteristics. If the same method of construction was used at Fort Boonesborough, its archaeological footprint should be the same as those documented elsewhere.[24]

Surprisingly (and disappointingly), no definite evidence of stockade sections was found. The simplest explanation is that excavation was not placed where the sections were preserved. Another possibility is that archaeological evidence of the stockade was not preserved or was unrecognizable. The stockade only stood for a few years, from 1776 to 1784. Within this short time frame, there were periods when the stockade had collapsed or was missing in places. When the Revolutionary War concluded, the stockade disappeared from the site within a year. The log pickets were probably salvaged for use elsewhere, leaving no wood to decompose in place and set down the distinctive, dark, circular stains that identify the former

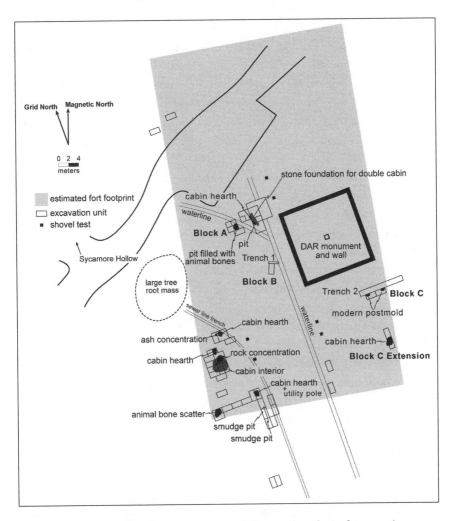

Fort Boonesborough site plan, as constructed from archaeological excavations. Note that the fort was situated slightly to the northwest, rather than due north.

presence of posts. Finally, the stockade may not have been consistently built by sinking the vertical log posts into a trench. Daniel Boone offered a slim clue about stockade construction when, referring to preparations for the Great Siege of 1778, he said, "We immediately proceeded to collect what we could of our horses and other cattle, and bring them through the posterns in the fort." By "posterns," he meant the vertical logs that formed the stockade. The ability to remove stockade posts was mentioned in accounts of Bryan's

Station, and the stockade at Fort Harrod was shallow enough for settlers to dig under it to allow access. Additional excavations in the future may determine whether stockade features are preserved at Fort Boonesborough.[25]

Since stockade was not definitively identified, the outline of the fort walls had to be determined by other evidence. The distribution of four cabin hearths, a feature interpreted to be an interior corner of the southwestern bastion, and plotted locations of late eighteenth-century artifacts on the site offered evidence for an estimated fort footprint. The discovery of cabin hearths was essential to delineating the fort's west, south, and east wall lines. Two hearths marked cabins along the westerly wall (or what was considered the front wall) of the fort. These hearths were only 6.5 feet (2 m) apart and anchored the southerly and northerly end walls of two cabins standing adjacent. A modern sewer line trench barely missed cutting through the northernmost hearth on its northerly side. If this hearth anchored the south end of a cabin, then the cabin interior would have been to the north, and the sewer line trench disturbed the cabin midden that accumulated in front of the hearth. This hearth was similar to others found on the site. It was constructed by digging a shallow circular pit about 6.5 feet (2 m) in diameter to contain the fire. Successive fires and wood fuel consumption produced an ashy soil in which animal bone, charred wood, and a few artifacts accumulated. No intact stone chimney base was present. Immediately adjacent, on the westerly side of the hearth, was a shallow circular soil deposit that may have been the remnants of a post that framed the hearth opening and supported a mantel shelf.

The hearth on the northerly wall of the adjacent cabin was a circular pit of fire-reddened and ashy soil located next to the edge of a midden stain that was strewn with animal bone elements, limestone rocks of various sizes, and other artifacts. The midden stain covered an area approximately 10 feet (nearly 3 m) in diameter and contained several domestic artifacts and a fairly heavy concentration of scattered stones. The stones were not large pieces, but the quantity suggests that they were remnants of a crudely built stone base that may have been dismantled. Local oral tradition claims that Samuel Halley used chimney stones from the fort site to build a water gap in the nineteenth century. The location and orientation of the midden stain relative to the hearth identifies it as an interior floor in the center of the cabin where domestic activities such as cooking, hearth cleaning, and other tasks took place. Organic midden that darkened the soil was more likely

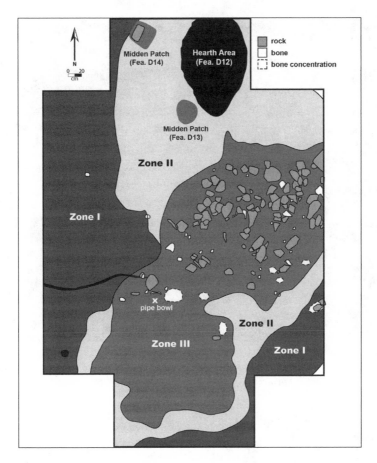

Hearth and interior of the Luttrell kitchen. Richard Henderson's plan placed Luttrell's kitchen on the westerly wall adjacent to his cabin at the southwest corner of the fort.

to accumulate here rather than along the interior walls of the cabin where beds and other furniture were probably placed. The intensity of the midden in color and content did indeed diminish at its edges. The concentration of limestone was intermixed with a large quantity of animal bone, including some large elements. The hearth itself was similar in size and content to the other hearths identified at the site. The southerly wall of the fort was identified by one hearth and a surface feature at the juncture of the southerly and westerly walls. The hearth was probably on the westerly wall of the cabin. It was similar in size and shape to others on the site. It did not have

Photo of the cabin hearth on the southerly wall of the fort. Courtesy of the William
S. Webb Museum of Anthropology at the University of Kentucky.

a recognizable stone chimney base nor were there large quantities of rock
associated with it.[26]

Another feature was discovered in the southwesterly corner of the fort,
most likely within what was the corner bastioned structure. This feature was
a scatter of animal bone and rock lying on top of organically enriched cultural
midden. Beneath the bone but still within the feature was a small, shallow
concentration where there had been intense burning. The concentration was
not large enough to have been a hearth like the others found elsewhere. The
entire feature was identified within the northeast quadrant of two adjacent 1
by 2 m units in which the remaining three quadrants were virtually devoid of
any artifacts or cultural midden. This was an "inside-outside" situation: the
edge of the bone and rock scatter marked the inside corner of the southwest
corner blockhouse and the culturally sterile area lay outside the fort
enclosure. Moses Boone said that the bastion on the southwest corner was
built quickly in 1778, just before the siege, and had no roof initially. John
Gass agreed, but neither man clarified if the bastion was a completely new

structure or if a protruding second story was added to an existing structure. The latter explanation makes more sense given the location of the cabin hearth found on the southerly wall of the fort, which must have been built by 1777 when the fort enclosure was complete. James Hall's rendition of Richard Henderson's fort plan places John Luttrell's cabin at the southwest corner and his kitchen in the adjacent cabin on the westerly wall.[27]

If the southwest corner structure was Luttrell's cabin (later expanded to include a bastion on the second story), then the two hearths along the westerly wall mark the two cabins next to the southwest corner blockhouse. The proximity of the two hearths suggests that two separate cabins stood adjacent, and the chimney of the southernmost cabin occupied its north wall, while the chimney of the northernmost cabin stood on its south wall. The cabin closest to the corner bastion would have been Luttrell's kitchen. Alternatively, the hearths could have been part of a double cabin in which they shared a chimney built between two log pens.

The hearth found on the southerly wall line was most likely the first cabin on the easterly side of the southwestern corner bastion. None of the sketch plans of the fort identify any of the occupants in the cabins along the southerly wall. The placement of the hearth and its associated chimney was on the westerly wall of the cabin about six or six and a half feet from the blockhouse. Two small circular patches of burned material were found in what appears to have been the southwesterly corner of the cabin or just outside it. One of the features contained burned corncobs. Small burn features, particularly if they contain corncobs, are usually identified as smudge pits. Their exact purpose is uncertain. One possible use was for insect control. The fort's location close to the Kentucky River may have attracted mosquitoes naturally occurring in a humid riverine environment in hot weather. Small smudge pits could have been employed to produce smoke that discouraged mosquitoes and other annoying insect pests. Another possible purpose was for smoking hides. Tanned deer and other animal hides were smoked over a smoldering fire to color them.[28]

The easterly wall of the fort was identified by a hearth that was first discovered in 1987. At that time the hearth was identified as a scatter of animal bone within a matrix of ashy soil. Only one artifact other than bone—a glazed redware rim with a green-and-cream-colored stripe applied just below the lip—was recovered. When the feature was reopened and excavation completed in 2012, only a few more bones were recovered and

Photo of the cabin hearth on the easterly wall of the fort. Courtesy of the William S. Webb Museum of Anthropology at the University of Kentucky.

virtually no other artifacts except for three wrought nail fragments and three glass fragments. Further excavation revealed an ashy pit very similar to the other hearths found at the site; it too lacked an intact chimney base. The distribution of animal bone on top of and outside of the ashy pit resembled the cabin interior floor and associated hearth from the Luttrell kitchen on the westerly wall line.

Occupants of all but three of the cabins along the easterly wall of the fort were identified by Bland Ballard based on his visit in 1779. The structure on the northeasterly corner where Richard Henderson lived was labelled "large house jutted over" to indicate that it was a blockhouse. Henderson had given up his dreams for Boonesborough by 1779, and the blockhouse may not have been occupied or Ballard did not remember who was living there in the spring of 1779. The next two spaces on the sketch are blank. The third cabin from the blockhouse was occupied by Jacob Baughman, who had come to Kentucky to serve as a chainman for John Floyd. The fourth cabin, located between Baughman and the rear gate of the fort, was occupied by Capt. John Holder, Ballard's commanding officer. The widow Thomas lived in the fifth cabin on the other side of the gate. Next to her, in the sixth cabin, was Col. Richard Callaway. The seventh cabin was probably occupied by Estill. (The legend lists him but omits the letter designation used to denote other occupants.) Finally, Capt. David Gass occupied the cabin next to the southeasterly blockhouse. If the Gass family lived here, they must have moved from the double cabin complex in the center of the fort where they were living during the 1778 siege. The hearth found on the easterly wall line of the fort may have been part of the cabin in which David Gass and his family lived following the siege of 1778 to the spring of 1780, when they moved to Estill's Station.

Of the five plans, only Henderson's plan shows the total number of cabins and bastions he intended to build. Assuming that Hall faithfully rendered Henderson's sketch, Henderson intended a symmetrical arrangement of cabins on each wall. Ballard's total of eight cabins on the easterly wall between the corner bastions agrees with Henderson's plan. In contrast, Moses Boone indicated many more spaces on the easterly wall than either Henderson or Ballard. Furthermore, Boone's plan does not show an equal number of cabin spaces on the easterly and westerly walls as Henderson's does. However, Boone's plan shows six spaces between the corner bastions on the northerly and southerly walls, which agrees with Henderson's plan if two of the spaces were intended to be stockade sections. If aspects of Boone's and Ballard's plans are considered together, even allowing for some discrepancies and omissions, they seem to corroborate Henderson's plan as the template for the fort.

The distribution of the hearths made measurement of the easterly-westerly dimension of the fort possible. The distance between the hearth on the easterly wall and a hearth more or less opposite it on the westerly wall was approximately 125 feet (38 m), which suggests that Bedinger's estimate of the size of the fort enclosure was more accurate than Hall's calculation. Bedinger's estimate was based on a visit to the site when the fort stockade was still standing, while Hall estimated the size by assuming that each cabin and the space adjacent to it was twenty feet.

The discovery of the cabin hearths along the fort walls also settled the question of whether the chimneys were on the inside or the outside of the enclosure. The debate about placement centers on arguments concerning fire hazard vs. avenues for breaching the fort walls. One line of reasoning holds that placing chimneys on the outside lessened the potential for collateral damage to the cabins should a chimney catch fire and flare out of control.

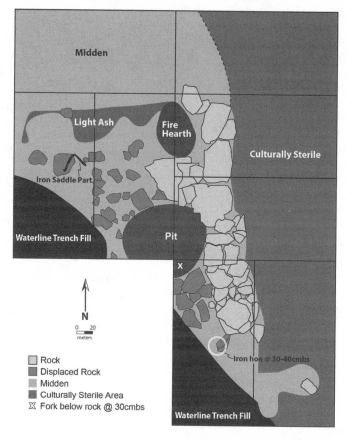

Plan of the stone foundation wall and associated features of the central cabin complex.

The opposing view argues that chimneys on the outside of the enclosure posed a threat because they could be pulled down, thereby breaching the fort wall. The answer was found in the association of interior floor midden relative to the hearth. In all cases the chimneys were on the inside of the fort enclosure.

Once the wall lines of the fort were established, the identity of the only dry-laid stone foundation found by excavation became clear. This feature consisted of several courses of dry-laid limestone that formed the partial remains of a structural foundation. A single, large piece of limestone protruded from the center of the foundation in a westerly direction and may be the remnant of a perpendicular wall line or, alternatively, a displaced stone from the stacked foundation wall. On the northerly side of the limestone protrusion was a hearth, and a small storage/trash pit was located on the south side. Artifacts were concentrated on the westerly side of the foundation within a midden stain marking the interior of the building. The location of the wall relative to the fort walls identified by other cultural features clearly placed it inside the central area of the fort and identified it as part of the central cabin complex drawn by Moses Boone—the double cabin and gunsmith shop that stood in the center of the fort.

Dimensions of the foundation allowed for an estimation of its original length. The wall extended 11 feet (3.4 m) and ran approximately 30 degrees west of magnetic north. It may have extended further in a southerly direction, but a park waterline trench truncated it. The northern terminus of the foundation was difficult to determine since the foundation was apparently dismantled and the rocks removed. Artifact density in the excavation units on the north and west side of the foundation was low, but the artifacts were varied. Given the variety, it seems likely that the units were inside the cabin. Assuming that the hearth feature adjacent to the stone foundation was centered on the wall, as was customary, the stone foundation likely once continued to the north for a distance as least as long as the extant foundation on the south side of the hearth. By this reasoning, the wall length was approximately 20 feet (6 meters).

Establishing which wall of the structure the foundation represented was more challenging, but the dogtrot floor plan offered some clues. John Gass and Moses Boone each drew the central cabin complex a little differently. Gass's sketch showed two pens of equal size with no space between them for a gunsmith facility. The wall dividing the two pens ran parallel with the long axis of the fort enclosure. Boone's sketch showed a smaller cabin to the east and a larger cabin to the west with a breezeway or narrow space between them where Squire Boone carried out his gunsmithing. Since Moses was Squire's son, his recollection of his father's shop was probably more accurate. The archaeological deposits on the easterly side of the foundation were essentially devoid of late eighteenth-century artifacts, midden, or any strong evidence of an interior floor, suggesting that this area was outside the structure. If this is correct, the stone foundation may represent the easterly wall of the central cabin complex.

One of the most unusual features found during excavation was a large pit filled with the partial carcass of a horse as well as bones identified as pig,

Photo of the pit that contained a partial horse carcass and other animal bones.

bison or cow, elk, and turkey. The feature was located 9.8 feet (3 m) west of the stone foundation remnant that was part of the structural complex in the center of the fort. If the stone foundation is the remnants of the easterly cabin of the central structural complex, the pit was probably inside one of the structural components. Unfortunately, the modern waterline trench ran diagonally between the pit and the foundation, clipping the edge of the pit and destroying archaeological evidence that might better explain the relationship of the pit to the central structural complex.

The contents of the pit were overwhelmingly dominated by animal bone; only a few artifacts were found that were not bone, notably a possible horseshoe nail and an expended large caliber (around .50 caliber) bullet. The pit was tightly packed with animal bones, many of which showed signs of butchering. Buffalo (or cow), elk, pig, and horse were identified. The horse bones in the pit had been deposited as an articulated partial carcass. Analysis of the pelvis identified the horse as female and fully mature. No bones from the head, neck, or legs below the femur were recovered, and butchering scars noted on some of the bones indicate that the meat was removed for consumption. Horses were prized animals and generally were not eaten; however, if a horse was accidentally killed, it would not have gone to waste as a meat source.

The location of the buried bones inside the fort enclosure suggests an intriguing possibility. Discarding bone or other food detritus could have been accomplished by burning or disposal outside the fort enclosure, perhaps in the river. Bones were also routinely fed to dogs, and some of the recovered bone showed evidence of carnivore gnawing. Digging a fairly large pit inside the fort suggests a different discard strategy may have been practiced during conditions that prevented or constrained disposal outside the fort. Such conditions prevailed during the Great Siege of 1778. This siege was the longest period during which fort occupants had limited freedom of movement outside their protective stockade. After the failure of the treaty negotiations on the third day, the large Indian force subjected the fort to heavy gunfire, continuing even into the night. Informants writing to Lyman Draper about their knowledge of the siege and the events that happened during it often made mention of casualties, although they generally were talking about human ones. Evisa Coshon, Daniel Boone's great-granddaughter, wrote that Col. Richard Callaway had a "fine gray mare" that was killed by spent balls during the siege. John Gass commented that stray bullets shot from a hill on the opposite side of the river killed a few horses and cattle and that the settlers butchered and ate the meat, "poor as it was."[29]

The combination of archival and archaeological information proved to be a powerful tool to uncover the secrets that the site of Fort Boonesborough holds within its soil. Archival sources provided important clues about the layout and construction of the fort, but archaeological excavation provided much more specific information about its dimensions, the spacing of the cabins, the arrangement of chimneys, and the kinds of activities carried out within the fort confines. Excavations at Fort Boonesborough identified key cultural features that delineated the south end of the fort and established conclusively exactly where the fort stood. Moreover, the dry-laid stone masonry foundations first identified in 1987 were determined to be part of the center double cabin used as both a residence and a gunsmith shop. Archaeological research on defensive Revolutionary War sites in the trans-Appalachian west has offered important insights and clarifications on how people responded to the threats they faced as they participated in the process of western expansion. Continued research in this area has great potential to deepen and enhance knowledge of this critical growth phase as the United States developed into and took its place in the world as a sovereign power.[30]

8

PACKING FOR THE WILDERNESS

Many scholarly disciplines study human culture and cultural behavior, and each has its particular perspective and approach. Archaeology is unique among the social sciences and humanities in its focus on material objects, the distributional patterning of those objects, and how they inform our understanding of the ways in which past cultures lived, worked, fought, thought, and managed their lives. The study of archaeological artifacts offers insights into the past that may confirm or reinforce conclusions drawn from the study of historic documents. Artifacts also may lead to conclusions that cannot be drawn any other way or obtained from other kinds of information. As archaeologist Leland Ferguson put it as long ago as 1975, "Archaeology need not, and should not, be the handmaiden of ethnology, history or any other field of study."[1]

The historical period in North America from the seventeenth century onward witnessed a burgeoning proliferation of material things that people made from the resources of their physical world. New inventions, improvements in technology, and the expansion of raw material sources and innovations over time often make the past seem more primitive to our modern perceptions. Yet people living in the past were faced with the same fundamental challenges of survival—procuring food, building shelter for protection from the elements, defending themselves—as modern societies face. After all, a moccasin worn by a settler fulfilled the same essential purpose as a modern sneaker; the difference is largely in the details of material, construction, durability, and comfort. Likewise, people living in past cultures purposely shaped their physical environment according to culturally dictated plans, just as modern society does. That commonality draws the student of human culture to the study of the past. Archaeology provides an entrée to that world.

Settlers preparing for life on the Kentucky frontier faced the challenge of transporting their material goods under difficult travel conditions over very long distances. Travelers to Fort Boonesborough usually entered Kentucky via the Wilderness Road through the Cumberland Gap and the eastern mountains. The trail was not improved enough for wagon traffic. Settlers rode horses or walked while driving their livestock. Pack animals, generally horses, carried household goods and tools. The trip took several weeks traversing little more than a blazed trail that snaked through dense forests and across mountain streams. Larger river floodplains often were choked with dense cane brakes. Crossing the Cumberland River and larger streams meant swimming horses, pack animals, and other livestock across swift water.

Settlers needed to bring clothing; bed linens; tools for agriculture; equipment for food processing, cooking, and serving; implements for sewing, spinning, and weaving; tools for constructing a cabin or other buildings and furniture; seed for crops; and weapons and ammunition. Within these basic needs stretched a wide variance in the types and quantities of supplies that were conveyed by individuals or families. Many settlers brought the bare minimum simply because they could not afford more. Single men coming to Kentucky generally carried very little beyond clothing, a gun and ammunition, an all-purpose knife, and perhaps a few other personal belongings. Many items could be fabricated when settlers reached their destination, particularly items made from wood or other natural resources. Examples include deer and buffalo skins tanned for leather, cane and reeds used for basketry, buffalo hair woven with flax or wool to produce linsey-woolsey, and wood turned to form bowls, trenchers, and other serving vessels and utensils. Metal tools and food processing, serving, and storage containers and other manufactured goods had to be brought in, and pack animals had limits on how much weight they could carry without breaking down. The result of these decisions and restrictions creates archaeological assemblages that are not large in terms of total artifact frequencies, particularly compared to later times when material goods were more plentiful and easier to replace.

Archaeological investigations at Fort Boonesborough and other late eighteenth-century sites recovered a wide variety of artifacts. For the sake of analysis, the artifacts were organized into functional groupings: architecture and hardware, personal belongings, agriculture and subsistence implements and residue (crops, meat, and wild foods), household items, arms and ammunition, and equine equipment. Analysis of artifacts associated with the fort offers insights into many aspects of colonial life from defensive strategies to everyday household activities to matters of dress and personal habits to foodways.

Architecture and Hardware

Artifacts associated with architecture and hardware are items used in construction of the fort cabins, stockades, stables or other buildings, and furnishings. Fort Boonesborough was constructed entirely of logs; the use of stone was minimal. An enduring myth of frontier history claims that settlers did not use iron nails when constructing their cabins. Archaeological investigations at Fort Boonesborough and many other settlement-era sites prove otherwise. While it is possible to build a log cabin entirely without the use of nails, they do make installing doors or facing windows much easier. Iron hinges also need nails to be securely fastened to the gates. The Fort Boonesborough architecture group is dominated by iron nails. All of the nails in this functional class are common nails that have heads that project from the shaft on at least two and usually all sides. While wooden pegs were still used more frequently as fasteners, the settlers at Fort Boonesborough recognized the efficacy of nails for many construction uses, and nails were desirable enough to warrant making room in pack trains for a supply of them. For people with blacksmithing skills, making nails was fairly easy, and some may have brought nail rod with them to make nails as needed. Rudimentary blacksmithing was common on the frontier. No nail rod was found at the fort site, but nail rod was identified at the Hugh McGary Station in Mercer County, which was occupied at the same time as the fort.[2]

Most of the nails from the fort are hand-shaped individually from wrought-iron nail rods. Wrought nails were made from the time of Rome to the late eighteenth century with virtually no change in the technology. Around the time of the American Revolution, cut nails were invented. They were made by cutting triangular nail blanks into flat strips and heading the blanks, a cheaper process. Cut nails quickly outcompeted wrought nails even though they were inferior in some ways to the earlier nails. Wrought nails could be bent or clinched sharply without breaking, while cut nails were more brittle. Clinching was employed in contexts like batten doors and shutters. When clinching was not required, cut nails worked just as well

Wrought-iron nails dominated the Boonesborough site. Note the example at the right, which has been clinched.

as wrought nails and were cheaper because more could be made in a given period of time.[3]

The fact that wrought nails are more frequent than cut nails in the Fort Boonesborough assemblage is an indication of the early date of the fort and the relatively short duration of its habitation. Had it continued to see intensive use into the nineteenth century, the proportion and frequency of cut nails dating after c. 1790 would be much higher. Cut nails accounted for only 15 percent of the nails used for construction. Hand-wrought nails dominated the category, accounting for 68 percent.[4]

Settlers brought different kinds of nails for different uses. The length of a nail, its pennyweight, is loosely correlated to its intended use. Of the forty nails whose length could be measured, all but three measured between 3d and 8d (1.25–2.5 in.). The three longer nails measured 10d (two examples) and 12d (one example). The shorter pennyweights were useful for many contexts, fastening such items as puncheon boards, floor joists, shingles, door and window facings, and furniture. Heavier nails were used for hardware such as gate hinges.

Identifying the heads of nails offers insights on the context of their use, since particular types were preferred for specific purposes. Headless, expanded, or T-head nails were preferred for fastening floorboards because they were easier to pound in so that the heads were flush with wood (lowering the risk to bare feet). Rosehead nails performed well in situations where the wooden piece being nailed was fastened in a vertical position, such as a door or window facing. In this context, particularly if shutters and hinges were being used, the protrusion of the nail head would help keep the nail from working out of the hole as doors or shutters were opened and shut. Other contexts in which nails might have been useful include bed frames, tables, and chairs. Nail head types that were identified in the fort assemblage include, in order of highest to lowest frequency, irregular or distorted, rosehead, expanded, T-head, ovate, and headless. Nails with irregular heads far outnumbered other types and reflect the effects of pounding on the head when the nail was driven into the wood and possibly denote further distortion if the nail was pulled from the wood for some reason. The presence of expanded, T-head, and headless nails may indicate flooring.

Wrought nails were recovered from every excavated area of the fort site; the highest density occurred in the central cabin complex where excavations were the most extensive. The widespread wrought-nail distribution suggests that nails were routinely brought to the site and used in many contexts. In contrast, the less numerous cut nails were concentrated in or near the central cabin complex where the only substantial stone foundation was found. Their concentration here suggests that this structure was occupied and maintained over a longer period after the fort had ceased to function as a defensive site.

Lime mortar, or daub, in association with the stone foundation located in the center of the fort site attests to other construction techniques. Its occurrence there is no surprise, since this feature was the only substantial example of stone masonry found at the site. The foundation itself was dry-laid, but lime mortar may have been used between the structure's logs. Archival references document that gaps in the cabin walls and the stockade were plugged with clayey mud that would not have been preserved in an archaeological context, particularly if the cabins and stockades were dismantled. However, the central cabin complex contained artifacts that suggest that it may have been occupied for some time after the end of the Revolutionary War. Properly chinking the log members of the structure would have improved the construction and made it more weather tight.

Several iron tacks and a brad were found in the central cabin complex, in the southwesterly blockhouse, in the Luttrell kitchen, and in the neighboring cabin on the west wall. These fasteners may have been used on portable storage boxes or as part of furniture. Storage boxes, trunks, and chests were multipurpose and were used to store important papers such as deeds and to hold clothing, linens, or other household goods.

Personal Belongings

Personal artifacts include such items as clothing fasteners (buttons and straight pins), shoe buckles, sewing equipment, jewelry, mirror glass, and smoking pipes. Clothing-related artifacts are the most common category in the personal group. Beyond the practical considerations of clothing choices (such as warmth and durability) was the social statement that clothing made. People often assessed social status or position using clothing cues. Historian Elizabeth Perkins perceptively observes, "Personal appearance, especially clothing, played an important role in the rapid appraisal of strangers. . . . Those passing the test of dress and manner . . . could expect preferential treatment. . . . Reading the language of dress became part of the social expertise of every border inhabitant." On a trip to Kentucky in 1788, Mary Dewees and her companions were given beds to sleep in at a rough tavern, a concession she attributed to their "dress or adress or perhaps Boath." Dress and appearance also reflected ethnic and cultural backgrounds.[5]

The concept of dress and undress is a useful way to think about colonial clothing. Dress refers to the total look conveyed by a combination of garments. Undress refers to everyday, utilitarian clothes used for work and usually involves fewer garments. Since laundering clothing was an arduous task, reducing wear and tear on clothing encouraged wearing a minimum unless conditions called for more formal attire. Adding or subtracting specific garments depended on factors such as weather, the formality of the occasion, one's social class, and the task at hand. Women living on isolated stations might only wear a shift in warm weather, particularly if they did not expect to be seen by outsiders. Likewise, men might just wear a pair of breeches and a shirt, adding leggings if they thought they would need leg protection. Settler Jacob Stevens referred to his clothes while describing his experiences at the Battle of Blue Licks in 1782. Since the battle took place in August, the pioneers who went to fight wore clothing suitable for hot weather. As he fled from the battlefield, Stevens crossed the Licking River on foot, emerging soaking wet. "When I got over, I stopped and drew off my buckskin breeches. . . . The buckskins, when wet were so heavy we codn't run, having them on. So then had on my short leggings, moccasins and shirt." As he proceeded, he lost his leggings, which left his legs unprotected when he encountered stinging nettles, "green and breast high." A man fleeing with him "gave me a linen hunting shirt to tie about me to keep the nettles from killing me." Jacob's loss of first his breeches and then his leggings meant he was left with perhaps a pair of underdrawers, a breechclout, or even nothing underneath his shirt. His description also highlighted a negative feature of wearing buckskin breeches; wet leather sagged and became very heavy.[6]

Late eighteenth-century clothing for men on the frontier is often stereotyped as being made of buckskin in the form of hunting shirts, breeches, and leggings. Joseph Doddridge's memoir described the hunting shirt as the universal dress of men, worn with breeches and/or leggings. The hunting shirt was a "loose frock, reaching halfway down the thighs, with large sleeves, open before, and so wide as to lap over a foot or more then belted. The cape was large, and sometimes handsomely fringed with a ravelled piece of cloth of a different color from that of the hunting shirt itself." This garment may have had buttons only at the sleeve cuffs since it was held closed by a belt. Knee- or full-length breeches were made with a drop front that fastened to the waist with metal buttons usually made of brass (sometime gilded) or a yellow metal alloy. Leggings were simply rectangles made of leather or cloth that laced around the leg. They protected the lower legs but could be made long enough to cover the thigh as well.[7]

In reality, clothing choices were more varied than the stereotype implies. While leather was very durable and protective, cloth garments were much more comfortable and were preferred over leather. Probate inventories that include a list of clothing are good sources of information on wardrobe choice and variety. William Stuart's inventory, recorded in the Lincoln County Court on March 19, 1783, listed his clothing in detail. A pair of drawers was the only undergarment listed. He owned two pairs of breeches (one made of leather) and four linen shirts over which he could choose among three waistcoats. Protective clothing included a pair of overalls and a pair of cloth leggings. He owned four stocks to wear at his neck, a handkerchief, eight pairs of stockings, a pair of half-hand gloves, a pair of silver knee buckles, and a watch. For footwear he had his choice of two pairs of shoes and a pair of "shoe boots" but no moccasins. A greatcoat kept him warm.[8]

James Wright's inventory, filed a month earlier, revealed a smaller wardrobe but showed similar variety. His coat, cloak, and two jackets were all described as old, as were his shoes and stockings and his two hats. But he followed the styles of the day in his suit of cotton and linen, a precursor to the modern three-piece suit, to be worn with his shirts and stocks. A pair of buckles adorned his shoes. He also had spare buttons, some fulled cloth (a type of felt), and some silk for future garments. Noteworthy for their absence were moccasins and hunting shirts. Like William Stuart and many others, Wright preferred English-style clothing.[9]

Women's clothing began with a shift, usually made of linen, that had either a drawstring or plain neck and drawstring or cuffs at the elbows. Women also wore stays, the precursor of a foundation garment that was later called a corset. Stays were most often worn by the middling and gentry classes. Working women and slave women also wore stays but more often for support than to produce a fashionable body shape. Stays varied considerably in the materials used to construct them, in the flexibility of their boning, and in the fabric that covered them. They were laced to the body and so did not require metal fasteners.[10]

Basic outerwear was a linsey petticoat (skirt) and a gown. The gown took several forms; the front could be open or closed, and the back was either a sacque (with loose fabric gathered in the back in pleats) or English style. The bodice and skirt were joined together and usually fastened across the front with hooks and eyes. The skirt was open at the front below the waistline, and the petticoat worn beneath was revealed in this open space. The petticoat was a skirt and was not considered an undergarment. It could have a waistband that fastened with a button or ties or it could be fitted around the waist with a drawstring. Several styles of loosely fitting gowns were also common informal or working wear for women. Other articles of clothing or accessories included a stomacher (a triangular piece of fabric used to hold the front of the gown together), a jacket or cape in colder weather, a mobcap (sometimes worn with a hat), mitts or a muff, and heeled shoes.[11]

Textile production was one of the most time-consuming and labor-intensive tasks done by colonial settlers on the frontier. Growing and harvesting flax and hemp, shearing sheep, tanning leather—these were just the beginning steps of a long process that occupied many hours of labor. Linen, wool, and cotton were all common fabrics used for colonial clothing. Frontier life was hard on clothing, and replacing garments was often difficult. Women spent a significant amount of their time spinning and weaving linen and wool, then sewing the cloth into clothing. But other fibers were also used, specifically buffalo hair combined with linen to form a variant of linsey-woolsey, and even nettles, which were collected and processed into fiber. Settler Mrs. Morrison mentioned that some women used nettle thread as a warp and buffalo hair for the weft as a stopgap solution to shortages of more desirable fibers. Flax cultivation was important for the production of linen. Likewise, hemp fiber could be woven into a durable, utilitarian cloth that was good for work clothes. Cotton did not grow well at Kentucky's latitude and saw less use than other fabrics that could be produced from locally available domesticated or wild plants and animals. Sheep were more difficult to raise than other livestock because they were vulnerable to predators such as wolves and required more shelter than cattle or pigs. Nevertheless, sheep were introduced at least by the mid to late 1780s and probably earlier in small numbers. Sheared wool could also be brought in as packing material and then spun and woven into fabric.[12]

One of the first nonfood crops grown was flax for linen. Flax seed was identified in the midden soil associated with the Luttrell kitchen. Flax tends to be a spring crop because the fiber cannot endure very hot weather. The leaves wilt, the stems turn yellow, and the seeds turn brown when it is time to harvest. The entire plant, roots and all, is pulled from the ground, since cutting the plant causes it to lose its sap which affects the quality of the linen. Once the settlers harvested flax, the fiber had to be separated from the woody stalks. First, a process called rippling used coarse iron wire combs to strip the seeds and leaves from the plant. Next, the stalks were retted to loosen the pectin or gum that attaches the fiber to the stem. Retting was accomplished by either submerging the stalks in water or spreading them on the ground and allowing dew to loosen the adhesion of the bark to the fiber. After retting, the plants were squeezed and allowed to dry before they were broken on a flax brake. A flax brake chopped away at the straw or chaff, freeing the fiber. More chaff was removed with a scutching knife and board, then the fiber was drawn through hackles (boards with protruding nails) to comb and straighten the longer fibers prior to spinning. This process also separated the shorter fibers used for tow, or coarse linen, from the finer, longer strands that resemble masses of blond hair and make the finest linen. Only after this labor-intensive process is completed is the flax ready to be spun into thread and woven into cloth used for garments and bed and table linens.[13]

Hemp was another fiber crop that was planted early in the settlement of Kentucky. Although no archaeological evidence of hemp was found at Fort Boonesborough, it was grown by Archibald McNeill in 1775 near Danville, and other settlers followed suit whenever they could procure the expensive seed. Hemp fiber makes a sturdy utilitarian cloth that is well suited for work clothes. In frontier Kentucky it also was fashioned into rope and served as a medium of exchange when money was scarce. The process of separating hemp fiber from the woody stalk resembled that done with flax—it was labor-intensive and physically demanding.[14]

Although sheep were present only in small numbers in the earliest years of settlement, their wool was valued for making a durable, warm fabric. Wool was produced by a less arduous process than linen but still entailed intensive labor. Once the sheep were sheared, the raw wool was scoured by washing, rinsing, and drying to remove dirt, grease, and sweat. Fuller's earth, a fine clay powder, was often used to remove lanolin, a natural grease found in sheep's wool. Once cleaned, the fleece was dyed using various natural products like indigo, madder, cochineal, goldenrod, and pokeberry. The fleece was then carded using carding combs set with wire teeth; carding straightened the fibers and removed any remaining matter that scouring left behind. Carded wool was then ready for spinning into fabric suitable for knitwear or bulkier items like carpeting. Another combing process removed the shorter fibers to make worsted cloth suitable for garments. A spinning wheel twisted the fibers into a long, continuous thread or yarn. The yarn was then woven on a loom to produce wool fabric, or it was knitted. Wool was fulled by trampling the cloth in a tub of warm, soapy water, a process that shrank the wool and locked the woven fibers closer together. The cloth was then stretched on tenter frames and allowed to dry. All of these processes were eventually mechanized, but the early settlers of Kentucky had no choice but to process their products by hand until conditions allowed them to build fulling mills and other facilities that employed machines to automate the process. Unsurprisingly, peddlers bringing in goods to sell and early storekeepers on the Kentucky frontier stocked fabrics as one of their major commodities. But tens of thousands of yards of wool and other cloth were produced at home by Kentucky women from homegrown raw materials.[15]

One of the useful byproducts of hunting wild game was leather. The production of leather was a specialized skill that usually was performed by men. First, hides were washed and soaked in a lime solution to burn off the top layers of skin. After removing hair and epidermis with a scraper, workers washed the hide again in a solution of urine, feces, stale beer, or rotting scraps of hide to remove the lime and soften the hide. The leather was then tanned by soaking in tannic acid, derived from crushed black oak or white hemlock bark, to remove the gelatin and toughen the hide into leather. The resulting product was dried and made pliable by treating it with tallow and neat's-foot oil or other lubricants and then burnishing it with an iron slicker and scouring stone. While not as exacting a skill as joinery, the process was long, laborious, and back-breaking. An inexperienced tanner could easily ruin a hide. An accomplished tanner quickly found customers for his services.[16]

Once the fabric and leather production processes were complete, clothing construction could begin. Sewing equipment is often recovered during archaeological excavation since the tools are usually made of metal. The fort excavations yielded a pair of large shears (missing one of its loop handles) suitable for cutting fabric pattern pieces, and a blade of a smaller pair of scissors that would have been useful for snipping thread, trimming seams, or other routine sewing tasks. The small scissors blade was bent at a 90-degree angle, obviously as a result of using them to pry something free. The same action might have also separated the two scissors blades, rendering the tool useless. Both the scissors and shears were made of iron and had pivoted blades. Two thimbles, one a fragment made of very thin metal and one a complete child-sized example, were also found. Both are made of brass and were probably manufactured in England. The complete child's thimble has dents in the crown or top that indicate heavy use. Thimbles to protect fingers from needle or pinpricks during hand sewing were a common component of every woman's sewing box. Little girls were taught to sew at an early age. Five straight pins with wound wire heads could have been used to hold fabric pieces together to facilitate sewing a seam or, alternatively, to pin a neckerchief or apron pinafore in place. Straight pins were often used to attach parts of women's garments to each other. Other uses for straight pins included pinning multiple pages of a document together, functioning as guides for making lace, and, in a departure from practical uses, used in conjuring or deflecting magic spells.[17]

While the textiles used to construct clothing rarely survive in archaeological deposits, fasteners such as buttons and buckles are frequently collected at archaeological excavations. Commercially marketed buttons were commonly made from metal but also were produced from horn, wood, and shell. Buttons recovered from the excavations are of several sizes and made of a variety of metals. All five pewter buttons recovered at the Boonesborough excavation are medium-sized, ranging in diameter from .54 to .625 in. (13.7–16 mm). They may have been sewn to sleeve cuffs or the

(*Left*) Sewing equipment recovered in excavations (*clockwise*): thimble, shears missing one of its loop handles, and one-half of a small pair of scissors with a bent blade. (*Right*) Various examples of clothing fasteners were recovered. (*Left column, top to bottom*): pewter button (two views), brass breeches button, pewter button; (*right column, top to bottom*): brass buckle, large brass button, domed button.

placket of a waistcoat. Pewter is a tin alloy to which copper and antimony are added to produce a stronger metal. It is light in color and has a relatively low melting point that allows it to be easily cast in a mold. Owning a button mold meant that buttons could be manufactured at home to replace lost or broken ones. One of the buttons recovered was cast in a mold that formed a wedge-shaped shank that was then drilled for sewing. However, this particular button has an incompletely drilled shank and was unusable. It also has a molded design on its face. The design is difficult to identify but might be a face, possibly in profile, surrounded by a decorative border. Its presence indirectly suggests that someone at Fort Boonesborough owned a button mold. Another pewter button also has decorative molding of an unidentified motif. The other buttons have plain faces. Plain-faced buttons are the most common type in use during the late eighteenth century, primarily on men's garments. By the time Fort Boonesborough was established, pewter buttons were worn primarily by people of limited means.[18]

The remaining buttons are made of brass or white metal: one exception is an unidentified dark metal that is pitted on the button face. This latter button has a wire eyelet for attachment and measures .63 in. (16 mm) in diameter, placing it in the medium-sized category. One of the buttons is made of white metal, has a spun back, and once had a soldered wire eye that has broken off. This type of button was made between 1760 and 1785. Its diameter of .7 in. (17.5 mm) places it near the uppermost limit of medium-sized buttons. Another button of equivalent size is made of brass and has a wire eyelet that was crimped into a metal foot soldered to the back. All three of these buttons could have been fasteners for waistcoats or breeches. The largest button recovered is a brass button with a wire eyelet and a stamped band around the perimeter of the face. At 1 in. (25.4 mm) in diameter, it falls within the category of a large button, such as one that was usually attached to a coat.[19]

Finally, a two-piece button was found in three fragments. The face and back of the button are made of very thin brass. It probably had a wire eyelet attachment, which is missing. The button face is slightly domed. Its diameter of .7 in. (18 mm) identifies it as a medium-sized button such as those often used on waistcoats or breeches. This button probably was not made until after 1812, or even later, well after Fort Boonesborough's primary occupancy period. While the precise date by which all the fort cabins were abandoned and eventually demolished is unknown, the most intensive period of occupation of the fort was from 1775 to approximately 1790. The button was found near the cabin foundation in the center of the fort. One fragment was found in the soil level above the top of the foundation, and the two other fragments were recovered from a later animal burrow where they had been carried sometime after their original deposit. The button could have been lost during cultivation of the fort site in early to mid-nineteenth century after the last of the cabins had been removed.[20]

A brass buckle frame was also recovered from the excavations. It is rectangular and has molded decoration. The chape that formed the fastening mechanism is missing. The two longer sides of the frame each have a central hole that held the chape in place. The two shorter sides each have two holes placed symmetrically. These holes served no functional purpose and may have once held small gemstones. The buckle may have also been plated to resemble silver or gold. Measuring 1 by 1.3 in. (2.5 by 3.3 cm), the buckle may have once adorned a shoe. It was found in association with the stone foundation wall in the center of the fort.

Although jewelry is a relatively rare find on archaeological sites, the fort site excavations recovered three beads and a gemstone. Another bead was found at some distance from the fort and is included in this discussion because of its possible trade bead identification. The two seed beads, one white and one black, could have been sewn onto textiles or leather or strung to decorate small pieces of jewelry. They were found in two different features and probably were not part of the same item or piece of jewelry. Beadwork on garments is usually considered to be Native American in origin but does not exclude use by settlers. Given the fort context, these beads could have once adorned leggings or other garments that may have been obtained during a raid of Indian villages, in a captive situation, or by sale or trade. For example, the Fort Boonesborough men who were captured in early 1778 when they were processing saltwater at Blue Licks could have been provided beaded clothing (such as leggings or moccasins) during their capture, and they brought the items back with them after they escaped or were released. Plunder taken on raids against the Indian villages might also have included clothing items that were then auctioned off. John Redd told historian Lyman Draper that he recalled seeing Daniel Boone at a meeting of the Virginia assembly dressed "in real backwoods stile" in a "common jeans suit, with the buckskin leggings neatly beaded. His leggings were manufactured by the Indians." Archival and archaeological evidence of beadwork in colonial, non–Native American sites underscores the mixture of different clothing traditions, transformed through cultural exchange.[21]

The other bead is larger and made of translucent glass in a faceted spherical shape; it is .4 in. (10 mm) in diameter. It resembles Czech faceted glass beads still made today and could have been part of a necklace. A circular green paste gemstone measuring .3 in. (8 mm) in diameter may have been set into a ring or a brooch. This gemstone, the larger bead, and the white seed bead were all found in association with the stone foundation and internal pit and hearth features that marked the cabin complex in the center of the fort. The seed bead was recovered from the base of a pit that was the

Although most of the items settlers carried to the frontier were utilitarian, bits of jewelry were found at the site. (*Top to bottom*): green paste glass gemstone, turquoise glass trade bead, faceted translucent glass bead.

earliest dated feature associated with the foundation wall. The larger bead and gemstone were recovered from general cultural midden, the former at a lower level than the latter. That stratigraphic position suggests that they were lost at different times, possibly by different people over the length of time the central cabin complex was in use. The black seed bead was recovered from hearth deposits that were associated with a cabin on the south wall of the fort.

A turquoise glass bead was found outside the fort site during the 1987 investigations. It is a wire-wound bead measuring .35 in. (9 mm) in diameter and is very similar to fur trade beads. It was found within the area where the Shawnees and their allies camped during the 1778 siege. It cannot be unequivocally attributed to Native Americans at the siege because it could have been dropped by a settler or even by a modern reenactor, but its provenience in or near the enemy encampment is suggestive.

Five fragments of flat, light green to aquamarine glass probably are from small hand mirrors, commonly called "looking glasses" in the eighteenth century. Ranging in thickness from .06 to .08 in. (1.4–2 mm), mirror glass was identical to windowpane glass except for having a painted reflective backing that created the mirror effect. All of the backing has flaked off the examples from the fort, and their identification as mirror glass is based on the lack of glass-paned windows in the fort cabins. Most of the flat glass is associated with the cabin complex in the center of the fort.

The recovery of a pipe stem, a pipe bowl fragment, and a ribbed pipe bowl and stem fragment, all made of white ball clay, points to tobacco consumption and, by inference, tobacco production. Tobacco consumption was a common personal habit by the time Fort Boonesborough was established. Tobacco was an important source of income for small and large farmers alike; it was one of the earliest nonfood crops grown in Kentucky. Identification of a single tobacco seed from the ashy hearth fill in the central cabin complex indicates that tobacco was grown in the fields around Fort Boonesborough as well.

The settlers at Fort Boonesborough raised small crops of tobacco for personal consumption and as a medium of exchange, but the tobacco industry did not begin to grow until the occupation of the fort itself was in its waning years. Thus it is not surprising that evidence of tobacco in the form of pipes and seed is very limited. But even their limited presence is significant because they acknowledge the important role tobacco played in the agricultural economy that developed in Kentucky as well as the social role tobacco consumption filled. As people struggled to place the town of Boonesborough on a secure economic footing in the 1780s and 1790s, tobacco and the New Orleans market played a role. The earliest tobacco warehouse at Boonesborough was authorized in 1787, and a second warehouse was built by 1810. These buildings were located southwest of the fort site on a higher terrace where the present entrance to the park is located on State Highway 388. Once viable transportation options (mostly roads suitable for wagons for the internal trade) allowed shipping tobacco to market, the tobacco industry at Boonesborough as elsewhere could thrive.[22]

The pipe fragments are from two types of pipes made in the eighteenth century. A short section of stem and a bowl sherd are from at least two different elbow pipes that were broken and discarded in the central cabin complex and in the Luttrell kitchen. A ribbed pipe bowl and stem fragment was also found in association with the Luttrell kitchen. This fragment is too small to tell much about what the pipe looked like. The bowl and stem

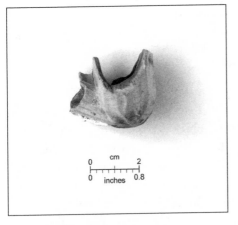

A portion of a stub stem tobacco pipe was found during excavations. The settlers at Fort Boonesborough raised small crops of tobacco for personal consumption, but the Kentucky tobacco industry did not begin to grow until the fort's waning years.

fragment is from a stub stem pipe of a style made between 1770 and 1840. Stub stem pipes have short stems into which a hollow cane or reed stem was inserted. The Fort Boonesborough example has molded ribbing that ran vertically from the base of the bowl to the rim. The stem also has molded ribbing that ran parallel from the base, possibly to the rim of the stem. It is made from an off-white ball clay. The angle of the bowl to the stem is 90 degrees. This angle orients the bowl opening toward the smoker and facilitates lighting the tobacco in the bowl, a process that was usually done with an ember held by tongs or with a lit candle.[23]

Although the personal artifact group does not include a large number of objects, what was collected documents how the settlers brought items with them that helped establish their identities and softened the rigors of the frontier experience. In spite of the hardships of frontier life, there were opportunities to don more formal apparel for a special occasion or to have a quiet smoke at the end of a long day. Pioneers interviewed many years later made little mention of these small, satisfying rituals, but artifacts like beads, pipes, buttons, and buckles are testimony to them.

Crops, Livestock, and Wild Resources

The settlers of Fort Boonesborough employed a combination of strategies that provided them with food, fuel, and raw materials. Cultivating crops and raising livestock replicated long-practiced patterns of food production in their newly adopted country. Wild resources such as local wood species provided fuel for cooking and heating, and edible and useful wild plants and game animals augmented settlers' diets as well as furnishing ingredients for folk remedies or other nonculinary needs.

HARVESTING NATURE'S BOUNTY

When settlers arrived at the site of Fort Boonesborough, they saw a wooded landscape with grassy openings and canebrakes punctuating the forest. The fort site was located in the Hills of the Bluegrass, a physiographic zone between the gently rolling, fertile land of the inner Bluegrass and the hillier, less fertile land of the outer Bluegrass. Its transitional location offered convenient and ready access to diverse animal and plant resources.[24]

Forested upland ridges and creek valleys offered abundant wood resources. Settlers encountered many familiar wood species and applied their prior knowledge of those species to appropriate uses. Construction (of buildings, stockades, and furniture) and manufacturing (of trenchers, bowls, buckets, and tool handles, for example) were the principal uses for wood, along with fuel. Flanking the river bottomland, Sycamore Hollow (also known as the Lick Branch) was named for the numerous sycamores that grew there. The ridge overlooking the Boonesborough bottomland was called Hackberry Ridge for a similar reason. The inference is that the creek drainage and uplands were wooded. Analysis of charred wood samples from the chimney hearths provided information on seventeen locally available wood species the settlers used. Hickory, oak, and walnut top the list, followed by elm, buckeye, and possibly mulberry and ash. Sycamore, American chestnut, honey locust, black cherry, and possibly catalpa, persimmon, Kentucky coffeetree, sassafras, and hackberry were all identified in minor amounts in the cabin hearths. Some trees bore edible fruits such as walnuts, hickory nuts, persimmons, chestnuts, and mulberries, while others found different culinary uses, such as sassafras for tea and Kentucky coffeetree pods as an alternative to coffee. The open hearths of the cabins were wasteful consumers of wood, requiring settlers to harvest lots of wood fuel for cooking and heating. Trees unsuitable for construction found a ready use as firewood as did the branches removed from wood intended for construction or deadwood collected from the forest floor.[25]

The local environment supported many species of fauna from large game to smaller mammals, birds, amphibians, fish, and shellfish. Large game animals such as buffalo, bear, deer, and elk provided the greatest amount of meat per animal killed, but settlers ate many other wild animal species. Bones collected from the fort site indicate a mix of wild and domestic animals were common to the settlers' diet.

One of the most important game animals for Kentucky settlers was the buffalo. The vast buffalo herds native to the Great Plains did not expand east of the Mississippi until the late 1500s, largely in response to human intervention. Widespread death from European diseases depopulated areas formerly occupied by native peoples. Overhunting encouraged by the fur trade led to declines in the numbers of deer and other desired animals, which in turn reduced hunting pressure in some areas. The Indian practice of burning off land to create openings for agricultural plots created savannas that presented desirable buffalo habitat. Buffalo herds east of the Mississippi never reached the teeming numbers that roamed the Great Plains, but they were nevertheless an important source of meat for incoming settlers. At Fort Boonesborough they were attracted to the mineral springs that rose in Sycamore Hollow and to the grassy browse on the adjacent terrace. Felix Walker, who arrived at Boonesborough in 1775, commented in his later memoir that he saw two to three hundred "buffaloes of all sizes . . . some running, some walking, others loping slowly and carelessly, with young calves playing, skipping and bounding through the plain."[26]

Buffalo provided large quantities of meat per animal as well as other raw materials that were made into useful items. The fresh meat was prepared in various ways for meals; it also was salted and dried to make jerky or rendered for tallow. Femur and shank bones were roasted, split, and scraped for their marrow, a delicacy that substituted for butter. The thick pelts were tanned into durable leather. Fleece was woven with linen to produce a sturdy variation of linsey-woolsey cloth, or it was wound with nettle to make a tumpline called a hoppus (or sapper's string) to carry large bags. Tough sinew was stripped from the spinal column for use as lacings or stout thread. Fresh skins were cut into long, hairy strips to form ropes called tugs that were virtually indestructible and had many uses. Buffalo horns were useful for holding gunpowder. Bones could be fashioned into knife or utensil handles.[27]

The bones that were discarded at the fort site are largely from the meatiest or choicest parts of the animal: the front and back legs, haunch, hump, ribs, shoulder, neck, and lower jaw. Buffalo were so large that they had to be butchered at the kill site and the meat packed on a horse for

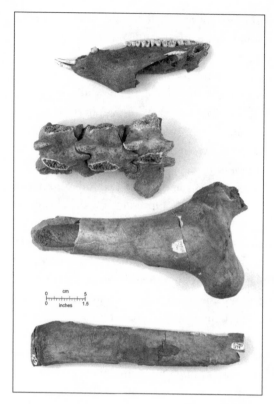

Bone fragments from both domestic and wild animals were recovered in the midden pits. (*Top to bottom*): pig mandible, horse vertebra, cow femur, buffalo thoracic vertebrae.

transportation. The bones indicate that the animal was dismembered by detaching the front and back legs, the shoulder and neck, the ribs and the hump. The head was quite large and may have only been harvested for the horns and the tongue (the latter suggested by the presence of teeth). Thoracic vertebrae formed the hump at the top of the buffalo's back. The hump meat was considered a delicacy, as were the tongue and tenderloins. Other meaty cuts came from the shoulder and haunch. Roasted ribs and marrowbones provided a succulent meal. Many of the bones have chop, knife, and even fork marks, indicating the harvesters used hatchets or tomahawks, knives, and forks for butchering and eating. Gnaw marks made by domestic dogs attest to the use of bones for dog food.

Richard Henderson mentioned in his journal on May 9, 1775, that nobody wasted any bear that was fit to eat, but they did not worry about them becoming scarce as they did for deer and buffalo. He wrote of eating "fat bear" and a "little spoiled buffalo and elk" on May 17, 1775, and washing it down with coffee. An adult black bear weighs more than four hundred pounds and has many pounds of harvestable meat. Butchering at the place of kill and leaving most of the bones behind lessened the burden of transporting the meat, but some cuts such as the haunch or shoulder were detached at the shoulder or hip and transported bone-in. The settlers found many uses for bear. The fatty meat was eaten, but it was also rendered for its tallow. Daniel Trabue found that he could render twenty-eight pounds of tallow from a single adult bear. Tallow not only made a superior cooking oil but was also used as a lubricant and as fuel for tallow lamps. Salting the meat produced succulent bear bacon that required less salt to cure than beef or pork. The tongue, heart, and kidneys were considered delicacies. The skin made a warm bedcover.[28]

Only a few bear bones were identified among the Fort Boonesborough bones. All of them came from the front (humerus and ulna) or back (femur) legs. All of them show knife cuts, and some were gnawed by domestic dogs. Elk bones are similarly sparse in the Fort Boonesborough collection but were distributed among three different cabins. Elk probably were not killed as often as buffalo and deer, but settlers took advantage of opportunities when they arose.

Deer provided a major source of wild meat and hides. The Kentucky landscape supported huge numbers of white-tailed deer, and commercial hunters supplied a large international market with skins. Aside from meat, deer provided raw materials similar to those obtained from buffalo for manufacture into useful and necessary items. Deer bone elements from the excavation are from many parts of the body, from head to torso to legs. Depending on their size, deer might be butchered into more manageable parts or simply slung whole onto a packhorse for transport from the kill site. Meat cuts indicated by the bones are also similar to those for buffalo: the rump, round, and shank from the back of the animal; ribs from the middle; and the chuck, brisket, and foreshank from the front. Antler was fashioned into handles and other items. Bones associated with the jaws as well as teeth were probably detached along with the tongue.

Bones from gray squirrel, raccoon, and gray fox were identified in small quantities. The raccoon and fox may have been taken mostly for their pelts. The raccoon, represented by a lower right jawbone with a cut mark on the outer side, was probably skinned for its pelt and its remains thrown to a dog that left gnaw marks on the bone. "Coon hunting" has a long history that dates back to Native Americans who hunted raccoons for their fur and meat. English settlers took up the practice and added dogs such as foxhounds to the hunt to improve their chances. Fox were prized for their pelts, while squirrel meat was considered good eating by backcountry settlers.

Although domestic poultry was brought to Fort Boonesborough as early as 1775, wild birds were hunted as well. Settlers spoke of sandwiching fatty bear meat between two slices of wild turkey breast when bread was unavailable. Several wild turkey bones were identified as well as a bone that probably was from a Canadian goose.[29]

Food sources from the Kentucky River and its tributaries were not ignored. Bowfin, bullhead, channel, and flathead catfish varied the diet with the added benefit of providing a pleasant pastime with a fishing pole. Coming from the eastern seaboard, many settlers were familiar with edible marine shellfish such as clams and mussels. Freshwater mussel shells from at least eight species, all from riverine environments typical of the Kentucky River, were found in sufficient quantity to conclude that the settlers were gathering them for food or, possibly, for bait.[30]

Familiar wild plant sources also augmented domesticated crops for food and other needed commodities. One story relates how the women followed their cattle to see what they ate as a means of identifying sources of edible and medicinal plants. Nuts, berries, and fruits from wild sources were gathered in season to supplement cultivated foodstuffs. Settlers' interviews mentioned that other plants, such as ginseng, spicebush, sassafras, and mint, provided useful medicines and teas, and Kentucky coffeetree supplied a coffee substitute. Sassafras and Kentucky coffeetree were both identified among the botanical samples at Fort Boonesborough. Many edible or usable wild plants are unlikely to be preserved in the archaeological record because of their method of preparation and ingestion. However, botanical analysis of the Fort Boonesborough samples identified elderberry, mulberry, persimmon, and black cherry as wild sources of berries or fruit. Walnuts, hickory nuts, and possibly butternuts were also consumed.[31]

Five species of wild plants that have culinary or medicinal uses were also identified by the botanical analysis. Their preservation in archaeological features is due to charring within cabin hearths that prevented them from decomposing naturally, but that context also suggests that they were purposefully gathered. Two of the plant species, wood sorrel (*Oxalis stricta*) and purslane (*Portulaca oleracea*), are edible. The leaves and flowers of wood sorrel have a distinct, tangy flavor. The plant can be eaten in a salad or chewed raw as a thirst quencher. It can also be brewed as a tea, boiled to produce an orange dye, or made into a poultice for dry mouth and swelling. Wood sorrel is native to North America. Purslane is not generally thought to be native to North America, but it may have been introduced in pre-Columbian times. The slightly sour and salty taste of the raw greens lends flavor to a salad, and it can be cooked like spinach or added to soups and stews. American bittersweet (*Celastrus scandens*) has been used in folk remedies to treat liver ailments, skin problems, arthritis, childbirth pain, diarrhea, and dysentery. All of its parts have toxic qualities, and modern medicine does not recommend its use medicinally.[32]

Two species, goosegrass (*Eleusine indica*) and common chickweed (*Stellaria media*), may also have been gathered by the settlers. Goosegrass has edible seeds but the yield is low. Its presence in a single feature in the central cabin complex may be due to its having been gathered for livestock feed or for some other nonculinary purpose. Chickweed was recommended as a treatment for mange or other skin conditions as early as the seventeenth century. It also was used to treat pulmonary symptoms or joint pain. Chickweed was naturalized to North America at an unknown date. It is a common plant in the British Isles, and settlers were probably familiar with it.[33]

The contributions that wild animal and plant sources made to the diets of the Fort Boonesborough settlers were essential in the early years of settlement. The strategies of hunting, wild plant gathering, crop cultivation, and livestock husbandry formed a multipronged approach that helped to lessen the effects of times when Indian attacks and raids restricted movement outside the fort and curtailed normal food procurement. The approach was not entirely new to the settlers, since many wild plant sources and game animals such as deer, small mammals, and fish were familiar. Nevertheless, the greater dependence on wild meat and plants introduced more variety in their diets and, at times, could mean the difference between being fed and going hungry.

WORKING THE LAND

Agricultural production was a primary occupation of the settlers at Fort Boonesborough; their survival depended on their ability to raise food crops and livestock. This was no small task under wartime conditions that made working in their fields very dangerous. In such perilous times wild foods,

This trapezoidal iron draw-hoe blade was fairly large at eight inches wide. It would have been suitable for chopping out weeds and other cultivation tasks.

particularly game animals, provided badly needed sustenance. Even so, the settlers suffered periods of food deprivation, as was the case during 1777 and early in 1778 when Indian attacks and raids were particularly frequent and violent.[34]

Once the land was cleared of trees and underbrush, the ground had to be readied for planting. Plowing was the preferred means to break up the soil but was not always feasible if a settler lacked a plow and horse to pull it. Hoes were used most frequently in the early years until a farmer could afford a plow and horse. As the crops grew, they were kept free of weeds by hoeing. An iron draw-hoe blade was found in the central cabin complex. A draw-hoe is used by pulling the blade through the soil. The blade from the fort site is trapezoidal, with rounded shoulders, and was hafted at a right angle to its wooden handle. At 8 in. (20.3 cm.) wide, it is a fairly large broad hoe suitable for chopping out weeds. The blade edge is very worn, and the blade was probably longer when it was new. The blade has a hole that may indicate a repair to the spine that reinforced the attachment of the eye to the blade.[35]

Settlers brought seeds for a variety of crops. Corn was one of the most important grain crops because it is so versatile, providing early corn for general consumption and dried corn that could be made into hominy or ground into meal for bread or livestock feed. A corn crop also served as proof that a settler had fulfilled one of the requirements for filing a land claim with the Virginia legislature. But other grains such as wheat, rye, and barley were also raised. Not surprisingly, corn was the most common grain identified at Fort Boonesborough, followed by wheat, barley, and possibly rye. Corn, barley, and rye were commonly used to make whiskey as well.

Several varieties of corn were grown in the colonies at the time Fort Boonesborough was settled. All were derived from prehistoric grains grown by Native American groups. The northeastern states grew Northern Flint varieties, while Southern Dent varieties such as Gourdseed (also called She-corn or White Dent) and Shoepeg were preferred in the southern states. Charred corn kernels, cobs, and cupules collected from the small feature along the south wall of the fort are mostly from a variety of Southern Dent corn. This variety was grown in the Great Plains prehistorically and at the time of contact between native tribes and settlers was being cultivated in the South as well, and its use gradually moved northward. Southern Dents are so called because the long, relatively thin kernel has a deep dent on the back. It was grown in Virginia at least by the early eighteenth century. A hallmark of the Gourdseed variety is the large number of kernel rows on the cobs, which denotes a greater yield, but its longer maturity time sometimes meant it was not dried on the cob before winter set in. Evidence of corn kernels typical of Northern Flint corn were also identified at Fort Boonesborough. It would not have been unusual for more than one variety of corn to be grown, particularly as settlers came in and out and brought seed corn with them from various places. Over time, Southern Dents were crossed with Northern Flints many times to produce the modern corn varieties commonly grown today.[36]

In addition to growing corn, vegetable gardening was a high priority. Richard Henderson mentioned garden crops several times in his journal. When the settlers had a lottery for town lots in late April 1775, Henderson considered himself fortunate to obtain four half-acre lots for the fort garden. He planted "small seed" and cucumbers on April 26. Archaeological evidence of seeds from the squash family corroborate Henderson's journal. Bottle gourds, which were not eaten but dried, emptied of their seeds, and fashioned into dippers and other containers, were also an important crop. In mid-May 1775 Henderson wrote of checking his garden in the hope that his greens were mature enough to harvest. By mid-June, corn planted in late April had tasseled, and the snap beans and peas were ripe. Beans and bacon made for an "excellent dinner." The settlers were probably also eating squash by this time. Settler accounts mention many other domestic plants that were grown at an early period. Fruit orchards, particularly apples and peaches, were planted from the first years of settlement. Potatoes, watermelons, cabbages, turnips, pumpkins, and a type of squash called simblins were just a few of the vegetables the settlers raised.[37]

Raising Livestock

Accompanying the settlers into the Kentucky frontier were their animals. Horses, cattle, and pigs are frequently mentioned in settler accounts (sheep and poultry less often), but all of them were brought to Kentucky from the earliest years of permanent settlement. Settlers brought a keen interest in domestic breeds that eventually led to nationally important developments in breed improvements. Domestic animal bones from Fort Boonesborough were definitively identified as horse, cow, pig, and, less certain, poultry. No evidence of sheep was identified among the bones found.

Horses were essential for the transport of people and goods. Indians appreciated their value and conducted regular raids to steal them. Settlers in turn went on retaliatory expeditions to steal them back. Settlers' accounts often mention losing horses, trading for them, and admiring particularly handsome stallions. Horses, like cattle, were commonly belled so that they could be more readily found if they wandered off, but losses to Indians took a high toll. All but one of the horse bones found at Fort Boonesborough were from an adult female whose partial, articulated carcass was buried in a pit inside the fort enclosure. Some of the bones show cut marks that are clear evidence that the animal was butchered and eaten. The buried carcass included the upper half of the torso from the shoulder to the rump and both thigh bones. No bones from the head, neck, front legs, or lower back legs were found in the pit, and only part of the rib cage was present.

Maintaining cattle herds was an important component of the settlers' agricultural strategy. Cattle provided milk and meat for food; hides for leather; and bone, horn, and hooves for powder horns, utensil handles, glue, and other products. By the time Fort Boonesborough was settled, the cattle brought in by the settlers were the result of many years of internal breeding. A dominant breed in Virginia was a variant of what later became known as the Devon breed. North Carolina became well known as a source of cattle by the early seventeenth century. Stray livestock notices in the late 1780s issues of the *Kentucky Gazette* list cows of many colors, including black, brown, dun, red, white, and various color combinations indicated by the term "brindle." The wide variety of animals described suggests that cattle at Fort Boonesborough probably were similarly diverse in their genealogy. Cow bones are outnumbered three to one by buffalo bones. While cattle were definitely slaughtered for food, the females were highly valued as a milk source, and settlers also retained them to build their herds. As long as wild game was available, cattle may have composed a smaller proportion of the meat diet. However, cattle were often killed by Indians during their raids. Settlers made the best of the situation by eating slain cattle and salvaging their hides when possible.[38]

Raising pigs was a third prong of the livestock strategy practiced by settlers. Pigs were allowed to run freely in the local woods, where they fattened on acorns and other natural resources. In the fall they were rounded up, slaughtered, and turned into smoked hams, bacon, jowl, souse, sausage, and lard. The pigs brought to Kentucky by the Fort Boonesborough settlers were tough, hardy, hairy animals that were similar to the feral pigs found today on Ossabaw Island, Georgia. Colonial pigs had thick, generally black coats, long snouts, and upright ears. Bone elements recovered by the excavation are from all parts of the animal, head to tail. The old saying about using every part of the pig except for its squeal certainly applies to the Fort Boonesborough collection. The bones came from pigs of all ages, from suckling to fully adult, and were distributed all over the fort, indicating the settlers were consuming pork regularly. Pork was likely the most common domesticated meat that the settlers ate.[39]

Poultry is rarely mentioned in settler accounts, but ducks and chickens were brought in with the other domesticated stock. The Callaways and the Poagues brought domestic ducks and chickens to the site as early as the fall of 1775. The principal evidence for poultry at the site is eggshell that was found in the central cabin complex. A single bone that might be duck also came from the same location.[40]

Once gardens and orchards were established and livestock began to reproduce, settlers suffered less from food insecurity. The settlers practiced a mixed strategy of procuring food from wild and domestic sources, raised a diversity of edible plants, and worked toward assuring food security despite wartime conditions that made their task much harder. The food remains from Fort Boonesborough testify to these efforts.

Household Goods

Artifacts relating to the kitchen and household are ubiquitous on residential archaeological sites of all ages. Fort Boonesborough settlers brought a complement of food processing, storage, and serving vessels, and metal utensils with which to prepare, serve, and eat their meals and store various food commodities. Household artifacts made of nonperishable materials such as iron, brass, copper, ceramics, and glass are the most common categories recovered from archaeological sites. Wooden and pewter artifacts tend to be rare or absent in household assemblages: in the case of wood, decomposition destroys all evidence, and pewter's durability and resale value for recasting meant even pieces were too valuable to discard.[41]

Transporting household goods was challenging, given the ruggedness of the trail into Kentucky that prevented the passage of wagons, the weight limitations of packhorses, and the vulnerability of glass and ceramic items to breakage. The need for other essential tools and equipment further limited the amounts of household goods, particularly luxury items. Artifact frequency is affected by the fact that many of the settlers who visited Fort Boonesborough stayed only for brief periods and so had limited opportunities to lose or discard items that might have become part of the archaeological record of the site. The variety of household goods found at Fort Boonesborough mirrors archaeological assemblages from other late eighteenth-century Kentucky station sites. Even given the constraints of transport, settlers brought household items that were not limited to practical, useful, and durable goods but also included fashionable tea wares, heirlooms, and other prized possessions.

Household artifacts that turn up in archaeological assemblages reflect the many mundane, routine tasks that were carried out daily. For example, milking cows, a task usually performed by women, required a pail to catch the milk and then vessels to process it. Red-clay earthenware milk pans were used to separate the cream for churning into butter or for souring to make clabber. A collared rim made of glazed red-clay earthenware found in the central cabin complex probably came from a milk pan or similar wide-mouth pan. Utilitarian pottery such as milk pans, crocks, porringers, and other vessel forms were commonly made from red-clay earthenware in the eighteenth and early nineteenth century until supplanted by more durable stoneware. The pottery was likely made back in the eastern colonies and

Ceramic and glass artifacts recovered at the Boonesborough site range from utilitarian crockery to fine china. (*Top, left to right*): collared redware rim, black glass bottle rim; (*middle*): striped redware rim; (*bottom, left to right*): scratch blue stoneware, green glazed Wedgwood teapot handle.

brought in with the settlers. All of the coarse earthenware found at the site was made from red clays common to many regions. The red-clay earthenware found at the fort is mostly lead-glazed on the interior of the vessel only; a few sherds are glazed on both surfaces. The extent of glazing relates to both function and price. Interior glazing renders a vessel waterproof, while glazing only one surface lowers the cost of manufacture. Most of the red-clay earthenware artifacts from the fort are very plain, undecorated fragments from the bodies of vessel forms like crocks and jars used for storing and processing food rather than from serving dishes. An exception is a rim from a shallow dish like a pie plate that has cream-, green-, and brown-colored bands along the inside of the rim. A nearly identical rim was found at Ingles' Ferry in Virginia.[42]

Settlers' accounts occasionally mention household goods, but generally archaeological evidence offers a better idea of what people used. William Clinkenbeard, a settler at Strode's Station not far from Fort Boonesborough, told Reverend Shane and he and his new wife only had a butcher knife when they first set up housekeeping. They got a "little pot" from John

Strode and bought more from him after he returned with a supply from a trip back east. Clinkenbeard meant a metal pot for cooking. The settlers at Fort Boonesborough used cast-iron pots and pans and sheet-metal skillets like the one missing its handle found in the central cabin complex. The skillet was large, measuring nearly a foot in diameter. Its missing handle was probably quite long, perhaps as much as three feet. This skillet did not have legs attached to its base that would have allowed it to stand above coals. Rather, it would have rested on a three-legged stand, or trivet. Molly Hancock, wife of William Hancock, made creative use of a detached skillet handle that she owned. She used it as a weapon of defense and was even said to sleep with it during the Great Siege of 1778.[43]

Fort Boonesborough settlers made room in their supplies for imported ceramic serving wares and bottles made of glass and English stoneware. Fragments of serving wares are from cups, saucers or plates, and a Wedgwood teapot, made around 1760, with green glazed molding on its handle. "Taking tea" was a popular ritual among frontier women that reinforced social ties and offered a welcome respite from the rigors of frontier life. Mrs. Phillips recollected her mother taking tea with Mrs. John Todd at the Lexington fort even though they only had dried buffalo jerky as an accompaniment. Surveyor John Floyd's estate appraisal listed four teacups and saucers and a teapot as well as a copper tea kettle and four tin canisters. Likewise, the inventories of Nathaniel and Sarah Hart, who died in the 1780s while living in the fort, included a diverse collection of utilitarian Dutch ovens, pots, and pans as well as "china ware," tea and brass kettles, teapots, a sugar pot, a cream pot, teaspoons, cups and saucers, and wine glasses.[44]

Given the social positions of the Transylvania Company partners—a judge, merchants, affluent farmers—it is not surprising that artifacts reflecting more elite status would occur at the fort. While the inexpensive, coarse red-clay earthenware crocks and pans were probably all made in potteries back east, the refined earthenware and stoneware dishes were made in England and exported to the colonies. Ceramic dishes tend to be used over many years. The ceramics from Fort Boonesborough reflect this curation pattern by the range of ware types: from English salt-glazed stonewares produced from the 1720s to cream-colored earthenware (creamware or Queens' ware) made from the 1760s to a bluish-white earthenware (pearlware) that was developed by 1780. A few porcelain sherds reflect trade between China and the United States beginning in the 1780s. Most of the sherds are undecorated or have minimal molded decoration along the rim. The two sherds from the handle of an elaborately molded and painted Wedgwood cauliflower teapot are an exception. How vexed the owner must have felt when a clumsy move chipped the handle of her treasured teapot! In fact, there may have been more than one teapot. One of the sherds was found in the cabin on the south wall, and the other came from the center cabin complex. Two tiny sherds were from at least one piece of "scratch blue"—salt-glazed stoneware that was made in the first half of the eighteenth century. Scratch blue designs were incised into the unfired clay, and blue pigment was rubbed into the incisions. It was made into teapots, bowls, plates, mugs, and other utilitarian forms and was very popular until it was supplanted by the creamwares in the 1760s. One of the sherds came from the cabin on the south wall while the other was nearer the Luttrell cabin on the west wall, but they could have been from the same vessel.

One of the creamware plate rims had a raised, molded design called feather edge that was made from the 1760s through the 1790s. A more elaborate feather edge variation graced another dish. Much smaller quantities of later pearlwares and porcelains dating after 1780 offer more evidence for the short occupation of the fort site. Nearly all the porcelain sherds were found in higher levels closer to the surface and may have been among the last artifacts discarded at the site before it was abandoned altogether.

Glass bottles and tablewares are common and inexpensive today but not so in the eighteenth century. Glass bottles were expensive enough to warrant keeping them even when they were damaged as the "2 Crak'd Bottles" in Sarah Hart's 1786 inventory attests. The glass fragments in the Fort Boonesborough assemblage were probably from bottles made in England and shipped to the colonies. Glass bottles were created individually by blowing air into a blob of molten glass affixed to a pontil rod, creating a glass bubble that could be manipulated with various tools into the desired shape. They generally were produced to hold alcoholic beverages or medicines, but because they were expensive to replace they were used for other purposes once their original contents were consumed.

Glass bottle fragments at Fort Boonesborough are from vessels of many colors, from clear to aquamarine to brown to various shades of green. Most common were cylindrical bottles that held alcoholic spirits such as wine or distilled liquors. One of the bottle rims is similar to a Canadian example dated to 1794. Two fragments are from a flask and a bottle with an oval body form.

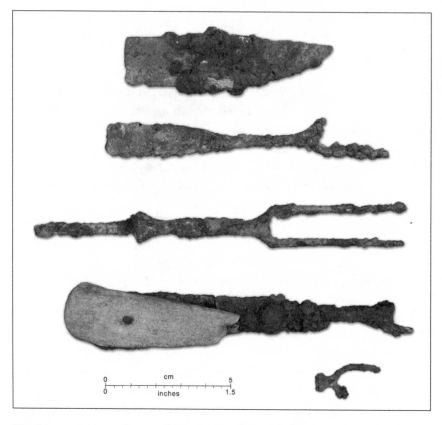

Matching eating utensils were becoming more common by the early years of Kentucky's settlement. (*Top to bottom*): knife blade and four examples of doubled-tined forks.

All of the bottles would have been closed with a cork. Bottle glass was found in every excavated part of the fort, although in very small quantities. Most families of limited means probably would not have owned any glass bottles.[45]

The use of matching knives and forks at mealtimes, although far from universal, was becoming more common in the late eighteenth century. A knife blade and several two-tined forks among the Fort Boonesborough artifacts attest to the popularity of these utensils. Knives were absolutely essential for butchering meat and myriad other cutting tasks. Men carried knives on their persons, particularly when hunting, and women used them in the kitchen. William Clinkenbeard considered his knife important enough to mention to Reverend Shane when he described the modest household goods he and his wife possessed at the beginning of their married life. The fragmentary utensils from Fort Boonesborough were typical of mid- to late eighteenth-century styles. One of the forks had a rat-tail tang that was originally inserted into a bone or wooden handle. More commonly, utensils were given handles by riveting a wedge-shaped piece of bone called a scale on each side of a metal plate. The bone scales were often crosshatched, as one of the Fort Boonesborough utensils is. All of the forks from Fort Boonesborough are two-tined. Most of the utensils from the fort were found in the center cabin complex. A stone fragment that might have served as a whetstone to sharpen knife blades was collected from the hearth of the cabin on the south wall.[46]

The diversity of household artifacts in the fort assemblage reflects the diversity of people who came from different places, who stood low, middle, and high on the social ladder of the times and made calculated decisions about what to bring with them. Practicality and necessity dictated many of their decisions, emphasizing the durable and utilitarian, but they did not eschew bringing with them some luxury and treasured objects. Faced with shortages and limited choices and access, social rituals such as drinking tea from refined ceramic teacups and saucers softened the rigors and uncertainty of frontier insecurity. Thus, someone at Fort Boonesborough carefully carried a fancy Staffordshire teapot over the Wilderness Road. Mrs. Hart brought her "large Chinai bowl" and a full tea serving equipage along with her Dutch ovens and a large cracked pot. While the truly destitute owned very little, many settlers could afford a few luxury items and brought them along to recreate some semblance of the homes they left.

Arms, Ammunition, and Horses

Horses, guns, and ammunition took on a special importance on the Kentucky frontier. Horses were used for transportation, hauling goods, and plowing. They also were essential for hunting, since large game had to be packed in on horseback or left to spoil. Horses often figured in trades of various sorts. Settlers admired and commented on particularly handsome specimens. Most families probably owned at least one horse.

A saddle frame, metal staples for leather straps, a brass tack ornament, part of a horseshoe, and several horseshoe nails point to the presence of horses at Fort Boonesborough. The saddle frame is made of iron, and it

Examples of horse tack found during excavations include
(*clockwise*): saddle frame, two saddle staples, decorative bridle
ornament.

formed the framework of a pommel with a high arch. The angle of the frame
is approximately 70 degrees. It was of a style commonly used on English
hunter/jumper saddles of the eighteenth century. Two brass staples that
would have been fastened to the saddle and used to guide leather straps
were also found near the frame in the central cabin complex. One of the
staples is engraved with Xs and circles. The circular brass tack ornament
has a molded floral pattern and was probably attached to a piece of horse
tack like a bridle. It was found in the Luttrell cabin on the west wall of the
fort.[47]

Like other ubiquitous artifact types, horseshoe nails were widely
distributed across the fort. A fragmentary horseshoe was recovered in 1987
at a depth that yielded other late eighteenth-century artifacts in the center
cabin complex. Fitting a horse with horseshoes was not a universal colonial
practice. A sample of stray horse advertisements published in the *Kentucky
Gazette* in the 1780s reveals a little more than 5 percent of the strays were
shod, suggesting that the practice was not yet common. Nevertheless, the
presence of horseshoe nails and a horseshoe indicates that some owners
shoed their horses.

Arms and ammunition played a vital role in settlers' lives, from hunting to defense. (*Top, left to right*): spall type gunflint, Brandon flint, French honey gun flint; (*middle, left to right*): two lead bullets with sprues, chewed lead bullet, small caliber bullet; (*bottom, left to right*): two sprues, two lead scraps.

Equal to his horse, a man's other prized possession was his gun. The famed Kentucky long rifle with its lengthy, internally grooved barrel that directed the bullet more accurately is the best-known gun of the period, but it was joined by smoothbore British muskets, French fusils, and other gun styles also in common use. All of the guns in use on the Kentucky frontier required gunflints, round lead bullets, and gunpowder to function. While gunflints could be manufactured from local cherts in a pinch, lead and gunpowder shortages were chronic on the frontier.

Gunflints are commonly found in early historic period sites because gun owners usually kept a supply of them on hand, and they were discarded when they wore out. During the Revolutionary War, French honey flint was the most common flint used to produce gunflints. These flints were exported to the colonies by the thousands. English gunflints made from the Brandon flint quarried from the cliffs of Dover became dominant after 1790, although their manufacture began a decade or so earlier. The French honey flint and

131

the English Brandon gunflints were made using a prismatic blade technology first developed in France and introduced in England between 1770 and 1800. Both types were found at Fort Boonesborough. The prismatic blade technology replaced the older wedge or spall technology. An example of the older gun spall type of flint was also found at Fort Boonesborough. One gunflint is made from local Haney Formation chert. The use of local cherts to make gunflints was a fairly common practice among Native Americans, but colonists also resorted to making their own when necessity demanded it.[48]

Like gunflints, lead bullets are common artifacts on early historic sites because large quantities were needed for hunters killing wild game for food or settlers defending themselves against Indian attack. Bullets were made in many different sizes by pouring molten lead into bullet molds designed to form bullets of a particular caliber. A bullet mold was a necessary accoutrement of any gun owner. Bullets found at the fort site ranged from small to large calibers. Several had small circular flat places on the surface where a sprue was sliced off. Sprues are formed at the opening of the bullet mold when the mold chamber is slightly overfilled with molten lead. A few of these detached sprues were also found. Some of the bullets were distorted, abraded, or flattened, all of which indicate that they had been shot, perhaps by Native Americans attacking the fort. Several have deformations that suggest they ricocheted after hitting a solid surface like the side of a cabin. During the siege of 1778, the gunfire from the Indian side was so heavy that afterwards the settlers picked up 125 pounds of expended lead bullets along the outside walls and clustered at the portholes. Some over-shots landed inside the fort as well. Evidence of alteration after the bullets became buried suggest that rodents and possibly swine modified two bullets by chewing them.[49]

The diameter of the smallest caliber bullet found was only .2 in. (5 mm); five others had diameters ranging from .3 to .35 in. (7.6 to 8.9 mm). These small bullets would have made up part of a buck-and-ball load used in smoothbore muskets. A buck-and-ball load combined small shot with a larger bullet to increase the gun's hit probability and lethality by combining the deadly impact of a larger bullet with the spreading pattern of a shotgun. Muskets were the common weapon used during the Revolutionary War by colonial militiamen and were particularly favored by Gen. George Washington.[50]

The larger bullets had calibers in the 40s and 50s and could have been used in rifles or, in the case of the highest caliber, as the large bullet in a buck-and-ball load. The range of calibers among the measurable bullets confirms that, as archival evidence states, both smoothbore and rifled guns were commonly used. Rifles were much more accurate than smoothbore muskets, but they were also more expensive. For example, John Floyd's 1783 estate inventory listed a rifle valued at £4 and two smoothbore guns valued together at only £1.[51]

The excavation recovered small pieces of lead that varied in size and shape. Some look like drips from the bullet molding process where molten lead was accidentally spilled. Others are more irregular and angular and probably were the remnants of bullets that blew apart when they hit a resistant surface. One piece of lead is flat and may have been folded around one end of a gunflint to hold it more snugly in the jaw of the lock.

Artifacts from sites like Fort Boonesborough not only reflect the needs of the settlers who used them but also are a product of the circumstances that brought them to the site. The Fort Boonesborough settlers represent a range of social classes and economic statuses, from more affluent men like the Transylvania Company partners to middling settlers of modest means to truly impoverished people who owned few material goods. People who had access to more resources had the capability to bring in more goods such as household metal, ceramic and glass receptacles, clothing and personal accoutrements, tools and utensils, guns and ammunition. These goods were packed in by horses that were highly valuable possessions in their own right.

The artifact classes identified in the Fort Boonesborough assemblage mirror what is typically found in residential sites, differing largely in the limited variety and quantities of goods that the average settler owned. Yet even given the constraints placed on the amounts of goods that could be transported into the Kentucky frontier, the fort artifacts include practical, utilitarian objects mixed with items that can be considered luxury goods or at least items of better quality. The privations of frontier life limited access to market goods, forced crowded living arrangements, required a "make do" approach, and delayed the accumulation of wealth, but these drawbacks were tempered in some respects by small, symbolic acts. A treasured English teapot for taking tea, a formal or more fancy garment to be worn on special occasions, or even ornamentation for one's horse reminded settlers of who they were and of the orderly society they could look forward to enjoying in the future.

9

FORT BOONESBOROUGH AS A COMMEMORATIVE SITE

Fort Boonesborough occupies a special place in the hearts and minds of Kentuckians whose ancestors sought refuge behind its stockade or stayed there briefly on their way to a new life. Unlike privately owned stations controlled by the owner of the land on which the site was built, Fort Boonesborough was a place where anyone could come and stay. Hundreds of settlers passed through its gates; everyone knew of it even if they had not visited. Its hybrid design offered both defense and residence at a tumultuous time in American history when security and sanctuary were essential for survival on the western frontier.

Fort Boonesborough was one of the principal sites of the early settlement era in the trans-Appalachian west. It witnessed the hostilities of 1776 that marked the onset of the American Revolution on the western frontier. It survived the "year of the bloody 7s" (1777), when it was one of only three occupied frontier sites in Kentucky, and it withstood the Great Siege of 1778, when it was defended for nine tense days against a force of several hundred Indians. It hosted many of the new settlers who streamed into Kentucky in 1779–1780. When the Treaty of Paris formally ended hostilities with Great Britain in 1783, the need for defense passed, and Fort Boonesborough no longer served a useful purpose. For a time after the end of the Revolutionary War, the fort cabins remained and were sometimes used as landmarks for surveys; perhaps a cabin or two was sporadically occupied for brief periods. Ironically, the failure of the town of Boonesborough to thrive, combined with environmental factors, contributed to the fort's preservation as an archaeological site. Eventually, the logs used to build the cabins and stockades and the stones that formed the chimney bases were salvaged for use elsewhere, and visible traces of the fort gradually disappeared. The Kentucky River flooded periodically, and each episode covered the site with another thin layer of silt until the residue of discarded and lost artifacts, the ashy organic soil that marked the old cabin hearths, the abandoned wells and pits dug for various purposes—all disappeared beneath a mantle of soil nearly a foot (30 cm) thick. The years passed and the Kentucky River gave and took away, sometimes eroding sediment along its banks and tributaries, sometimes dumping it. This process of erosion and sedimentation affected the fort site by burying at least half of it and washing away the northerly end of the site nearest Sycamore Hollow.

Fort Boonesborough lived on in memory even as visual evidence of it disappeared. The name Boonesborough still appeared on Kentucky maps throughout the nineteenth century, marking not a bustling town but merely a sleepy hamlet hosting a few houses, a ferry across the Kentucky River, a tobacco inspection facility, a tavern, a wool factory, and a store or two widely dispersed along the old Log Lick Trace that became State Road 388. In 1840 a celebration of the sixty-fifth anniversary of the settlement of Kentucky was held at the fort site, complete with military parades by volunteer corps from eight counties and an oration by Gov. James T. Morehead. Even as late as 1876, the site (incorrectly labelled as "Boons Fort") was shown on a county map. The US Postal Service had a post office there from 1826 until 1866. At least two of the five known postmasters (Samuel Halley and John Stephens) lived in Boonesborough at known sites within the town limits.[1]

Fort Boonesborough's pioneer history was celebrated in 1901 when the Filson Club published George Washington Ranck's book, *Boonesborough: Its Founding, Pioneer Struggles, Indian Experiences, Transylvania Days, and Revolutionary Annals.* This book remains the most comprehensive history of the earliest years of Boonesborough published to date. Its publication reflected an era of intense interest in historical commemoration in the United States that celebrated the country's past with such events as the Centennial International Exposition of 1876 that marked the one-hundredth anniversary of the signing of the Declaration of Independence and the erection of local monuments to mark significant historical locations.

Allied with commemorative efforts were organizations such as the Daughters of the American Revolution. In 1896 Mrs. Sara Gibson Humphreys Chenault and fifteen other local women organized the Boonesborough chapter of the DAR. One of their first projects was to raise funds to purchase and place a monument at the fort site, which they achieved in 1907. A stone wall marking the small square plot of land the chapter had purchased was built around the monument in the 1930s during another period of monument building. A monument to the Transylvania Company was erected by the Transylvanian Society of Henderson, Kentucky, near the fort site in 1935. Dr. Willard Rouse Jillson orated a dramatic panegyric on a Louisville radio station to publicize the unveiling of the monument on October 12, 1935. His radiocast emphasized in heroic terms Richard Henderson's dream of empire and downplayed the entrepreneur's failure. He claimed that if not for Fort Boonesborough's endurance throughout the Revolutionary War, the other "lesser" forts and settlements in Kentucky would have collapsed, Virginia's and North Carolina's influence west of the Cumberlands would have ceased, and George Rogers Clark's campaign to secure the Northwest Territory never would have happened. Similar hyperbole to promote heritage tourism was published in several articles about the Transylvania Company and Boonesborough in the *Kentucky Progress* magazine during the same period.[2]

In 1907 the celebration of Fort Boonesborough as an important agent of Kentucky's role in the settlement of the west and the success of the Revolutionary War took center stage at the Jamestown Ter-centennial Exposition. The Kentucky Jamestown Exposition Commission unanimously voted to build a reproduction of Fort Boonesborough for the event. Even though a "faithful adherence to pioneer requirements . . . [was] made subservient to modern conveniences" by using electric lights and carpets instead of tallow candles and puncheon floors, the intent was to evoke a sense of the opening of the frontier. Reenactment of the kidnapping of Jemima Boone and the Callaway girls provided dramatic entertainment. The implicit comparison to Jamestown as a founding settlement was unmistakable.[3]

Heritage tourism and capitalist ambition combined in 1909 when an enterprising pharmacist took advantage of Boonesborough's place in local memory, its river location, and its nearby mineral water springs to build a resort. David Williams built a series of ten cabins along the second terrace above the Kentucky River, beginning with a cabin on either side of the DAR monument and extending south nearly to Boonesborough Beach. He built a hotel/dancehall that he called Boonesboro Hotel and improved the sulfur water spring enclosure in Sycamore Hollow so the water could be easily collected. People came for the medicinal qualities of the springwater and

Hot and Cold Water   *Newly Furnished*

Boonesboro Beach Hotel

and Cottages

Kentucky's Most Popular Bathing Beach

Black and White Sulphur Wells

Chalybeate and Lithia Waters

An advertisement for Boonesboro Beach Hotel, a resort that capitalized on the memory of Fort Boonesborough site during the first part of the twentieth century. Courtesy of the William S. Webb Museum of Anthropology at the University of Kentucky.

for recreation and relaxation. The resort was featured in one of the driving tours outlined in *The WPA Guide to Kentucky*, a publication that encouraged road tourism and, not coincidentally, boosted local businesses and tourist attractions during the Great Depression. The guide described the venue as "a small resort of stilted red and green frame cottages, a hotel, and a bathing beach on the Kentucky River." A hotel ad touted the black-and-white sulfur wells and the chalybeate and lithia waters available for the patrons' use. David Williams's children, David Jr. and Sara F., inherited 255.98 acres of the tract on September 22, 1923, and continued to operate the resort through lease agreements until the 1950s or 1960s.[4]

The Daniel Boone Bicentennial Commission was established in 1934 with the purpose of furthering plans for the celebration of the bicentennial anniversary of Boone's birth. The commissioners were tasked with organizing an appropriate observance, endorsing the publication of books on Boone and the state's pioneer history, and acquiring three sites associated with him—Fort Boonesborough, Boone's Station, and Bryan's Station. An all-day celebration was held at Boonesborough on September 3, 1934, that attracted a crowd of more than six thousand to hear addresses by Gov. Ruby Lafoon, Sen. Alben W. Barkley, Congressman Virgil Chapman, and other speakers.[5]

The acquisition of sites associated with Boone was one of the more challenging tasks of the commission. The Pioneer National Monument Association was created with the goal of acquiring and developing the three sites as parks and connecting them by a national highway with the Blue Licks Battlefield. Thirty-two acres of the battlefield had been purchased by the state in 1928, and the acreage was already part of the state park system. The sale of Boone half-dollar coins raised about $30,000, and David Williams Jr. was contacted about selling Boonesborough in 1935. His initial asking price was higher than the association wanted to pay, and negotiations went on for years. In the meantime additional acreage was purchased to increase the size of the Blue Licks park, but efforts at the time failed to acquire Boone's or Bryan's Stations. By the 1950s the association focused their attention on acquiring Boonesborough. Intense lobbying efforts and feasibility studies resulted in a bond issue in November 1960 that raised $10 million to develop state parks. Finally, in 1963 the David Williams heirs sold 57.47 acres to the Commonwealth of Kentucky for the establishment of Fort Boonesborough State Park. With this purchase, the Pioneer National Monument Association was disbanded at the end of 1963.[6]

Two booster organizations have taken on the job of promoting Fort Boonesborough as a heritage tourist attraction. The Fort Boonesborough State Park Association was established in 1965 when the Fort Boonesborough State Park was dedicated and opened to the public. This association raised funds for building the fort replica currently standing at the park, developed a historical walking tour, and partially funded the archaeological study carried out in 1987. The association disbanded and was replaced by the Fort Boonesborough Foundation in 2010. The current foundation raised funds for some of the fort site excavations, sponsored this book, and still supports the park's living history program.

10

THE FRONTIER EXPERIENCE IN RETROSPECT

The frontier experience of the Fort Boonesborough settlers played out in an arena of armed conflict in which the British American colonies were taking control of their destiny by violently severing ties to their mother country. An unfamiliar western location far away from settled areas fostered insecurity and isolation that dominated the settler experience. Common frontier experiences were shared by everyone, regardless of their cultural background, social status, or wealth. The real and present danger of injury and death during Indian raids and attacks made no distinctions between an impoverished settler and a rich one. Everyone went hungry during food shortages occasioned by periods when settlers were unable to safely cultivate and harvest crops, hunt for wild game, or gather edible wild plants. Replacing and replenishing necessary material goods such as clothing, lead, gunpowder, and salt was a collective challenge. Kentucky settlers devised strategies to combat the challenges and problems they faced, resulting in a frontier culture that addressed safety concerns, food shortages, and replenishment of necessary goods and commodities.

Settlers came to Kentucky from many different areas and varied widely in their social and economic backgrounds and circumstances. Some were gentry who had the financial resources to bring material goods, livestock, and land warrants, while others came into the country with very little. Class distinctions meant that the elite tended to dominate socially and politically. As early as 1784 John Filson acknowledged "a diversity of manners, customs, and religions" among the late eighteenth-century migrants and guardedly suggested that the frontier settlement experience would eventually homogenize the differences into a population of similar outlook. Historian

Frederick Jackson Turner made the idea of a homogeneous population a centerpiece of his frontier thesis, and many historians followed suit. Recent research on the ethnic, economic, and racial dimensions of early settlers documents a greater cultural pluralism and the persistence of differences than were previously supposed. The fluidity of frontier conditions made individual social interactions "contingent, ready to be verified, muted, or altered by actual experience" even as people held on to their values, attitudes, and prejudices and directed their actions and reactions accordingly.[1]

Practicing cooperation and mutuality was a strategy that paid off even as it required trust among strangers. Differences and distinctions of class, background, socioeconomic status, political affiliation, and race that the Kentucky settlers recognized in each other made trust difficult, at times, to achieve. While distrust or wariness was often rooted in unequal social standing, discord could arise even among social equals. While Richard Henderson complained that some of the men who came to Kentucky with him were "scoundrels who scarcely believe in God or fear a devil," so did he also wonder why Nathaniel Hart, his partner and social equal, was so standoffish and discontented. Misunderstandings and resentments on the part of Benjamin Logan and Richard Callaway fueled their insistence that Daniel Boone be court-martialed after the Great Siege of 1778. Boone was vindicated by an acquittal and received a promotion that did not likely completely appease his accusers. Yet there were many examples of cooperation, collaboration, reciprocity, and even risk-taking for the collective benefit. Settlers understood the necessity of combined effort and teamwork as they negotiated the unfamiliar and often dangerous conditions of the frontier.[2]

The Structure of Defense on the Kentucky Frontier

Personal safety concerned everyone, regardless of background, since a bullet or arrow fired by an adversary did not distinguish among people of different social ranks. The settlers employed two principal strategies to address the issue of personal safety: local militia units and defensive construction in the form of stockaded forts and stations. Militia service was an ancient British tradition that colonial governments adopted in place of a professional standing army. Twelve of the thirteen original colonies passed laws that made militia organization and service compulsory. Every able-bodied man between sixteen and sixty was obligated to participate in training each year, to equip himself with a weapon and ammunition, and to be at the ready for service as needed. Militia units were administered at the county level, colonial assemblies usually appointed district colonels, and local officers were selected by members of their company. This practice generally resulted in officers of higher social status, but popularity and leadership qualities also played a role. For example, Daniel Boone was not considered part of the gentry class, yet he fulfilled an important leadership role as a militia officer.[3]

The Kentucky frontier posed particular conditions that complicated recruitment and assembly of militiamen to meet specific threats: the Appalachian Mountains physically separated the Kentucky frontier from more settled areas to the east. When the Virginia General Assembly formed Kentucky County out of Fincastle County, effective January 31, 1777, one of their motivations was the organization of a local militia to more effectively counter Indian attacks. Militia commissioners named David Robinson county lieutenant, John Bowman colonel, George Rogers Clark major, and Daniel Boone, James Harrod, Benjamin Logan, and John Todd captains. Daniel Boone was the ranking officer for the fort at Boonesborough and led a company there. At the time only twenty-two riflemen were available. The militia rolls changed often as men cycled on and off tours of duty or moved to different sections of the country.[4]

The second strategy for collective safety was the construction of defensive residential forts and stations. Originally conceived as part of a scheme to establish a royal colony in 1775, the construction of Fort Boonesborough was the first step in establishing control of the Kentucky territory and beating out other competitors by physical possession. The onset of the revolution and the rejection of the Transylvania Company's plans by the Virginia General Assembly squashed the idea of a royal colony by 1778. The fort continued to exist because its presence was a critical element in the militia-based defense of the Kentucky frontier against British-financed Indian raids and attacks.

Fort Boonesborough was part of a collective of defensive residential sites that began in 1775 and expanded over the next few years to form a network of large forts and smaller stations scattered over Central Kentucky like nodes on a spider web. Initially, the settlers did not perceive a significant military threat, even as the Revolutionary War ensued, and they did not exert much effort in defensive construction for their protection. An attack at Leestown (in present-day Frankfort) in April 1776 and the capture of Jemima Boone and Frances and Betsy Callaway the following July awakened the settlers to the prospect of increased Indian attacks. The construction of defensive structures became a priority. John Floyd wrote to his employer, Virginia surveyor William Preston, on July 21, 1776, that "if the war becomes general, which there is now the greatest appearance of, our situation is truly alarming. We are about finishing a large fort and intend to keep possession of this place as long as possible. They are, I understand, doing the same at Harrodsburg, and also on Elkhorn at the Royal Spring."[5]

In their use of stockade, blockhouses, and bastions, builders of defensive structures on the Kentucky frontier borrowed architectural features from earlier and contemporary forts in places like the backcountry of the Greenbrier and New River valleys. The Greenbrier and New River forts differed from many Kentucky forts and stations in that they generally served as places of refuge to which settlers resorted during times of danger. Fort Arbuckle, for example, was a two-bastioned, diamond-shaped fort enclosed completely by stockade with a blockhouse inside. Fort Donnelly was similar, except that the Donnelly house and kitchen were located at one of the corners. Settlers took refuge there when it was too dangerous to stay at their outlying cabins, but they returned to their homes as soon as the danger passed.[6]

Fort Boonesborough, on the other hand, supported a year-round population, thus elevating the importance of the residential aspects of the fort's design. The fort plan employed four larger structures at each corner that had protruding second stories, or bastions; a total of twenty-six cabins forming the walls of the enclosure; and a central double cabin. All of these structures served primarily as residences. Some of the cabins were connected. Gaps between cabins were filled with stockade. Stations constructed during an emigration surge in 1779–1780 in Kentucky followed similar architectural plans that emphasized the residential function. In general, forts and stations on the Kentucky frontier tended to serve as the primary residence of settlers until conditions were safe enough for them to move out to their own land and build a permanent house.[7]

The architecture of Fort Boonesborough maximized the amount of residential space relative to the size of the area that was enclosed against the external threats of attack. The tradeoff was privacy and comfort. Accommodating the numbers of people and animals in the fort's relatively compact square footage meant sacrificing considerable privacy. If each of the cabins was occupied by a family, the population density of the fort would have been at times quite high. Absolute population numbers are difficult to determine, but families tended to be quite large in the late eighteenth century generally, and families known to have lived at Fort Boonesborough were no exception. Daniel and Rebecca Boone, for example, brought six children with them when they moved to the fort in 1775. Richard Callaway and his wife arrived in the same year with five children. David and Sarah Gass's family included nine children when they arrived in 1777. Nathaniel Hart brought his wife and family of nine children to the fort in 1779. Many other families, an undetermined number of militiamen, and slaves added to the fluctuating totals.[8]

The combination of residential and defensive functions at Kentucky forts and stations was not a new response to dangerous frontier conditions, but the architectural plan that combined cabins and stockade to form a protective enclosure for year-round occupation was unique. The cabin/ stockade combination was employed at places where more than one family lived and varied from a few cabins to larger sites such as Bryan's Station, which housed as many as forty-four families in 1782. After the Revolutionary War the plan was adopted at such places as Bledsoe Station in Tennessee as an effective means of mounting a protective shield against Indian incursions.[9]

Investigations at Fort Boonesborough underscore the ephemeral nature of the archaeological deposits and architectural evidence of late eighteenth-century defensive residential sites. Five oval hearth pits filled with charred wood and ash-stained soil marked the locations of cabins in the center and along the south, west, and east walls of the fort. Intact dry-laid stone foundations were found only in the central cabin complex. The hearth and cabin interior midden documented on the west wall and the hearth on the east wall contained fairly dense scatters of displaced rock that could indicate the remnants of chimney bases that were salvaged for their largest stones. The other two hearths, one adjacent to the hearth and cabin interior on the west wall and the other on the south wall, had very little associated rock. The presence or absence of rock used to build chimney bases suggests that cabin chimney construction was not consistent at the fort. Building a stone chimney base to a height of three or four feet was advisable because the stone kept the fire in the hearth from igniting the stick-and-daub chimney shaft above it. However, it was possible to build a chimney completely out of stick-and-daub as long as the inside of the chimney was plastered with clay mud to a sufficient height to absorb the heat of the fire. In effect, the fire in the hearth fired the clay plaster in the same way that a kiln fires clay into pottery. The method was not optimal, but a chimney could be built more quickly if a stone base was eliminated.[10]

The locations of the chimney hearths where evidence of stone occurred or where stone may have been employed in the construction of the bases are associated with cabins for which occupants are known. The center cabin complex was occupied by Squire Boone and his family from 1775 to 1778. Their neighbors in the adjoining cabin were either the David Gass or Richard Callaway families. The cabin hearth and interior midden on the west wall may have been John Luttrell's kitchen from 1775 to approximately 1776. The hearth on the east wall may be the cabin where Bland Ballard said the David Gass family was living in 1779. These were the households of prominent men who played significant roles in Fort Boonesborough's history. They may have preferred cabins that were more substantially constructed than others at the fort, both for greater comfort and as a measure of their social class or leadership positions. The two hearths with no evidence of a stone chimney base seem to have been among the number of anonymous cabins built with no particular family in mind. They probably had a sequence of various occupants over time, such as single men assigned to militia duty, short-term visitors, or slaves. Their construction was relatively rapid compared to cabins with stone chimney bases.[11]

The archival record hints at social distinctions expressed in visual terms. Richard Henderson's cabin was the largest structure in the fort and had a bastioned second story and a shingle roof. There was also a size difference between the two center cabins as depicted in Moses Boone's sketch; he placed the Callaway family in the larger cabin. The archaeological evidence for cabin size is equivocal because the use of logs in construction and the lack of continuous durable foundations did not leave clear measurable footprints of the cabin floorplans. However, some inferences are possible. The location of the hearth in the stone foundation marking the central cabin complex suggests that the wall was originally twenty feet long; twenty feet was a common wall dimension for log buildings. The distributions of artifact and midden associated with a cabin hearth on the west wall suggests a slightly smaller cabin, perhaps sixteen feet.

Another aspect of cabin construction at the fort suggested by the archival record is the presence of some double cabins. The structure in the center of the fort was a double cabin, built on a dogtrot plan, and it incorporated a gunsmith shop in the narrow space between the two log pens. The two hearths on the west wall are approximately six feet apart, suggesting that they were part of two separate cabins that were quite close to one another or that they were part of a double cabin.

Although archaeological evidence proved elusive, the archival record clearly indicates that Fort Boonesborough had a stockade. However, the sections were short and the settlers may have taken shortcuts by not consistently seating each individual picket in a deep trench. Archival evidence indicates that the stockade was not strongly constructed and that it required frequent repair. A possible factor hindering the discovery of stockade is the short amount of time that the stockade was in place. The fort was not fully enclosed by cabin walls and stockade until late in 1776. The stockade remained in place through 1777, but by June 1778 stockade was missing along one wall of the fort enclosure and had to be quickly reinstalled before the siege. The end of the war in 1783 made a defensive posture unnecessary, and the stockade was dismantled by 1784. Thus, stockade only stood at the fort for about seven years, was not extensive or substantial, and was in disrepair for at least a few months during that time. If the stockade was not solidly built and its upright members did not decompose in place, its archaeological detection becomes much more difficult. However, future excavation may shed light on the occurrence of stockade at Fort Boonesborough.[12]

While the aim of the defensive construction was to put up a formidable appearance of impregnability, the log forts and stations were not designed for sustained military onslaughts. Kentucky settlers experienced armed conflict during the Revolutionary War primarily as short-term raids and attacks by Indian warriors rather than as prolonged offensives by British regiments as occurred back east. The principal mode of Indian warfare utilized surprise and ambush. Classic European modes of warfare such as frontal assaults or extended sieges were rare on the Kentucky frontier. While sheltering inside a log fort did not prevent casualties entirely, the tactic worked well for most engagements.

The Great Siege of 1778 was the last major military engagement to take place at Fort Boonesborough. That same year Kentucky militiamen led by Gen. George Rogers Clark captured Kaskaskia; the following year

Clark captured Vincennes and British governor Henry Hamilton, seriously compromising British power in the Ohio Valley. The 1779 passage of a land law that spelled out the requirements for legally claiming land in Kentucky spawned a surge of emigrants. The increase in permanent population led to many more defensive stations being built to house new settlers. A higher density of defensive sites improved the security coverage of the Kentucky frontier, but it also introduced points of vulnerability at less effectively defended stations. While Fort Boonesborough was not the target of any major attacks for the rest of the war, the taking of Ruddell's and Martin's Stations in June 1780, the deaths of Richard Callaway and Pemberton Rawlings (1780) and Nathaniel Hart (1782) near Fort Boonesborough, the Battle of Blue Licks, and numerous skirmishes, raids, and attacks kept the entire frontier on edge.

. The signing of the Treaty of Paris in 1783 brought more peaceful conditions to the Kentucky frontier, although Indian hostilities did not cease entirely until the Battle of Fallen Timbers in 1794. By the end of the revolution, however, a defensive posture at Fort Boonesborough was no longer considered necessary. Nonetheless, its tenacity and perseverance in the military defense of the western theatre of war from 1775 to 1783 stands as an accomplishment worthy of national recognition, to which its designation as a National Landmark attests. Its remarkably brief eight years of existence as a defensive site witnessed frequent Indian incursions and the longest siege ever carried out on Kentucky soil. The fort housed residents for one or more years and accommodated short-term visitors on their way elsewhere and militiamen assigned to brief periods of protective service. In a time of severe turmoil, able leaders aided by determined settlers intent on holding the line against their British and Indian enemies were essential to a success that was by no means assured.

Even as the Revolutionary War raged around them, the settlers at Fort Boonesborough were looking to the future. Judge Henderson and most of his partners in the Transylvania Company had decamped by 1779 when a group of settlers petitioned the Virginia General Assembly for a town charter. From the moment the charter was signed, the effort to create a prosperous, thriving town met serious challenges even as Kentucky experienced phenomenal population growth, established a robust agrarian economy, and founded strong political institutions. Finding a place for Boonesborough within this period of rapid settlement and in the face of the territory's maturing political arena was hampered by diverse forces: early leaders such as Callaway and Hart were killed, town trustees refused to serve, and attempts to be named the county seat in 1786 or the state capital in 1792 failed. Environmental factors made a significant portion of the town claims untenable for building. Boonesborough survived as a small town for several decades by serving as a tobacco inspection point, hosting a local post office, and accommodating a few businesses, but its resident population continued to decline.[13]

Coping with Shortages and Deprivations

Crowded conditions at the fort compromised comfort by forcing people to live in close quarters in hastily built cabins with no amenities, but crowding also fostered miserable conditions exacerbated by periods of food shortages and other deprivations. The challenge of obtaining sufficient food supplies was acute on the Kentucky frontier. Settlers brought seed stores and livestock with them so that crops could be planted as soon as possible and herds established. Nevertheless, reliance on wild game and indigenous edible plants was absolutely necessary to ensure a regular food supply. Salt was equally necessary to preserve meat for times when food was scarce or difficult to procure. Procuring salt from local salt springs was a dangerous endeavor, as Daniel Boone and his salt boilers learned in early 1778. The effects of food shortages were grave. Periods of near starvation led to significant declines in health and hygiene that were further exacerbated by crowding and dirty conditions; in turn, these hardships fostered infectious diseases and other afflictions such as body parasites.

Animal bone and plant remains collected by the archaeological excavations at Fort Boonesborough demonstrate how wild food sources subsidized domestic food stores. The long journey to Kentucky limited the numbers of domestic animals emigrants could realistically bring with them. Keeping livestock alive and healthy on the frontier was challenged by Indian raids that killed cattle and other stock. Settlers faced difficulties in replacing domestic animals that died or were stolen.

Managing domestic animals was a skill that most settlers brought with them, but hunting game was another matter. Hunting was a dangerous occupation: Indian warriors preyed on settlers who strayed from their places of sanctuary. Large game animals that were injured but not killed could in turn injure the hunter, and other accidents could easily disable or kill.

Overhunting emptied the area around the fort of game and necessitated longer, more dangerous hunting forays. Some settlers traded their skills in other areas for meat from more proficient hunters. Single young men assigned to the forts and stations for militia duty often hunted for the greater good as part of their duties.

Sufficient food stores had to be packed in to cover the time required for crops to mature. Wild plants augmented cultivated sources as settlers tended their crops and waited for harvest. Wild plant sources identified at Fort Boonesborough speak to the use of such plants as medicine as well as food. Folk medicines were commonly used to treat all sorts of ills, from digestive upsets to cuts and abrasions to sprains or muscle strain. In the absence of doctors, settlers with skill in folk medicine were valued, as were midwives who assisted with childbearing.

Consumer Behavior on the Kentucky Frontier

An American colonist contemplating a permanent move to Kentucky in the 1770s and 1780s had to contend with the difficulties of transport that limited the amount and, to some degree, the types of material goods they could bring. The most direct route to Fort Boonesborough from the east, and the one most commonly used, crossed the Cumberland Gap on what eventually came to be known as the Wilderness Road. The road was in actuality no more than a trail that traversed steep, dangerous mountain country, crossed many streams, and wound through dense forests and undergrowth. Wagons could not negotiate the trail, which left horses the most suitable mode of transportation, carrying humans as well as baggage and supplies. Material goods had to be packed in saddlebags or loaded on a packhorse in panniers, thus precluding the transport of large items like furniture. Since most settlers moved to Kentucky with the intention of claiming land on which they would establish farms, high priority was given to tools, equipment, livestock, and other stores that furthered that goal. Cattle, pigs, and sheep made the trip on their own power, but poultry probably had to be contained in some way. Agricultural tools such as hoes and plow shares were most efficiently transported without their wooden handles or other components, and these would be fitted out and made usable upon arrival. Tools such as axes, froes, adzes, hammers, and saws were brought for the construction of cabins and other necessary structures. Firearms and their accoutrements (powder horn, pouch, bullet mold, lead, flints, and gunpowder) were necessary for hunting and defense. Work clothing and sturdy footwear were a necessity. Iron pots and pans for cooking; utilitarian crockery for food processing and storage; knives, forks, spoons, and other utensils; pewter and ceramic plates for serving food; disassembled spinning wheels and looms—all items that anticipated the needs of a household far from sources of replacement and replenishment.[14]

In addition to the material goods people brought with them, there were limited opportunities to acquire goods in Kentucky. Richard Henderson, the principal partner in the Transylvania Company, established a store at Fort Boonesborough shortly after he arrived in the spring of 1775. He sold gunpowder, lead, osnaburg cloth (a kind of coarsely woven flax or linen fabric), metal buttons, and salt. He accepted various payments: an elk skin or services such as "ranging," improving the trail into Kentucky, bringing a canoe upriver, hunting game, shoeing horses, and traveling to Powell's Valley for sulfur and saltpeter (ingredients for making gunpowder). Peddlers bringing consumer goods to Kentucky for resale provided another means of acquisition; in addition, settlers took periodic trips back east. A less common source of goods derived from raids on Native American villages north of the Ohio River. Settlers launched retaliatory raids that sometimes resulted in the taking of "plunder" such as silver trade jewelry, blankets, guns, and horses. Militia campaigns conducted raids with the primary purpose of retrieving stolen horses, and leaders dangled the prospect of plunder as a recruiting tool. Typically, captured goods were either divided among the men or auctioned off and the proceeds divvied up.[15]

The trans-Appalachian frontier was settled at a time in American history when the capitalist world economy was expanding and consumer demand for manufactured items was high. The economic ideology the Fort Boonesborough settlers carried with them reflected a transition to capitalism that had taken place earlier, but their full participation in market exchange was not immediately possible in Kentucky. The distance from established towns, cities, seats of government, and mercantile systems forced settlers to practice a level of self-sufficiency and mutuality until living conditions improved. Nevertheless, participation in a consumer culture is evident in the wide variety of commercially produced artifacts that occur in frontier assemblages.[16]

The artifacts recovered from Fort Boonesborough were owned by an unknown number of people, but most of them were probably discarded or lost during the eight years that the fort actively served a defensive role. Fewer artifacts were discarded after the Revolutionary War had ended and the stockade was dismantled, but the cabins still were occupied for a few years. The short period during which the artifacts were discarded or lost at the site explains the relatively low frequencies but still offers a glimpse of the kinds of material goods settlers used. The artifacts recovered from the excavations at Fort Boonesborough as well as other Revolutionary War–era Kentucky sites indicate that refined and utilitarian ceramics and glass, cooking implements, and personal items were commonly brought to the frontier.

Ceramic artifacts from the site included coarse crockery made in the colonies and exported British refined creamware and pearlware tea services. English salt-glazed plates were exported from Britain for sale. Sarah Hart's inventory taken in 1785 lists numerous examples of the household items she owned when she died at the fort. Among them are "Chinai" tea cups and bowls, which may have been English made, refined ceramics with Chinese inspired painted decoration (or what potters in the Staffordshire, England, area called "China glaze"). Other items listed in her inventory that could end up as fragments in an archaeological assemblage include wine glasses, cracked bottles, iron cooking pots and Dutch ovens, pots that might have been redware storage or processing vessels, and a mirror. Although the Hart cabin was not excavated, similar artifacts from nearly all these categories were found at the cabins in Fort Boonesborough.[17]

Historian Elizabeth Perkins's analysis of Kentucky probate inventories concludes that capital goods (livestock, firearms, and agricultural tools and equipment) were more prominent than "the genteel trappings of bed and board." She also concludes that a high desire for manufactured goods encouraged the establishment of mercantile stores as soon as conditions allowed. The brisk trade in British imports, particularly English ceramics, reflected a genteel attitude concerning bodily privacy in the shift from using communal wooden trenchers to individual plates. Likewise, taking tea was a habit shared by people of low to high incomes as reflected in the pots, kettles, cups, and saucers listed in inventories and often represented in artifact assemblages. Imported fabrics of all kinds were also in high demand in spite of post–Revolutionary War warnings that wearing imported lace and silk reinforced social class distinctions and undermined the principle of equality embodied in the American republican model.[18]

This frontier consumption did not come cheaply; transportation costs of consumer goods were high, and, after adding a small profit for the merchant, the Kentucky consumer could expect to pay 50 percent more for goods from the principal market at Philadelphia. High costs generally restricted consumer purchasing to more affluent families. The scarcity of currency in Kentucky complicated payment for consumer goods since merchants had to have cash to replenish their stock on annual buying trips back east. While merchants accepted all forms of currency from Spanish reales to English pounds, shillings, and pence, they also accepted a wide variety of commodities in trade, from country produce and hides to land warrants to livestock on the hoof; women could barter with merchants by offering their butter, cheese, eggs, and homespun linen.[19]

Artifacts recovered from early historic settlement sites like Fort Boonesborough and other defensive stations such as Hugh McGary's at Shawnee Springs, Logan's Station (St. Asaph's) in Lincoln County, and Daniel Boone's Station in Fayette County all attest to the "coexistence of capitalist commodity markets and local systems of mutuality and exchange." Carole Shammas asked the question in 1982: "How Self-Sufficient Was Early America?" She concluded that even if neighborhood reciprocity helped to create local self-sufficiency for some needs, the western consumer participated fully in the commercial world. In terms of American agrarian development, the world market was involved from the beginning, financing migration to the colonies, buying colonial surpluses, and providing manufactured goods to enthusiastic consumers. Even in late eighteenth-century Kentucky, before mercantile systems were well established, settlers made choices about what to bring based on what they wanted (tea cups and saucers, "Chinai bowls," jewelry, and the like) as well as what they needed (nails, tools, guns, lead, and gunpowder, for example), and many of these choices involved the purchase of manufactured goods. Once they were established in Kentucky, settlers began producing commodities both for their own use and for sale or trade while still buying or bartering for goods when available. The privations of the frontier and the distance to markets may have slowed their consumer behavior, but these difficulties did not eliminate it.[20]

Looking Forward

As hostilities ended and frontier conditions lifted, people abandoned the forts and stations that had sheltered them. They built houses, developed farms, established towns, and organized governmental, educational, religious, and civic institutions. They turned their attention to the future. The population expanded as people who had been unwilling to settle under adverse conditions streamed into a more peaceful Kentucky in search of a more prosperous life. At the national level the federal government put in place the institutions that made real and functional the words of the Constitution and the Bill of Rights as the thirteen former colonies struggled to resolve their differences regarding how the country was to be governed.

There were lessons to be learned from the Kentucky experience. One concerned the system by which vacant lands were allocated. The British metes and bounds system of surveying land was used by all thirteen colonies. The system had some inherent weaknesses—natural landmarks such as trees to mark corners or streams to show boundaries could change as trees died and streams shifted course, and irregular shapes made the description of the tracts more complex. The system broke down particularly when there was inadequate oversight in the recording of claims. As a result surveying groups operating independently in Kentucky frequently surveyed over other, earlier surveys, creating a maze of overlapping surveys that were called "shingled claims." When the Land Court of 1779–1780 convened in Kentucky, one of their duties was to sort out the problem of overlapping claims, but their success was limited and litigation over land boundary disputes persisted for decades in Kentucky courts.[21]

After the Revolutionary War ended, the new United States of America had to find a way to pay off its war debts, and land sales in the western territories was the answer. The original thirteen colonies ceded their western lands to the federal government to facilitate these land sales and allow western expansion to continue while paying off the war debt. The metes and bounds system of surveying was unsuited for mapping land that was sold sight unseen to buyers. The Land Ordinance Act of 1785 established the township and range system of surveying land, and the federal government took responsibility for the accurate recording of the surveys. Although not all of the former colonies adopted the new system, the land donated by Virginia that included the Northwest Territories was surveyed under the township and range system. In Kentucky the new method applied only to the Jackson Purchase region in the far western part of the state, which had been purchased in 1818 from the Chickasaws under the administration of Andrew Jackson; the remainder of the state had already been surveyed and transferred to private owners under the metes and bounds system.

Another legacy of frontier-era Kentucky concerned Native American relations with white settlers. Indian tribes had an antagonistic relationship with Euro-American settlers long before the settlement of Kentucky. The territory was a war zone that offered no accommodating middle ground of common interests as had been the case between Native Americans and the British. The war's end did not alter the anti-Indian sentiments many Kentuckians felt, particularly since raids north of the Kentucky River continued to occur until the definitive defeat of the Shawnees at the Battle of Fallen Timbers in 1794. As federal troops were marshalled to fight Native Americans for control of the Northwest Territory north of the Ohio River in the 1790s, Kentuckians supported the army by supplying livestock and food. The move stimulated the growth of the new state's emerging agrarian economy and furthered efforts to establish an American national state. The state also initiated internal improvements by opening roads from the Bluegrass region to Cincinnati and the Ohio River that facilitated the delivery of goods. Thus, Kentuckians' attitude towards Native American tribes and the role the state filled in supplying the army played into the eventual subjugation and expulsion of native peoples. Likewise, thousands of Kentucky militiamen willingly fought the British during the War of 1812, and the state's troops saw more combat and suffered more casualties than those of any other state. Their enthusiasm grew out of a patriotism that was a legacy from their Revolutionary War beginnings. "The earliest settlers of Kentucky were bonded by war, bred in war, and taught the values of war in a way that made military service a natural, self-evident expression of manhood."[22]

Early in the nineteenth century, the narrative of the nation's birth out of revolution was crafted into a public memory that emphasized and commemorated patriotism and heroism. The celebration of the American Revolution in the national collective memory is embedded in its identity as the key event that expressed the unity of the new nation. Belief in a national tradition of unity was particularly important in the antebellum period when controversies and cleavages associated with the Constitutional Convention of 1787, the Nullification Crisis of 1832, and other political quarrels threatened to repudiate the integrity and existence of the republic.

Fort Boonesborough fit neatly into the emerging ethos as a sterling example of stalwart resistance in the face of superior forces. Even while the town of Boonesborough struggled and failed to prosper, over the course of the nineteenth century Fort Boonesborough was celebrated as a place to be venerated and revered. The brief period when the fort was occupied as a defensive site is an example of "hot" chronology, a concept described by anthropologist Claude Levi-Strauss as a time "where in the eyes of the historian numerous events appear as differential elements." The "hottest" or most significant period of a society's past is its beginnings; in this regard Fort Boonesborough's significance is its role in the beginning of the United States of America as a sovereign nation.[23]

The Fort Boonesborough story has remarkable staying power. From the celebrations of the nineteenth century to the commemorative monuments and park of the twentieth century to the active living history programs that attract thousands of visitors each year in the twenty-first, Fort Boonesborough continues to appeal to a wide audience of genealogists, reenactors, archaeologists, historians, and other students of human culture.

APPENDIX
Boone's Road Cutting Team and Henderson's Party

Daniel Boone's Road Cutters

Daniel Boone
Squire Boone
Edward Bradley
James Bridges
William Bush
Richard Callaway
Samuel Coburn
Captain Crabtree
Benjamin Cutbirth
David Gass
James Hall
John Hart
William Hays, husband of Susannah Boone Hays
Susannah Boone Hays, Boone's daughter
William Hicks
Edmund Jennings
Thomas Johnston
John Kennedy
John King
Thomas McDowell (killed en route)
Joseph McPheeters (killed en route)
William Miller

William Moore
James Peeke
Bartlett Searcy
Reuben Searcy
Michael Stoner
Sam, male slave belonging to William Twetty (killed en route)
Samuel Tate
Oswald Towns
Capt. William Twetty (killed en route)
Unnamed female slave belonging to Richard Callaway
John Vardeman
Felix Walker

Richard Henderson's Party (A Partial List)

William Calk (joined en route)
William Cocke
Dan, slave belonging to Richard Henderson
James Durring
John Farrar
Nathaniel Hart
Nathaniel Henderson
Richard Henderson
Samuel Henderson
John Luttrell
Robert McAfee (joined en route)
Samuel McAfee (joined en route)
Thomas Slaughter
Enoch Smith (joined en route)
William Bailey Smith
Robert Whitledge (joined en route)

Source: Both lists were compiled from Belue, *Life of Boone,* 335–36, 356.

NOTES

Preface

1. Only the British Crown could create and sanction a new colony. A proprietary model gave full governing rights to an individual or group of people, such as was done for Pennsylvania.

2. Jim Kurz, "Looking for Daniel Boone's Fort" (Lexington, KY: unpublished manuscript, 1990), 1.

3. Archival research included many sources with archaic spellings and usages. These have mostly been retained without comment or, in a few cases, clarified if the meaning appears unclear to modern readers. The project area was selected to include all of the Kentucky River bottomland where alternative sites of the fort were suggested, including land outside the current boundaries of the park. The mouth of Otter Creek was once closer to the fort site than it is today. It was moved by the Army Corps of Engineers in 1914 to relieve pressure against the dam at Lock No. 10, located downstream. Nancy O'Malley, *Searching for Boonesborough*, Archaeological Report 193 (Lexington: University of Kentucky Program for Cultural Resource Assessment, 1989).

4. Prehistoric artifacts were found in small quantities at the fort site during the excavations. O'Malley, *Searching for Boonesborough*, 41–42.

5. O'Malley, *Searching for Boonesborough*.

6. My volunteers included: Marty Blackson, David Carper, Lisa Cheatham, Brian and Cheryl Cowell, Anita Drane, Oliver Frye, Marie Gregory, Joyce Hannen, Edna and Laura Harris, Molly, Tom, and Virginia Hentschel, Mark and Robin Hopkins, Hong Phan Huynh, Paul Jaquith, Fran Johns, Dwayne Keagy, Herbert Livingston, Roger and William Long, Charles Mallinkopf, Trina Maples, David, Kathy, and Mary McIntosh, Blaine Miller, JaNette Mullins, Delores Nelson, Gayle Osborne, Julie O'Shaughnessy, Maria Perry, Marie Rieber, "Robbie" Robbins, Bruce Ross, Eli and Mark Scarr, Charlie and John Schimmoeller, Adonis and Radford Spivey, Teresa Tune, Ann Marie Usher, Allan Wickersham, Patsy J. Wilson, Chip Winkler,

Notes

and Linda Young. Other people who aided in one form or another include Mrs. Sarah Morgan, Ote Lisle West, Dorothy Richards, William Eaton, Charlie Barton, Philip DiBlasi, Dr. Terrance Martin, Dr. Tom Dillehay, Dr. Mary Powell, Dr. Richard Jefferies, Dr. Steve McBride, Dr. Kim McBride, Dr. Tom Sussenbach, Andrea Allen, Barbara Gortman, Jo Staggs, Jo Stone, and Ed Winkle. Park manager Robert Wilson and his staff facilitated in many ways.

7. I am indebted to Walter Bloxson, Steven Brandenburg, Jim Haag, Allison Harnish, Arlis Johnson, Kayla Kidwell-Snider, Allison Layne, Steve LeBrun, Donna Maupin, Mike McMurtry, Robert Moody, John Morgan, Zach Morgan, Scott New, C. Martin Raymer, Mack Read, Matt Read, Bill Sharp, Wayne Sweezey, Teresa Tune, Hugh Tuttle, Hannah Weigle, Elizabeth Weyer, Joan Wood, and Chi Woodrich for their hard work during a punishingly hot and dry summer. The results of the ABPP grant are reported in Nancy O'Malley, *Drawing Battle Lines at Fort Boonesborough: The Siege of 1778* (Lexington, KY: American Battlefield Protection Program, 2012).

8. Students in the field school included Kristina Farr, Katherine Gamblin, Emma Gottbrath, Ashley Nugent, Alyssa O'Bryan, Trent Redmon, Allison Stevenson, Hannah Weigle, and Jessica Wise.

9. Wayna Adams, Michael Arthur, Steve Brandenburg, Rick Burdin, Justin Carlson, Matt Davidson, David Dejardins, John Dubose, Chris Dubose, Emily Elkins, Kurt Fiegel, Paxton Fiegel, Tristan Fiegel, Sharon Graves, Jim Haag, Wanda Henley, Joe Hewitt, Andrea Hunt, Bill Huser, Jim Kurz, Mae Marks, Michelle Massey, Donna Maupin, Jerry Raisor, Crystal Reedy, Caitlin Rogers, Katie Bales Sayer, Rick Seelhorst, Jim Tuttle, Hannah Weigle, and Ann Wilkinson contributed their labor to the excavations. Park manager Rob Minerich, curator Jerry Raisor, and other staff provided many helpful services.

1. Kentucky on the Cusp of Revolution

1. Alan Taylor presents a comprehensive discussion of the historic context of the late eighteenth-century developments that led to the American Revolution and set the stage for the settlement of Kentucky. Much of the summary in this chapter draws on his insights and conclusions. See *American Revolutions: A Continental History, 1750–1804* (New York: Norton, 2016).

2. Andrea A. Smalley, "'They Steal Our Deer and Land': Contested Hunting Grounds in the Trans-Appalachian West," *Register of the Kentucky Historical Society* 114, nos. 3, 4 (2016): 303–39; Taylor, *American Revolutions*, 61.

3. James Corbett David, *Dunmore's New World: The Extraordinary Life of a Royal Governor in Revolutionary America* (Charlottesville: University of Virginia Press, 2013), 57.

4. David, *Dunmore's New World*, 56–57.

5. John Mack Faragher, *Daniel Boone: The Life and Legend of an American Pioneer* (New York: Holt, 1992), 72–73; Taylor, *American Revolutions*, 73.

6. Taylor, *American Revolutions*, 64, 52.

7. Taylor, *American Revolutions*, 76; Smalley, "They Steal Our Deer," 320.

8. David, *Dunmore's New World*, 61.

9. The Kentucky territory was made part of Fincastle County when it was established in 1772. David, *Dunmore's New World*, 62–63; Craig Thompson Friend, *Kentucke's Frontiers* (Bloomington: Indiana University Press, 2010), 49; Neal O. Hammon, "Land Tenure in Kentucky" (Shelbyville, KY: unpublished manuscript, n.d.), 62; Neal O. Hammon and Richard Taylor, *Virginia's Western War, 1775–1786* (Mechanicsburg, PA: Stackpole Books, 2002), xvii–xix.

10. Hammon and Taylor, *Virginia's Western War*, xxii.

11. Eric Hinderaker, *Elusive Empires: Constructing Colonialism in the Ohio Valley, 1673–1800* (Cambridge: Cambridge University Press, 1997), 190–95; David, *Dunmore's New World*, 78, 89–90; Hammon and Taylor, *Virginia's Western War*, xxx.

12. Taylor, American Revolutions, 82.

13. For a description of the extent of the Transylvania Company's purchase, see chapter 2.

2. Richard Henderson and the Transylvania Company

1. Archibald Henderson, "Richard Henderson and the Occupation of Kentucky, 1775," *Mississippi Valley Historical Review* 1, no. 3 (1914): 343.

2. Henderson, "Henderson and the Occupation," 343.

3. Wallace L. McKeehan, "Archives: The Regulators and the Battle of Alamance," Sons of Dewitt Colony Texas website, www.tamu.edu/faculty/ccbn/dewitt/mckstmerreg1.htm; James P. Whittenberg, "Planters, Merchants, and Lawyers: Social Change and the Origins of the North Carolina Regulation," *William and Mary Quarterly* 34, no. 2 (1977): 215–38; Marjoleine Kars, *Breaking Loose Together: The Regulator Rebellion in Pre-Revolutionary North Carolina* (Chapel Hill: University of North Carolina Press, 2002), 183–84.

4. Archibald Henderson, "The Creative Force in Westward Expansion: Henderson and Boone," *American Historical Review* 20, no. 1 (1914): 102; Archibald Henderson, "The Transylvania Company: A Study in Personnel: James Hogg," *Filson Club History Quarterly* 21, no. 1 (1947): 11.

5. Henderson, "Creative Force," 99. John Luttrell married Susanna, daughter of John Hart, who was a brother to Nathaniel and Thomas Hart. Henderson, "James Hogg," 11; Henderson, "Henderson and the Occupation," 347–48.

6. George Washington Ranck, *Boonesborough: Its Founding, Pioneer Struggles, Indian Experiences, Transylvania Days, and Revolutionary Annals* (Salem, NH: Ayer Co. Publishers, 1986), 151.

7. Neal Hammon calculated the number of acres covered by the grant in Kentucky and Tennessee.

8. Ranck, *Boonesborough*, 151. The spelling of Cherokee names varies among different publications. Ranck cites Mann Butler's *History of Kentucky* as his source. Butler was provided the deed by James Alves, a descendant of two of the Transylvania Company proprietors, who possessed a copy of the original deed. A slightly different spelling for Oconistoto was used by Lyman Draper in his biography of Daniel Boone. Ted Franklin Belue, *The Life of Daniel Boone by Lyman C. Draper* (Mechanicsburg, PA: Stackpole Books, 1998), 333.

9. Henderson, "Henderson and the Occupation," 351; Ranck, *Boonesborough*, 148–49.

10. Ranck, *Boonesborough*, 181–82; Friend, *Kentucke's Frontiers*, 59.

11. Belue, *Life of Boone*, 335.

12. Taylor, *American Revolutions*, 6.

3. Establishing Fort Boonesborough on the Kentucky River

1. Friend, *Kentucke's Frontiers*, 59; Hammon and Taylor, *Virginia's Western War*, 3; Belue, *Life of Boone*, 357–58.

2. Nancy O'Malley, *Searching for Boonesborough*, Archaeological Report 193 (Lexington: Program for Cultural Resource Assessment, Department of Anthropology, University of Kentucky, 1989); Letter from George W. Stoner, Lyman Copeland Draper Manuscripts 24C55, Wisconsin Historical Society, Madison (hereafter cited as Draper Mss., WHS); Kathryn H. Weiss, *Daniel Bryan, Nephew of Daniel Boone: His Narrative and Other Stories* (Forbestown, CA: privately printed, 2008), 21; Ranck, *Boonesborough*, 176; Julian J. N. Campbell, *The Land of Cane and Clover: Presettlement Vegetation in the So-Called Bluegrass Region of Kentucky* (Lexington: University of Kentucky Herbarium, 1985).

Spelling variants for Boonesborough are common in the archival record. Felix Walker omitted the "e" in Boonesborough throughout his narrative, even though he spelled Daniel Boone's surname correctly when referring to him. He also misspelled James Harrod's surname as "Herod," despite his claim that Harrod was an "old acquaintance in North Carolina." He wrote his memoir in 1824, many years after the events he describes, and Walker simply may not have recalled the most common spellings. He uses the term "station" to indicate a type of privately owned, defensible construction adopted when earlier frontiers were settled in the Greenbrier River valley in what is now West Virginia. The term "station" was sometimes used synonymously with "fort," particularly by writers later in the nineteenth century, but eighteenth-century writers usually used the term "fort" to designate a public place of defense. While both terms refer to constructions that served dual purposes of defense and residence, forts were usually larger, housed more people, and were available to anyone who needed sanctuary, whereas stations were generally considered privately owned and controlled. See Ranck, *Boonesborough,* 165, 167; Nancy O'Malley, *"Stockading Up": A Study of Pioneer Stations in the Inner Bluegrass Region of Kentucky,* Archaeological Report 127 (Lexington: University of Kentucky Program for Cultural Resource Assessment, 1987); Nancy O'Malley, "Frontier Defenses and Pioneer Strategies in the Historic Settlement Era," in *The Buzzel about Kentuck: Settling the Promised Land,* ed. Craig Thompson Friend (Lexington: University Press of Kentucky, 1998), 57–76.

3. Another variant is "Boonesboro," which was commonly used in the late nineteenth century. It was the preferred spelling of a resort built by David Williams around 1909, and the spelling still can be seen on some highway directional signs. The enabling legislation for the state park in 1956 also adopted this spelling, although the park name is spelled "Boonesborough." The most common spelling, and the preferred variant in most publications, is "Boonesborough." George Washington Ranck preferred this spelling in his 1901 history, as did the Transylvania Company proprietors. See General Assembly of Kentucky, "An Act Relating to Establishment of Boonesboro State Park," House Bill No. 156, Frankfort, 1956; Ranck, *Boonesborough,* 172; Louise Phelps Kellogg, "A Kentucky Pioneer Tells Her Story of Early Boonesborough and Harrodsburg," *History Quarterly of the Filson Club* 3 (1928): 233; Interview of John Gass by John Dabney Shane, Draper Mss. 11CC11-15, WHS.

Richard Henderson's journal is transcribed in Ranck, *Boonesborough,* and Belue, *Life of Boone.* While Ranck's work remains the most comprehensive history of Boonesborough, he heavily edited Henderson's journal and left out numerous sections that he deemed unnecessary to his narrative. Some of the omitted sections, however, reveal much more anxiety on Henderson's part regarding the validity of his enterprise, particularly in his encounters with men who were surveying land and seeking to settle in Kentucky at the same time. Draper's biography of Daniel Boone quotes many of these omitted sections. Henderson went to great effort to persuade other settlers to join him in supporting his company, but he frequently encountered suspicion and skepticism concerning the validity of his claim and the terms of land transactions and governance. Belue, *Life of Boone,* 346.

4. The location of the lots laid out by Boone and his men ahead of Henderson's arrival is not precisely known. They may have focused on the area north of where Fort Boone was established. This area is now completely taken over by a large limestone quarry that has obliterated all evidence of previous occupation. Henderson's lots probably were located so that they did not interfere with the lots that Boone had laid out earlier.

5. Belue, *Life of Boone,* 351.

6. Ranck, *Boonesborough*, 173–74, 176; Belue, *Life of Boone*, 346–47. John Luttrell was married to Nathaniel Hart's niece, Susannah, who was the daughter of Nathaniel's brother John. Luttrell's conveying Nathaniel's criticism to Henderson is curious. Was he trying to avoid taking sides in a quarrel between the two men?

7. Belue, *Life of Boone*, 347.

8. Sarah S. Hughes, *Surveyors and Statesmen: Land Measuring in Colonial Virginia* (Richmond: Virginia Surveyors Foundation and Virginia Association of Surveyors, 1979).

9. Ranck, *Boonesborough*, 174; Belue, *Life of Boone*, 347; Neal O. Hammon, ed., *John Floyd: The Life and Letters of a Frontier Surveyor* (Louisville, KY: Butler Books, 2013) 23.

10. Belue, *Life of Boone*, 349–50, 359.

11. Belue, *Life of Boone*, 365. Although James Harrod helped to establish Harrodstown (now called Harrodsburg) in present-day Mercer County and was living there in 1775, he also claimed and improved land at the Boiling Spring (in present-day Boyle County). He did not take up permanent residency at Boiling Spring until 1778. The St. Asaph settlement served as John Floyd's headquarters when he was surveying in the Kentucky territory. Henderson's recognition of the three settlement areas seems to reflect his recognition of the factions that coalesced around particular leaders.

12. Ranck, *Boonesborough*, 198, 201–2, 211–12.

13. Ranck, *Boonesborough*, 176; Belue, *Life of Boone*, 350.

14. Kellogg, "Kentucky Pioneer," 233; Ranck, *Boonesborough*, 135.

15. Ranck, *"Boonesborough,"* 39. Luttrell was not destined to return to Boonesborough. He joined colonial forces and was killed at Cane Creek, North Carolina, in 1781. Luttrell had not been present during the siege of 1778; in 1779 Richard Henderson entered two land claims on his behalf at the land court held in December. The court acknowledged Luttrell's right to the claims by virtue of his having raised a corn crop in 1775 and his residency in Kentucky for a total of twelve months between 1775 and 1778. The latter condition he probably did not technically meet, since he arrived at Boonesborough in April 1775 and left around August. However, the land court granted his claim. Draper Mss. 2CC300-31, WHS; Kentucky Land Office, *Kentucky Doomsday Book, 1779–1780*, accessed September 18, 2018, https://sos.ky.gov/admin/land/non-military/settlements_preemptions/Pages/Kentucky-Doomsday-Book.aspx, 116.

16. Ranck, *Boonesborough*, 42–44.

17. Belue, *Life of Boone*, 389.

18. Belue, *Life of Boone*, 390; Ranck, *Boonesborough*, 44, 230.

19. Hammon, *John Floyd*, 105–6.

20. Ranck, *Boonesborough*, 54, 254.

21. Natalie Inman, "'A Dark and Bloody Ground': American Indian Responses to Expansion during the American Revolution," *Tennessee Historical Quarterly* 70, no. 4 (2011): 258–75.

22. Francois Furstenberg, "The Significance of the Trans-Appalachian Frontier in Atlantic History," *American Historical Review* 113, no. 3 (2008): 647–77; Inman, "Dark and Bloody Ground," 263; Colin G. Calloway, "'We Have Always Been the Frontier': The American Revolution in Shawnee Country," *American Indian Quarterly* 16, no. 1 (1992): 39–52.

23. John Filson, "The Adventures of Daniel Boon," in *The Discovery, Settlement and Present State of Kentucke and an Essay Towards the Topography, and Natural History of that Important Country* (Wilmington, DE: James Adams, 1784), appendix 1; Ranck, *Boonesborough*, 49–51.

24. Belue, *Life of Boone*, 439–40, 443.

25. Ranck, *Boonesborough*, 442–43, 446, 448–49.

4. Captivity, Escape and the Great Siege of 1778

1. The summary of the siege draws upon Ranck's account supplemented by primary documentation compiled by Anne Crabb. Crabb's main source of information was the Draper manuscripts, particularly interviews by John Dabney Shane and Lyman Draper, as well her genealogical research. Ted Belue's copiously edited transcription of Lyman Draper's biography of Daniel Boone also contributed to the summary. Belue, *Life of Boone*, 460; Ranck, *Boonesborough;* Anne Crabb, *And the Battle Began Like Claps of Thunder: The Siege of Boonesboro—1778—As Told by the Pioneers* (Richmond, KY: privately printed by the author, 1998).

2. Belue, *Life of Boone*, 462–63.

3. Ted Franklin Belue, "Terror in the Canelands: The Fate of Daniel Boone's Salt Boilers," *Filson Club History Quarterly* 68, no. 1 (1994): 3–34.

4. Belue, "Terror in the Canelands."

5. Upon his arrival he discovered that his wife and children had returned to North Carolina, believing him to be dead. Belue, *Life of Boone*, 480.

6. Ranck, *Boonesborough*, 73–74; Crabb, *And the Battle Began*, 70; John D. Barnhart, "Lieutenant Governor Henry Hamilton's Apologia," *Indiana Magazine of History* 52, no. 4 (1956): 383–86; Weiss, *Daniel Bryan*, 28. Bryan mentioned the presence of one or more Cherokee warriors.

7. Ranck interpreted the erection of two "blockhouses" as meaning the addition of second stories on cabins already built at the southwest and southeast corners of the fort. Both Moses Boone and John Gass stated that the fort was enlarged and new bastions built. Use of the term "bastion" rather than "blockhouse" (which refers to the entire building) may mean the construction of an overhanging second

story. Interview by Lyman Draper with John Gass, Draper Mss. 24C74; interviews by John Dabney Shane with Moses Boone and John Gass, Draper Mss. 19C8–57 and 11CC11-15, respectively, WHS. Keeping the fort in a state of defensive readiness was a constant struggle made worse by the lackadaisical attitude of many of the settlers. While the fort apparently had been completely enclosed by 1777, the stockade was already in disrepair less than a year later. Low-quality construction might account for part of the problem, but another possibility may have been a practice of removing the upright puncheons forming the stockade for other uses. Ranck, *Boonesborough*, 70–72.

8. One of the defenders, William Bailey Smith, estimated the male population of the fort at thirty men and twenty boys, while Ranck estimated forty-four or forty-five men based on his sources. Ranck, *Boonesborough*, 177. A surreptitious reconnoiter in early 1778 by French Canadians Charles Baubin and Louis Lorimier and forty Shawnees estimated the fort housed eighty men. A detailed list based on more recent research identified families and individuals by name. Using Anne Crabb's evidence, there may have been seventeen women, thirty-seven children, two slaves, and as many as seventy-six men. Crabb, *And the Battle Began*, 59–62, 66–68.

9. Hamilton's letters have not survived. Ranck, *Boonesborough*, 81; Belue, *Life of Boone*, 501; Nancy O'Malley, *Drawing Battle Lines at Fort Boonesborough: The Siege of 1778*, Report prepared for the American Battlefield Protection Program, Lexington, KY, 2012, p. 33.

10. Belue, *Life of Boone*, 502.

11. Ranck, *Boonesborough*. 82.

12. Ranck, *Boonesborough*, 83.

13. Ranck, *Boonesborough*, 84.

14. Ranck, *Boonesborough*, 85–87.

15. Ranck, *Boonesborough*, 506–7.

16. Moses Boone stated that the tunnel extended 25 feet into the bank from the river's edge. Daniel Trabue, who was not present at the siege and was merely reporting what he had heard about it, said the sound of digging could be heard and the tunnel nearly reached the fort. John Gass, who was present during the siege, said the tunnel was about 120 feet long and came within 10 feet of the fort wall. Daniel Bryan, who heard the story from his uncle, Daniel Boone, also estimated that the tunnel came within 10 or 15 feet of the countermine. These estimates seem wildly inaccurate given the distance from the fort to the river and considering the topography and difference in elevation between the fort and the water level of the river. John Gass gave the distance from the river to the fort as 210 to 240 feet. The tunnel began at river's edge and thus would have had to extend some 200 to 230 feet to come within 10 feet of the fort. Yet Gass's estimate of the tunnel's

length was half that distance. The difference in elevation between the edge of the river and the fort was 30 vertical feet. The tunnel would have had to been dug at an uphill angle to overcome the elevational difference. Bryan also said that the excavators dug up to the surface to see how close they were to the fort and that the interpreter, Pompey, stuck his head out of the hole and was killed. Pompey's manner of death was corroborated by Moses Boone. However, during the investigations in 2011, geophysical surveys were conducted using ground penetrating radar along the modern edge of the first terrace. They did not reveal any evidence of a tunnel. If the tunnel was 120 feet long, as Gass claimed, the remote sensing equipment should have detected a remnant of its western, higher end. If it was only 25 feet long, as Moses Boone reported, erosion would have washed away any remnants of disturbance in the early twentieth century. The truth may lie somewhere in the middle. Interviews with John Gass and Moses Boone by Lyman Draper, Draper Mss. 24C73 and 19C12, respectively, WHS; Weiss, *Daniel Bryan*, 29.

17. Ranck, *Boonesborough*, 95–96.

18. Interview with John Gass by Lyman Draper, Draper Mss. 24C73 (10), WHS; Belue, *Life of Boone*, 518. Two settlers were mortally wounded the third night of the siege. David Bundrin was stationed at a porthole when a bullet passed through and pierced his brain, leaving him speechless and miserable for two or three days before he died. Samuel Henderson's slave, London, died instantly from a shot in his neck while he sheltered in a ditch previously dug under Richard Henderson's kitchen cabin to extinguish a fence fire. Daniel and Jemima Boone were slightly injured, while Squire Boone and Pemberton Rawlings sustained more serious wounds. Daniel Boone thought that thirty-seven Native Americans were killed and many more wounded.

19. Ranck, *Boonesborough*, 97–99.

20. Jack M. Sosin, *The Revolutionary Frontier, 1763–1783* (Albuquerque: University of New Mexico Press, 1974), 117; Pioneer and Historical Society of the State of Michigan, *Pioneer Collections* (Lansing, MI: Thorp & Godfrey, 1886).

21. Ranck, *Boonesborough*, 15; Reuben Gold Thwaites, *Daniel Boone* (New York: D. Appleton and Co., 1913); Daniel Trabue, "The Journal of Col. Daniel Trabue: Some Account of His Ancestry, Life and Travels . . . ," in *Colonial Men and Times*, ed. Lillie DuPuy VanCulin, 3–160 (Philadelphia: Harper, Innes & Sons, 1916); Belue, "Terror in the Canelands," 33.

5. Establishing a Town

1. Ranck, *Boonesborough*, 253; James Rood Robertson, *Petitions of the Early Inhabitants of Kentucky to the General Assembly of Virginia 1769 to 1792*, Filson Club Publications 27 (Louisville, KY: John P. Morton & Co., 1914), 50.

2. William Waller Hening, *The Statutes at Large, Being a Collection of All the Laws of Virginia, from the First Session of the Legislature in the Year 1619* (Richmond, VA: George Cochran, Printer, 1822), 10:39.

3. The petitioners included the following signatures (in order signed): William Hancock, Edward Nelson, John Bullock, James Berry, Joseph Doniphan, Jesse Copher, Nicholas Procter, Nathel Baslock, John South, Senr., Charles (?) Procter, Rubin Procter, Michael Bedinger, Jesse Hedges, Samuel Estill, John Harbeston, John Hewly, James Doster, William Patterson, John Callaway (?), James Briant [Bryant], Walter Welch, Edmond Fair, Benjn. White, Edward Harrod, Jacob Starns, Peter Harper, Ambros Coffy, Thos. Noell, John South (Jr.), John Kelly, Benjamin Dunneway, Joshua P [illegible]. Legislative Petition from Inhabitants of Boonsfort, October 16, 1779, Accession no. 36121, Box 366, Folder 1, Virginia State Archives, Richmond (hereafter cited as Boonsfort petition). Robertson, *Petitions of the Early Inhabitants*, 189–232.

4. Of the five proposed trustees, Nathaniel Hart and Richard Callaway had been at Boonesborough (with occasional trips back east) since the Transylvania Company launched their settlement in 1775. James Estill arrived sometime after the siege of 1778 and was at Boonesborough by the spring of 1779. The petition may have been written before he arrived. George Madin and Robert Cartwright had no known connection to Boonesborough nor is their relationship to Hart or Callaway known.

5. Robertson, *Petitions of the Early Inhabitants*, 50.

6. Boonsfort petition, October 16, 1779.

7. Robertson, *Petitions of the Early Inhabitants*, 52; Hening, *Statutes at Large*, 10:196–97.

8. "An Act for Establishing the Town of Boonesborough in the County of Kentucky," in *The Statute Law of Kentucky: With Notes, Prœlections, and Other Observations on the Public Acts*, by William Littell (Frankfort, KY: William Hunter, 1809), 3:538–39; Hening, *Statutes at Large* 10:134–36; Robertson, *Petitions of the Early Inhabitants*, 256; Boonsfort petition, October 16, 1779.

9. Joan E. Brookes-Smith, comp., *Master Index Virginia Surveys and Grants, 1774–1791* (Frankfort: Kentucky Historical Society, 1976), 19, 176, 208, 213; Kentucky Land Office, *Kentucky Doomsday Book, 1779–1780*, 115, 165; O'Malley, *"Stockading Up,"* 233.

10. Hening, *Statutes at Large*, 9:560–61, 10:135–36.

11. Hening, *Statutes at Large*, 10:135. In 1779 Boonesborough was part of Kentucky County, Virginia, whose county seat was Harrodsburg (also known as Oldtown and Harrodstown). In 1780 Kentucky County was divided into Fayette, Jefferson, and Lincoln Counties. Boonesborough was in Lincoln County, which retained Harrodsburg as the county seat until 1785 when Harrodsburg became part

of Mercer County. Madison County (containing Boonesborough) was formed the same year and its first county seat was Milford; it was moved in 1798 to Richmond. William E. Ellis, H. E. Everman, and Richard D. Sears, *Madison County: 200 Years in Retrospect* (Richmond, KY: Madison County Historical Society, 1985).

12. The Calk family were in possession of several documents related to Boonesborough; family members also preserved William Calk's surveying equipment for many years, which included a compass manufactured by Edward Naime of London, England; a Jacob's staff to which the compass was attached; and a surveyor's Gunter's chain thirty-three feet long (or two poles, half the standard length of sixty-six feet). The two plats he surveyed for the Boonesborough trustees are also among his papers. The family donated the surveying equipment, numerous documents, and other family heirlooms to the Kentucky Historical Society in a series of gifts dating from 2003 to 2007. Lewis H. Kilpatrick, "The Journal of William Calk, Kentucky Pioneer," *Mississippi Historical Review* 7, no. 4 (March 1941): 369.

13. Brookes-Smith, *Master Index Surveys*, 29. Calk's tract was Patent 4988.

14. Robertson, *Petitions of the Early Inhabitants*, 48–52.

15. Harry Enoch, personal email with the author, August 2017.

16. Ellen Eslinger, "Migration and Kinship on the Trans-Appalachian Frontier: Strode's Station, Kentucky," *Filson Club History Quarterly* 62, no. 1 (1988): 52–66; O'Malley, *"Stockading Up,"* 311.

17. Henderson and other settlers who had purchased land under the Transylvania Company's terms were allowed to file their surveys under the new land law. The early date of the surveys conferred elder claim in many cases and thus allowed the claimant to acquire land that would otherwise have been lost. Kentucky Land Office, *Doomsday Book*.

18. Charles W. Bryan Jr., "Richard Callaway, Kentucky Pioneer," *Filson Club History Quarterly* 9 (1935): 35–50; R. Alexander Bate, "Colonel Richard Callaway, 1722–1780," *Filson Club History Quarterly* 29, no. 1 (1955): 3–20; Richard H. Hill, "Callaway Family Data," *Filson Club History Quarterly* 29 (1955): 331–38; John D. Shane, "The Henderson Company Ledger," *Filson Club History Quarterly* 21, no. 1 (1947): 22–48.

19. Ellis, Everman, and Sears, *Madison County*, 14.

20. "An Act to Explain and Amend the Act for Establishing the Town of Boonesborough, in the County of Kentucky," in Littell, *Statute Law of Kentucky*, 3:539–40. Deed to William Calk dated February 4, 1792, Land Grants and Documents Collection, Folder 2, Item 1, Eastern Kentucky University Special Collections, Richmond.

21. The trustees serving in 1792 included Peter Evans, James French, John Wilkerson, Nicholas George, William Bush, and John Holder. The deed indicated that they were appointed by an act of assembly that has not been found in acts passed

in Virginia when Kentucky was still a part of it, nor can it be found in the early acts passed after Kentucky became a state. J. T. Dorris, "A 1792 Offer for the Location of the Capital of Kentucky at Boonesboro," *Register of Kentucky State Historical Society* 31, no. 95 (1933): 174–75; Lowell H. Harrison and James C. Klotter, *A New History of Kentucky* (Lexington: University Press of Kentucky, 1997), 68.

22. Littell, *Statute Law of Kentucky*, 1:221; William Calk Papers, 50M25, University of Kentucky Special Collections, Lexington.

23. "An Act Appointing Trustees for the Town of Boonsborough, and for other purposes," in *Acts Passed at the First Session of the Thirtieth General Assembly for the Commonwealth of Kentucky* (Frankfort: Kendall and Russell, State Printers, 1821), 270–72; Madison County Circuit Court, Case 2856, Kentucky State Library and Archives, Frankfort.

24. Trustees serving in 1809 included John Moore, Daniel Bentley, Edward Bondurant, and P. Thomas Stephens. Richard Collins published a plat of Boonesborough that was based on a plat in the possession of John Stephens. John Stephens and his siblings inherited a small tract containing the ferry at Boonesborough from their father, James, in the 1830s. John acquired by relinquishment or purchase his siblings' undivided interests in the tract. He added to his holdings over the next few decades by buying adjacent parcels as they became available. Born in 1813, Stephens grew up in Boonesborough and was familiar with many of its former landmarks. Collins visited him on April 10, 1873, and was shown the site of the fort, the remnants of which he described as "a few stones which composed the foundations of two chimneys." Richard Collins, *History of Kentucky, Revised* (Covington, KY: Collins & Co., 1874), 515–16.

25. Trustees in 1817 included Green Clay, Daniel Bentley, Edward Bondurant, George Giddings, and Thomas Lindsay.

26. Elkanah Bush, Green Clay, Richard Oldham, Thomas Lindsay, and Jesse Hedges had been appointed trustees in October 1821. Clerk of Court, Madison County Order Book E:164, Richmond, KY. The act passed the following month confirmed only three of these men and appointed four different men for unknown reasons. Trustees named in 1824 included Edmund Baxter, Jesse Barnes, Joseph Bonnell, Elkanah Bush, Green Clay, and Elisha Williams. French Tipton Papers, Z Book, 141, Eastern Kentucky University Special Collections and Archives, Richmond. Trustees in 1825 included Edward Baxter, Joseph Bonnell, Elkanah Bush, Green Clay, Thomas Lindsay, and Elisha Williams. The deeds clearly state that the trustees regained the lots through repossession because Halley failed to pay the purchase price. This statement seemingly contradicts the 1821 act that mentions Halley buying forty-three lots and trying unsuccessfully to pay for them and procure deeds from the trustees. Clerk of Court, Madison County Deed Book R:21–25, 80; Tipton Papers, O Book, 51; Clerk of Court, Madison County Order Book F:280.

27. Ranck, *Boonesborough*, 178–79; Crabb, *And the Battle Began.*

28. Guy Carleton Dorchester, "No. 11—Observations upon the Colony of Kentucky," in *Report on Canadian Archives*, ed. Douglas Brymner, 118–20 (Ottawa, ONT: Brown Chamberlin, 1891); O'Malley, *Searching for Boonesborough.*

29. US Bureau of the Census, Population Census for Boonesborough, Madison County, Kentucky, 1810, www.ancestry.com/interactive/7613/4433398 _00251?backurl=https%3a%2f%2fsearch.ancestry.com%2fsearch%2fdb. aspx%3fdbid%3d7613%26path%3d&ssrc=&backlabel =ReturnBrowsing.

30. Carville Earle and Ronald Hoffman, "Staple Crops and Urban Development in the Eighteenth-Century South," *Perspectives in American History* 10 (1976): 7–78; Charles E. Gage, "Historical Factors Affecting Tobacco Types and Uses and the Evolution of the Auction Market," *Agricultural History* 11, no. 1 (January 1937): 43–57.

31. Hening, *Statutes at Large*, 258, 580; Clerk of Court, Madison County Order Book A:123; Tipton Papers, Z Book, 141; Ellen Eslinger, "Farming on the Kentucky Frontier," *Register of the Kentucky Historical Society* 107, no. 1 (Winter 2009): 3–32; Joe Russell Whitaker, "The Development of the Tobacco Industry in Kentucky: A Geographical Interpretation" (master's thesis, University of Wisconsin, Madison, 1923), 4–6.

32. The first warehouse was built on top of a Late Prehistoric Native American site (Site number 15MA41) attributed to the Fort Ancient culture. Fort Ancient people are considered ancestral to historic tribes such as the Shawnees. Native Americans that besieged Fort Boonesborough in 1778 set up camp just out of rifle range from the fort and probably occupied this site during the siege. O'Malley, *Searching for Boonesborough*, 65, 67. Harry G. Enoch, ed., *Bound for New Orleans! Original Journal of John Halley of His Trips to New Orleans Performed in the Years 1789 & 1791* (Winchester, KY: privately printed, 2005); Clerk of Court, Madison County Order Book B:420, 602; Order Book C:15.

33. Clerk of Court, Madison County Order Book C:457, 462.

34. Clerk of Court, Madison County Deed Book G:350; Order Book D:477.

35. Clerk of Court, Madison County Order Book D:375, E:239, 247; G:152; Madison County Deed Book X:30.

36. Thomas Spottswood Hinde was born in Hanover County, Virginia, in 1787 and moved to Kentucky with his parents, Dr. Thomas Hinde and Mary Todd Hubbard Hinde, in 1797. By 1807 he was employed as a clerk for the Ohio House of Representatives. He may have lived in the Boonesborough area for a short period as a boy or young man. He wrote two letters from Boonesborough that had to have been written during a visit. The map may date to that period. Map of Otter Creek, Thomas Hinde Papers, Draper Mss. 40Y113, WHS.

37. Robertson, *Petitions of the Early Inhabitants*, 53; John Patrick vs. Robert

Clark and John Sydebottom, Samuel M. Wilson Vertical File, University of Kentucky Special Collections 52W98; Clark County Deed Book 34, p. 362, Winchester, KY; Clarke and Sidebottom v. Calloway's [sic] Heirs, in *Decisions of the Court of Appeals of the State of Kentucky from March 1, 1801 to January 18, 1805, Inclusive*, ed. Harvey Myers, 46–48 (Cincinnati: Robert Clarke & Co., 1869.

38. Enoch, *Bound for New Orleans*, 1; O'Malley, *Searching for Boonesborough;* Clerk of Court, Madison County Deed Book U:248.

39. O'Malley, *Searching for Boonesborough*.

40. O'Malley, *Searching for Boonesborough*.

41. Lavinia H. Kubiak, *Madison County Rediscovered: Selected Historic Architecture* (Frankfort and Richmond: Kentucky Heritage Council and Madison County Historical Society, 1988), 49; Archibald Henderson, "The Transylvania Company: A Study in Personnel, 3. The Hart Brothers: Thomas, Nathaniel, and David," *Filson Club History Quarterly* 21, no. 1 (1947): 343; Clerk of Court, Lincoln County Will Book A:4, Stanford, KY; Nathaniel Hart to Lyman C. Draper, Draper Mss. 17CC207, WHS.

42. Clerk of Court, Madison County Deed Book R;24, 1:287, 2:459, 5:382, 26:555, 59:11, 68:555.

43. Clerk of Court, Madison County Deed Book R:21–23.

44. Clerk of Court, Madison County Deed Book X:30; Collins, *History of Kentucky*, 516.

45. In 1817 a major flood hit the Kentucky River and washed away thousands of pounds of tobacco stored in warehouses along its banks. This flood may have affected the warehouse at Boonesborough as well. If it did, the entire bottomland where the town in-lots were located would have been flooded. Whitaker, "Tobacco Industry," 16; Ranck, *Boonesborough*, 133n; Jacob F. Lee, "Whether It Really Be Truth or Fiction: Colonel Reuben T. Durrett, the Filson Club, and Historical Memory in Postbellum Kentucky," *Ohio Valley History* 9, no. 4 (Winter 2009): 27–47.

6. Evidence in the Earth

1. Ranck, *Boonesborough*, iii.

2. Leslie E. Wildesen, "The Study of Impacts on Archaeological Sites," in *Advances in Archaeological Method and Theory*, ed. M. B. Schiffer (New York: Academic Press, 1982), 51.

7. Designing a Fort for Defense and Residence

1. The protruding second story of a bastion allowed enfilading gunfire from within to prevent the enemy from scaling the fort walls. Portholes in the cabin walls on all sides of the fort provided more places for defensive gunfire.

2. Ranck, *Boonesborough*, appendix 1; Kellogg, "A Kentucky Pioneer."

3. Moses Boone, Draper Mss. 19C12, and John Gass, Draper Mss. 24C74, WHS. Moses was nine and John was fourteen at the time of the siege. Ranck, *Boonesborough*, 35; James Hall, *Sketches of History, Life and Manners of the West* (Philadelphia: Harrison Hall, 1835), 283; Sketch Plan of Fort Boonesborough by Bland Ballard, Draper Mss. 8J168, WHS; Interview of Josiah Collins by John Dabney Shane, Draper Mss. 12CC64-78, WHS.

4. Neither Shane nor Draper included their questions in the transcripts of their face-to-face interviews. Draper retained dated lists of some of the questions he asked of John Gass by letter. Gass's replies sometimes offered answers or recorded that he did not know the answer, but he often omitted responding to questions.

5. Danske Dandridge, *George Michael Bedinger: A Kentucky Pioneer* (Charlottesville, VA: Michie Company, Printers, 1909), 38.

6. James Alves to James Hall, Draper Mss. 2CC31, 38, WHS; Hall, *Sketches of History*, frontispiece.

7. Nathaniel Hart Jr. republished Hall's plan in 1843 but indicated north as parallel with the long axis of the fort. George Washington Ranck included Hall's plan in his 1901 history of Boonesborough with one critical change: he replaced the north arrow with a facsimile of Richard Henderson's signature. Knowing the orientation of the fort was critical to interpreting the distribution of cultural features uncovered by excavation. Henderson's plan was the most useful for comparative purposes. Josiah Collins labelled the Kentucky River as flowing east-west closest to the fort rather than its correct northwestwardly course. Bland Ballard drew the river running parallel to the correct wall but reversed the cardinal directions in his labels. Both Moses Boone and John Gass drew an arrow running parallel to the Kentucky River that could have been intended to indicate north, or the flow of the water, or both.

8. Hall, *Sketches of History*, 283; Trabue, "Journal," 37.

9. Josiah Collins, Draper Mss. 12CC74, WHS; Moses Boone, Draper Mss. 19C8-57, WHS.

10. Ballard seems to have been unaware that the "large house jutted over" had been formerly occupied by Richard Henderson. By 1779 Henderson had been absent from Fort Boonesborough for months, only returning briefly in December to file a claim with the land court commissioners. Bland Ballard, Draper Mss. 8J168, WHS; Harry G. Enoch, *Colonel John Holder: Boonesborough Defender and Kentucky Entrepreneur* (Morley, MO: Acclaim Press, 2009), 80–81; List of Boonesborough Lot Owners, William Calk Papers, M. I. King Library, Special Collections, University of Kentucky, Lexington.

11. Bland Ballard, Draper Mss. 8J168, WHS; Interview with Isaiah Boone, Draper Mss. 19C85, WHS.

12. Josiah Collins estimated that the stockade was ten or twelve feet high. Draper Mss. 12CC74, WHS.

13. Crabb, *And the Battle Began*, 35.

14. Ranck, *Boonesborough*, 183.

15. Crabb, *And the Battle Began*, 32.

16. Moses Boone, Draper Mss. 19C8-57, WHS; Crabb, *And the Battle Began*, 31.

17. Crabb, *And the Battle Began*, 39.

18. Ranck, *Boonesborough*, 212.

19. Nathaniel Hart Jr. explicitly told Mann Butler and T. Williams that he and his family lived in the fort from 1779 to 1785, during which time both of his parents died. Chenault reported that Nathaniel Hart Sr. built a small fortified site called White Oak Station in 1779 that was occupied by Hart and his family and several Low Dutch families from Pennsylvania. A survey of the Log Lick Trace by John Crooke in 1811 used the White Oak Station site and spring as a survey point. It was located sixth-tenths of a mile south of the fort on what is now State Highway 388, near a former log house traditionally (but probably erroneously) attributed to Nathaniel Hart Sr. This station was never mentioned by Hart Jr., and he further stated in a deposition that his father claimed only one settlement and preemption on Hart's Fork of Silver Creek. The station may have been where Hart Sr. first settled when he reached Boonesborough in 1775. He helped the Low Dutch families build a station at his old improvement, but he may not have lived there. The inhabitants of the station suffered many casualties from Indian raids, and they abandoned the site in 1782 and built another station in present-day Boyle County on James Harrod's Boiling Spring tract. Letter dated October 10, 1833, from Nathaniel Hart Jr. to Mann Butler, Draper Mss. 2CC25, WHS; Letter dated December 20, 1838, from Nathaniel Hart Jr. to T. Williams, Draper Mss. 2CC26, WHS; William Chenault, "The Early History of Madison County," *Register of Kentucky Historical Society* 30, no. 91 (1932): 133; J. T. Dorris, "Early Kentucky History in Madison County Circuit Court Records and Colonel William Harris Caperton's Account of Estill's Defeat (continued)," *Register of Kentucky Historical Society* 43, no. 145 (1945): 340; O'Malley, *"Stockading Up,"* 128–29.

20. Ranck, *Boonesborough*; Crabb, *And the Battle Began*; Kentucky Land Office, *Kentucky Doomsday Book*, 134.

21. Harry Enoch, personal email to author, 2017.

22. Housing militia for short periods may have taxed the space limits of the fort considerably. St. Asaph's (Logan's Station) had to accommodate nineteen men in a single cabin built for the purpose in 1778. Archival records do not often mention the accommodations provided for militia or what they entailed, but one can infer that all the major stations and forts periodically had to find housing for militiamen. The

tradeoff was the security and protection the militia presence offered. Kim A. McBride and W. Stephen McBride, *Archaeological Investigations at Logan's Fort, Lincoln County, Kentucky*, Research Report no. 3 (Lexington: Kentucky Archaeological Survey, 2000), 12; Ranck, *Boonesborough*, 60; Belue, "Terror in the Canelands."

23. The 1987 excavations identified two large postholes running parallel to the south side of the DAR monument wall. They were not definitively identified as part of the fort, although the evidence was too ambivalent to rule out the possibility. A photograph discovered many years later revealed that the postholes were part of the post foundations of a resort cabin built by David Williams in the early twentieth century.

24. W. Stephen McBride and Kim A. McBride, "Methods in the Archaeology of Colonial Frontier Forts: Examples from Virginia and West Virginia," in *Historical Archaeology of Military Sites: Method and Topic*, eds. Clarence R. Geier, Lawrence E. Babits, Douglas D. Scott, and David G. Orr (College Station: Texas A&M University Press, 2011), 123–33; Nancy O'Malley, "Field Investigations at Daniel Boone's Frontier Station, Fayette County, Kentucky," Paper presented at the Society for Historical Archaeology Annual Conference, Mobile, AL, 2002.

25. Daniel Boone, as narrated to John Filson, *The Adventures of Colonel Daniel Boon*, 13; O'Malley, "Frontier Defenses," 67.

26. William G. Eaton, personal communication with the author, 1987; Rick Allen, personal communication with the author, 2017. The absence of intact stone chimney bases for the hearths marking cabins along the fort walls is intriguing. Generic descriptions of chimneys in the forts and stations usually presume that all had dry-laid stone bases. Joseph Doddridge described his firsthand recollection of the construction as "a few stones [that] formed the backs and jambs of the chimney." Daniel Drake described the chimney in his father's cabin as "carried up with cats & clay to the height of the ridge pole. There cats & clay were pieces of small poles, well imbedded in mortar." A later historian, Alfred Pirtle, affirmed that stone was used to build a chimney if it was near and easy to procure, but in its absence the entire chimney was made by laying sticks of wood on one another with a thick coat of mud to bind them. Mrs. James Caperton and Katherine Phelps, "A Partial List of Those at Fort Boonesborough," *Register of Kentucky Historical Society* 23, no. 68 (1923): 144; Joseph Doddridge, *Notes on the Settlement and Indian Wars of the Western Parts of Virginia and Pennsylvania, from 1763 to 1783, Inclusive* (Pittsburg, PA: John S. Ritenour and William T. Lindsey, 1912); Daniel Drake, *Pioneer Life in Kentucky*, Ohio Valley Historical Series no. 6 (Cincinnati: Robert Clarke & Co., 1870); Alfred Pirtle, "Frontier Defence," *Register of the Kentucky Historical Society* 19, no. 57 (September 1921): 114.

27. Belue, *Life of Boone*, 672.

28. Steven Edholm and Tamara Wilder, "Brief Overview of the Wet-Scrape

Braintanning Process," in *Buckskin: The Ancient Art of Braintanning* (Boonville, CA: Paleotechnics, 2001), 16, http://paleotechnics.com/Articles/PDFs/Briefoverview. PDF.

29. Letter dated March 28, 1885, from Evisa Coshon to Lyman C. Draper, Draper Mss. 21C27, WHS; Interview with John Gass by John Dabney Shane, Draper Mss. 11CC11-15, WHS; Crabb, *And the Battle Began*, 42.

30. Archaeological research of forts and stations is slowly progressing but much waits to be explored. In Kentucky, my publication *"Stockading Up"* remains the most comprehensive work on Kentucky stations. I have also investigated several individual stations, as have other archaeologists. The work at Fort Boonesborough is the most detailed archaeological fieldwork that has been done on a large fort in Kentucky to date. Extensive archival research and limited archaeological investigation have focused on the short-lived Fort Jefferson in far western Kentucky. Many more sites await closer examination. See O'Malley, *"Stockading Up"*; *Frontier Life at Shawnee Springs*; *Searching for Boonesborough*; *Drawing Battle Lines*; *Daniel Boone's Frontier Station*; "Frontier Defenses." See also McBride and McBride, *Archaeological Investigations at Logan's Fort*; K&V Cultural Resource Management, *Constant's Station: Mitigation of Site 15CK461, Winchester, Clark County, Kentucky*, Report prepared for the Winchester-Clark County Industrial Park Authority, 2012; Kenneth C. Carstens, "In Search of Fort Jefferson: Past, Present, and Future Studies," in *Proceedings of the Symposium on Ohio Valley Urban and Historic Archaeology*," vol. 2, ed. Donald B. Ball and Philip J. DiBlasi (Louisville, KY: University of Louisville, 1984), 45–56; Kenneth C. Carstens, "Current Field Strategies and Hypothesis Testing: The Fort Jefferson Project Continues," in *Studies in Kentucky Archaeology*, ed. Charles D. Hockensmith (Frankfort: Kentucky Heritage Council, 1991), 165–75.

8. Packing for the Wilderness

1. Leland Ferguson, *Historical Archaeology and the Importance of Material Things*, Special Publications 2 (Rockdale, MD: Society for Historical Archaeology, 1977), 7.

2. Caperton and Phelps, "A Partial List," 144; Jay D. Edwards and Tom Wells, *Historic Louisiana Nails: Aids to the Dating of Old Buildings* (Baton Rouge: Geoscience Publications, Department of Geography and Anthropology, Louisiana State University, 1993), 2; Nancy O'Malley, "Frontier Life at Shawnee Springs: Archaeology and History of Hugh McGary's Pioneer Station, Mercer County, Kentucky" (unpublished manuscript, December 15, 2017), Microsoft Word file.

3. Edwards and Wells, *Louisiana Nails*.

4. Jacob Perkins invented a nail-making machine that could produce ten thousand nails per day around 1790. Edwards and Wells, *Louisiana Nails*.

5. Elizabeth A. Perkins, *Border Life: Experience and Memory in the Revolutionary Ohio Valley* (Chapel Hill: University of North Carolina Press, 1998), 85–88.

6. Interview with Jacob Stevens, Draper Mss. 12CC135, WHS.

7. Doddridge, *Notes on the Settlement and Indian Wars*, 140.

8. Clerk of Court, Lincoln County Will Book A:13–14, Stanford.

9. Clerk of Court, Lincoln County Will Book A:20–21.

10. "A Colonial Lady's Clothing: A Glossary of Terms," Colonial Williamsburg website, accessed April 30, 2018, www.history.org/history/clothing/women/wglossary.cfm; Linda Baumgarten, "Looking at Eighteenth-Century Clothing," Colonial Williamsburg website, accessed September 11, 2018, www.history.org/history/clothing/intro/clothing.cfm.

11. Kathleen A. Staples and Madelyn Shaw, *Clothing through American History* (Santa Barbara, CA: Greenwood, 2013), 269–80, 344–52.

12. Interview with Mrs. Morrison, Draper Mss. 11CC152, WHS.

13. Alice Morse Earle, *Home Life in Colonial Days* (reprint; Stockbridge, MA: Berkshire Traveller Press, 1974), 168–72.

14. James S. Hopkins, *A History of the Hemp Industry in Kentucky* (Lexington: University Press of Kentucky, 1951), 69, 71.

15. Earle, *Home Life*, 193–202. Although natural sources of Fuller's earth occur in Western Kentucky, supplies probably had to be brought into Central Kentucky in the late eighteenth century. John W. Hosterman and Sam H. Patterson, *Bentonite and Fuller's Earth Resources of the United States*, US Geological Survey Professional Paper 1522 (Washington, DC: Government Printing Office, 1992), 26.

16. Edholm and Wilder, "Wet-Scrape Braintanning Process."

17. Mary Beaudry, *Findings: The Material Culture of Needlework and Sewing* (New Haven, CT: Yale University Press, 2006), 8, 96.

18. Stanley J. Olsen, "Dating Early Plain Buttons by Their Form," *American Antiquity* 28, no. 4 (1963): 551–54; Carolyn L. White, *American Artifacts of Personal Adornment, 1680–1820: A Guide to Identification and Interpretation* (Lanham, MD: Altamira Press, 2005), 57, 64.

19. Olsen, "Dating Early Plain Buttons," 553; White, *Artifacts of Personal Adornment*, 57.

20. Olson, "Dating Early Plain Buttons," 553.

21. Belue, *Life of Boone*, 528, 181; Interview with John Redd, Draper Mss. 10NN101, WHS; Diana DiPaolo Loren, *The Archaeology of Clothing and Bodily Adornment in Colonial America* (Gainesville: University of Florida Press, 2010).

22. Whitaker, "Tobacco Industry"; Leland Smith, "A History of the Tobacco Industry in Kentucky, 1783–1860" (master's thesis, University of Kentucky, Lexington, 1950), 22; L. C. Gray, "The Market Surplus Problem of Colonial

Tobacco," in *Essays on American Colonial History*, 2nd ed., ed. Paul Goodman (New York: Holt, Rinehart and Winston, 1972), 240, 251.

23. Ivor Noel Hume, *A Guide to Artifacts of Colonial America* (New York: Knopf, 1978), 303 (Type 29).

24. P. P. Karan and Cotton Mather, *Atlas of Kentucky* (Lexington: University Press of Kentucky, 1977), 112–13.

25. Ranck, *Boonesborough*, 166, 176.

26. Ted Franklin Belue, *The Long Hunt: Death of the Buffalo East of the Mississippi* (Mechanicsburg, PA: Stackpole Books, 1996), 7–8; Ranck, *Boonesborough*, 166, 176, 205.

27. Belue, *The Long Hunt*, 226, 228.

28. Belue, *Life of Boone*, 350, 151.

29. Doddridge, *Notes on the Settlement and Indian Wars*, 130.

30. Identified mussel shells include species with the fanciful common names of Mucket, Elephant Ear, Pigtoe, Purple Warty Back, Ringpink, Rabbitsfoot, Black Sandshell, and Three Ridge.

31. Lucien Beckner, ed., "Reverend John Dabney Shane's Interview with Pioneer William Clinkenbeard," *Filson Club History Quarterly* 2, no. 3 (April 1928): 98, 113–14.

32. "*Oxalis stricta*," Wikipedia, https://en.wikipedia.org/wiki/Oxalis_stricta, last edited August 8, 2017; "*Portulaca oleracea*," Wikipedia, https://en.wikipedia.org/wiki/Portulaca_oleracea, last edited December 3, 2017; "American bittersweet," Medicinal Plants of the Northeast, accessed November 28, 2018, www.bio.brandeis.edu/fieldbio/medicinal_plants/pages/American_Bittersweet.htm.

33. "*Stellaria media*," Wikipedia, https://en.wikipedia.org/wiki/Stellaria_media, last edited September 30, 2017; "*Eleusine indica*," Wikipedia, https://en.wikipedia.org/wiki/Eleusine_indica, last edited December 2, 2017.

34. Settler Josiah Collins described the fort inhabitants in March 1778 as a "poor, distressed, half-naked, half-starved . . . dirty, lousy [and] ragged people" too afraid to hunt. Draper Mss. 12CC67, 74, WHS.

35. Gilbert Imlay, *A Topographical Description of the Western Territory of North America* (New York: Samuel Campbell, 1793), 147; Keith Egloff, *Colonial Plantation Hoes of Tidewater Virginia*, Research Report No. 1 (Williamsburg: Virginia Research Center of Archaeology, 1980), 26.

36. William L. Brown and Edgar Anderson, "The Northern Flint Corns," *Annals of the Missouri Botanical Garden* 34, no. 1 (1947): 1–20, 22, 29; William L. Brown and Edgar Anderson, "The Southern Dent Corns," *Annals of the Missouri Botanical Garden* 35, no. 3 (1948): 255–86.

37. Ranck, *Boonesborough*, 173, 177, 179; Interview with Mrs. John Arnold

by John Dabney Shane, Draper Mss. 11CC241–245, WHS; Interview with Mrs. Shanklin by John Dabney Shane, Draper Mss. 11CC217–224, WHS; Interview with John Gass, Draper Mss. 24C73, WHS; Lucien Beckner, "Rev. John Dabney Shane's Interview with Mrs. Sarah Graham of Bath County," *Filson Club History Quarterly* 9 (1935): 227; Kellogg, "A Kentucky Pioneer," 230.

38. G. A. Bowling, "The Introduction of Cattle into Colonial North America," Scientific Paper 277, *Journal of Dairy Science* 25, no. 2 (1942): 125–54.

39. E. Giuffra et al., "The Origin of the Domestic Pig, Independent Domestication and Subsequent Introgression," *Genetics* 154, no. 4 (2000), www.history.org/foundation/journal/winter10/pigs.cfm.

40. Belue, *Life of Boone*, 389–90.

41. Ann Smart Martin, "The Role of Pewter as Missing Artifact: Consumer Attitudes toward Tableware in Late Eighteenth-Century Virginia," *Historical Archaeology* 23, no. 2 (1989): 1–27.

42. Fred Lucas, personal communication with the author, 2012.

43. Beckner, "Clinkenbeard Interview"; George C. Neumann and Frank J. Kravic, *Collector's Illustrated Encyclopedia of the American Revolution* (Texarkana, TX: Rebel Publishing, 1989); Crabb, *And the Battle Began*, 38.

44. Perkins, *Border Life*, 103; Inventory and Appraisal of John Floyd's Estate, Jefferson County, Virginia Court Commissioners, June 7, 1783, Reuben T. Durrett Collection, Perkins Special Collections Research Center, University of Chicago; Inventory of Sarah Hart, Clerk of Court, Lincoln County Will Book A:134–38.

45. Olive R. Jones, "Cylindrical English Wine and Beer Bottles, 1735–1850," in *Studies in Archaeology, Architecture, and History* (Ottawa, ONT: National Historic Parks and Sites Branch, Environment Canada, 1986).

46. Pam Dunning, "Composite Table Cutlery from 1700 to 1930," in *Studies in Material Culture Research*, ed. Karlis Karklins, 32–45 (California, PA: Society for Historical Archaeology, 2000).

47. Kelly Ladd, Associate Curator of Archaeological Collections, Colonial Williamsburg Foundation, personal communication with the author, August 30, 2017. Ms. Ladd confirmed that the saddle frame, staples, and tack ornament were very typical of equine equipment of the late eighteenth century.

48. John Witthoft, "A History of Gunflints," *Pennsylvania Archaeologist* 36, nos. 1, 2 (1966): 12–49.

49. Belue, *Life of Boone*, 347; Daniel M. Sivilich, *Musket Ball and Small Shot Identification: A Guide* (Norman: University of Oklahoma Press, 2016), 104–6.

50. Sivilich, *Musket Ball*, 10–11.

51. Inventory and Appraisal of John Floyd's Estate, Reuben T. Durrett Collection, Perkins Special Collections Research Center, University of Chicago.

9. Fort Boonesborough as a Commemorative Site

1. "The Boonesborough Celebration," *Lexington Observer and Reporter,* Wednesday, May 27, 1840; D. G. Beers & Co., compiler, *Map of Madison Co. Kentucky from New and Actual Surveys* (Philadelphia: J. H. Toudy & Co., 1876); O'Malley, *Searching for Boonesborough,* 33.

2. Willard Rouse Jillson, "The Transylvania Memorial," *Register of the Kentucky Historical Society* 33, no. 105 (October 1935): 368–70; Susan Starling Towles, "The Founding of Boonesborough by the Transylvania Company," *Kentucky Progress Magazine* 6, no. 4 (1934): 181–83; Julia Alves Clore, "The Personnel of the Transylvania Company," *Kentucky Progress Magazine* 6, no. 8 (1935): 366–67, 400; "Kentucky's Historical Trees: No. 5—The Tall Sycamores at Boonesboro," *Kentucky Progress Magazine* 3, no. 6 (1931): 28–29, 49; Archibald Henderson, "Richard Henderson, President of the Transylvania Company," *Kentucky Progress Magazine* 6, no. 7 (1935): 357–59; J. T. Dorris, "The Transylvania Colony," *Kentucky Progress Magazine* 6, no. 4 (1934): 187.

3. C. C. Ousley, *Kentucky at the Jamestown Ter-Centennial Exposition April 26 to November 30, 1907: A Report from the Kentucky Jamestown Exposition Commission,* Kentucky Digital Library, accessed December 12, 2017, http://kdl.kyvl.org/?commit=search&f%5Bpub_date%5D%5B%5D=1907&q=C.C.+Ousley&search_field=all_fields.

4. The beach at Boonesborough was created in 1905 during the construction of Lock 10. The Kentucky River had frozen upstream, producing a thick ice layer that encased thirty thousand saw logs and clogged the channel from Beattyville to Irvine. A March thaw sent the logjam downstream to crash against Locks 9 and 10 and scour a new channel around them. At Lock 10, the scouring took place on the Madison County (Boonesborough) side, eroding bank sediments to a width of 240 feet and a depth of 40 feet and exposing a buried sandbar that became known as Boonesborough Beach. Erosion slowed further downstream but still washed away 80 feet of the terrace edge immediately east of the fort site. Leland Johnson and Charles E. Parrish, *Engineering the Kentucky River: The Commonwealth's Waterway* (Louisville, KY: US Army Corps of Engineers, Louisville Engineering District, 1999), 125; F. Kevin Simon and Federal Writers' Project of the Works Progress Administration for the State of Kentucky, eds., *The WPA Guide to Kentucky* (reprint; Lexington: University Press of Kentucky, 1996), 423.

5. "Boone Bicentennial," *Register of Kentucky State Historical Society* 33, no. 102 (January 1935): 64–69.

6. In 1991, Robert Channing Strader willed the site of Daniel Boone's Station to the state of Kentucky for use as a state park. Archaeological excavations in 1999 confirmed significant remains of the site. In 2018, the state, narrowly interpreting

a clause in the will, transferred Boone's Station to the David's Fork Baptist Church without public comment or input. Bryan's Station is still privately owned. Nancy O'Malley and Karen Hudson, *Cultural Resource Assessment of Boone Station State Park, Fayette County, Kentucky* (Lexington: Department of Anthropology, University of Kentucky, 1993); Charles Hay, comp., "History of the Pioneer National Monument Association and the Fort Boonesborough State Park Association" (Richmond, KY: typescript prepared by author, n.d.); Clerk of Court, Madison County Deed Book 202, p. 225, Richmond.

10. The Frontier Experience in Retrospect

1. Filson quote in Perkins, *Border Life*, 82; Frederick Jackson Turner, "The Significance of the Frontier in American History," in *The Annual Report of the American Historical Association* (Washington, DC: American Historical Association, 1894), 197–227; Perkins, *Border Life*, 85.

2. Belue, *Life of Boone*, 351, 520–21. Social discord among strangers was common in settlements like Lexington as well. Jane Stevenson moved her family from the greater safety of Lexington to a more remote, less secure station because she did not want to rear her children among "that sort of people." Mrs. Morrison, likewise, was concerned when she saw a "rough old Dutchwoman" among the strangers arriving. Perkins, *Border Life*, 198, 86. One way settlers mitigated potential social conflicts was to emigrate to Kentucky with family and friends and settle in the same place. Many of the smaller stations were enclaves of people related by blood or association. O'Malley, *"Stockading Up"*; Eslinger, "Migration and Kinship," 52–66.

3. Richard W. Stewart, ed., *American Military History*, vol. 1, *The United States Army and the Forming of a Nation, 1775–1917* (Washington, DC: Center of Military History, 2005).

4. Hammon and Taylor, *Virginia's Western War*; George M. Waller, "George Rogers Clark and the American Revolution in the West," *Indiana Magazine of History* 72, no. 1 (March 1976): 1–20.

5. Settlements included Fort Boonesborough, Fort Harrod, Logan's Station (St. Asaph's), McClelland's Station, Leestown, Boiling Springs (Harrod's Station), Hinkston's Station, and Bryan's Station. Leestown, Boiling Springs, Bryan's, Hinkston's, and McClelland's Stations were all abandoned after Indian attacks in the summer of 1776 and remained unoccupied through 1777, the year of the "terrible 7s." John Floyd to William Preston, July 21, 1776, Draper Mss. 33S300-305 and 4C20, WHS.

6. Kim Arbogast McBride and W. Stephen McBride, "Archaeological Investigation of Fort Arbuckle," *Journal of the Greenbrier Historical Society* 6, no. 6 (1998): 16–22; W. Stephen McBride and Kim Arbogast McBride, "Archaeological

Investigations of Fort Donnelly," *Journal of the Greenbrier Historical Society* 8, no. 2 (2006): 21–36.

7. Forts and stations were also sited to take advantage of nearby freshwater springs and arable land for cultivating crops. Occasionally, access to springs was protected by covered walkways, as at Fort Harrod. Most forts and stations could not employ that option, and visiting the springs for water was sometimes dangerous. Likewise, a guard was often posted to protect people working in the fields. McBride and McBride, "Logan's Fort"; O'Malley, *"Stockading Up."*

8. Neal O. Hammon, ed., *My Father, Daniel Boone: The Draper Interviews with Nathan Boone* (Lexington: University Press of Kentucky, 1999); Harry G. Enoch and Anne Crabb, *Women at Fort Boonesborough, 1775–1784* (Richmond, KY: Fort Boonesborough Foundation, 2014).

9. O'Malley, *"Stockading Up,"* 178–87; Kevin E. Smith, "Bledsoe Station: Archaeology, History, and the Interpretation of the Middle Tennessee Frontier, 1770–1820," *Tennessee Historical Quarterly* 59, no. 3 (Fall 2000): 174–87.

10. Local builders salvaging foundation stones for other uses after the fort was abandoned may account for their absence, but if so, the salvaging was thorough except for the foundation wall in the center cabin complex.

11. David Gass's son, John Gass, claimed that his family lived in the center cabin complex. Squire Boone's son, Moses, claimed that Richard Callaway and his family lived there. Bland Ballard placed the Gass family in the cabin next to the southeast corner bastion on the east wall. John Gass, 24C74, WHS; Moses Boone, 19C12, WHS; Bland Ballard, 8J167-168, WHS.

12. Stockade may have been erected by building a framework of log pickets split lengthwise and set vertically in the ground at intervals; horizontal members were pinned near the top and at ground level, to which were pinned pickets that did not extend below ground. The archaeological signature of a stockade built in this way would be limited to the post molds (filled postholes) of the upright pickets that were set in the ground.

13. See Ellen Eslinger, *Citizens of Zion: The Social Origins of Camp Meeting Revivalism* (Knoxville: University of Tennessee Press, 1999), introduction and chapter 1, for an insightful discussion of the process of western expansion in Kentucky, its extraordinarily violent beginnings, and its rapid postwar development.

14. A detailed description of the perils and dangers of the Cumberland Gap route into Kentucky is found in Ellen Eslinger, *Running Mad for Kentucky: Frontier Travel Accounts* (Lexington: University Press of Kentucky, 2004), 1–66.

15. John D. Shane, "Henderson Company Ledger," 22–48; Hart's Ledger, &c., Draper Mss. 17CC189-213, WHS; Ellen Eslinger, "'Elated by Success and Enriched with Spoils': Wartime Plunder on the Ohio Valley Frontier," Paper presented at the Organization of American Historians annual meeting, April 19, 2012.

16. Alan Kulikoff, "The Transition to Capitalism in Rural America," *William and Mary Quarterly* 46, no. 1 (January 1989): 120–44; Christopher Clark, Daniel Vickers, Stephen Aron, Nancy Grey Osterud, and Michael Merrill, "The Transition to Capitalism in America: A Panel Discussion," *History Teacher* 27, no. 3 (May 1994): 263–88.

17. Clerk of Court, Lincoln County Will Book A:134–38, Stanford; George L. Miller and Robert Hunter, "How Creamware Got the Blues: The Origins of China Glaze and Pearlware," in *Ceramics in America*, ed. Robert Hunter (Milwaukee, WI: Chipstone Foundation, 2001), 135–61. Similar types of artifacts excavated at the stations of Daniel Boone, Hugh McGary, and John Grant signify consumer behavior that relied on exported goods such as cooking, processing, and serving vessels and utensils, metal buttons and sewing tools, jewelry, and the like, as well as goods produced within the colonies like utilitarian crockery.

18. Elizabeth A. Perkins, "The Consumer Frontier: Household Consumption in Early Kentucky," *Journal of American History* 78, no. 2 (September 1991): 486–510.

19. A "piece of eight" was recovered from Hugh McGary's Station in present-day Mercer County. This is a fragment of a Spanish dollar that was cut into eight pieces, each worth one *real* or about 12.5 cents. This station was contemporaneous with Fort Boonesborough, having been occupied from 1779 to 1788. Spanish dollars were very common coin currency in the British American colonies and the United States until the Coinage Act of 1857 abolished their use. O'Malley, "Frontier Life at Shawnee Springs"; "Spanish Dollar," Wikipedia, accessed December 4, 2017, https://en.wikipedia.org/wiki/Spanish_dollar; Perkins, *Consumer Frontier*, 503.

20. Perkins, *Consumer Frontier*, 487; Carole Shammas, "How Self-Sufficient was Early America?" *Journal of Interdisciplinary History* 13, no. 2 (Autumn 1982): 247–72; Allan Kulikoff, "Households and Markets: Toward a New Synthesis of American Agrarian History," *William and Mary Quarterly* 50, no. 2 (April 1993): 342–55; Ann Smart Martin, "Makers, Buyers, and Users: Consumerism as a Material Culture Framework," *Winterthur Portfolio* 28, nos. 2, 3 (Summer–Autumn 1993): 141–57.

21. Samuel M. Wilson, *The First Land Court of Kentucky, 1779–1780* (Lexington: Privately printed, 1923).

22. William H. Bergmann, "A 'Commercial View of this Unfortunate War': Economic Roots of an American National State in the Ohio Valley, 1775–1795," *Early American Studies* 6, no. 1 (Spring 2008): 137–64; James P. Cousins, "The 'Free and Easy' Generation of Kentucky and the War of 1812," *Register of the Kentucky Historical Society* 111, no. 2 (Spring 2013): 133–39.

23. Barry Schwartz, "The Social Context of Commemoration: A Study in Collective Memory," *Social Forces* 61, no. 2 (December 1982): 374–402.

BIBLIOGRAPHY

Acts Passed at the First Session of the Thirtieth General Assembly for the Commonwealth of Kentucky. Frankfort: Kendall and Russell, State Printers, 1821.

Aron, Stephen. *How the West Was Lost: The Transformation of Kentucky from Daniel Boone to Henry Clay.* Baltimore: Johns Hopkins University Press, 1996.

Barnhart, John D. "Lieutenant Governor Henry Hamilton's Apologia." *Indiana Magazine of History* 52, no. 4 (1956): 383–96.

Bate, R. Alexander. "Colonel Richard Callaway, 1722–1780." *Filson Club History Quarterly* 29, no. 1 (1955): 3–20.

Baumgarten, Linda. "Looking at Eighteenth-Century Clothing." Colonial Williamsburg website. Accessed September 11, 2018. www.history.org/history/clothing/intro/clothing.cfm.

Beaudry, Mary C. *Findings: The Material Culture of Needlework and Sewing.* New Haven: Yale University Press, 2006.

Beckner, Lucien. "Reverend John Dabney Shane's Interview with Pioneer William Clinkenbeard." *Filson Club History Quarterly* 2, no. 3 (April 1928): 95–128.

———. "Rev. John Dabney Shane's Interview with Mrs. Sarah Graham of Bath County." *Filson Club History Quarterly* 9 (1935): 222–41.

Beers, D. G., and Co. *Map of Madison Co. Kentucky from New and Actual Surveys.* Philadelphia: J. H. Toudy & Co., 1876.

Belue, Ted Franklin. *The Life of Daniel Boone by Lyman C. Draper.* Mechanicsburg, PA: Stackpole Books, 1998.

———. *The Long Hunt: Death of the Buffalo East of the Mississippi.* Mechanicsburg, PA: Stackpole Books, 1996.

———. "Terror in the Canelands: The Fate of Daniel Boone's Salt Boilers." *Filson Club History Quarterly* 68, no. 1 (1994): 3–34.

Bergmann, William H. "A 'Commercial View of this Unfortunate War': Economic Roots of an American National State in the Ohio Valley, 1775–1795." *Early American Studies* 6, no. 1 (Spring 2008): 137–64.

Boone, Daniel. *The Adventures of Colonel Daniel Boon, Formerly a Hunter.* Edited by John Filson. Reprint, edited and expanded by Alvin Salisbury. Xenia, OH: Old Chelicothe Press, 1967.

"Boone Bicentennial." *Register of the Kentucky Historical Society* 33, no. 105 (1935): 64–69.

Bowling, G. A. "The Introduction of Cattle into Colonial North America." Scientific Paper 277. *Journal of Dairy Science* 25, no. 2 (1942): 125–54.

Boyd, Julian P. "The Sheriff in Colonial North Carolina." In *Essays on American Colonial History*, edited by Paul Goodman, 312–29. New York: Holt, Rinehart and Winston, 1972.

Brookes-Smith, Joan, comp. *Master Index Virginia Surveys and Grants, 1774–1791.* Frankfort: Kentucky Historical Society, 1976.

Brown, William L., and Edgar Anderson. "The Northern Flint Corns." *Annals of the Missouri Botanical Garden* 34, no. 1 (1947): 1–20, 22, 29.

———. "The Southern Dent Corns." *Annals of the Missouri Botanical Garden* 35, no. 3 (1948): 255–86.

Bryan, Charles W., Jr. "Richard Callaway, Kentucky Pioneer." *Filson Club History Quarterly* 9, no. 1 (1955): 35–50.

Calk, William, Papers. Photostat copies, Special Collections, M. I. King Library, University of Kentucky, Lexington.

Calloway, Colin G. "'We Have Always Been the Frontier': The American Revolution in Shawnee Country." *American Indian Quarterly* 16, no. 1 (1992): 39–52.

Campbell, Julian J. N. *The Land of Cane and Clover: Presettlement Vegetation in the So-Called Bluegrass Region of Kentucky.* Lexington: Herbarium, University of Kentucky, 1985.

Caperton, Mrs. James, and Katherine Phelps. "A Partial List of Those at Fort Boonesborough." *Register of Kentucky State Historical Society* 23, no. 68 (1925): 142–61.

Carstens, Kenneth C. "Current Field Strategies and Hypothesis Testing: The Fort Jefferson Project Continues." In *Studies in Kentucky Archaeology*, edited by Charles D. Hockensmith, 165–75. Frankfort: Kentucky Heritage Council, 1991.

———. "In Search of Fort Jefferson: Past, Present, and Future Studies." In *Proceedings of the Symposium on Ohio Valley Urban and Historic Archaeology*, vol. 2, edited by Donald B. Ball and Philip J. DiBlasi, 45–56. Louisville, KY: University of Louisville, 1984.

Chenault, William. "The Early History of Madison County." *Register of the Kentucky Historical Society* 91, no. 133 (April 1932): 119–61.

Clark, Christopher, Daniel Vickers, Stephen Aron, Nancy Grey Osterud, and Michael Merrill. "The Transition to Capitalism in America: A Panel Discussion." *History Teacher* 27, no. 3 (May 1994): 263–88.

Bibliography

Clore, Julia Alves. "The Personnel of the Transylvania Company." *Kentucky Progress Magazine* 6, no. 8 (1935): 366–67, 400.

Collins, Richard. *History of Kentucky, Revised.* Covington, KY: Collins & Co., 1874.

Cousins, James P. "The 'Free and Easy' Generation of Kentucky and the War of 1812." *Register of the Kentucky Historical Society* 111, no. 2 (Spring 2013): 133–39.

Crabb, Anne. *And the Battle Began Like Claps of Thunder: The Siege of Boonesboro—1778—As Told by the Pioneers.* Richmond, KY: privately printed by the author, 1998.

Dandridge, Danske. *George Michael Bedinger: A Kentucky Pioneer.* Charlottesville, VA: Michie Company Printers, 1909.

David, James Corbett. *Dunmore's New World: The Extraordinary Life of a Royal Governor in Revolutionary America—with Jacobites, Counterfeiters, Land Schemes, Shipwrecks, Scalping, Indian Politics, Runaway Slaves, and Two Illegal Royal Weddings.* Charlottesville: University of Virginia Press, 2013.

Doddridge, Joseph. *Notes on the Settlement and Indian Wars of the Western Parts of Virginia and Pennsylvania, from 1763 to 1783, Inclusive.* Albany, NY: Joel Munsell, 1876.

———. *Notes on the Settlement and Indian Wars of the Western Parts of Virginia and Pennsylvania, from 1763 to 1783, Inclusive, Together with a View of the State of Society and Manners of the First Settlers of the Western Country.* Pittsburgh: John S. Ritenour and William T. Lindsey, 1912.

Dorchester, Guy Carleton. "No. 11—Observations upon the Colony of Kentucky." In *Report on Canadian Archives*, edited by Douglas Brymner, 118–20. Ottawa, ONT: Brown Chamberlin, 1891.

Dorris, J. T. "Early Kentucky History in Madison Circuit Court Records and Colonel William Caperton's Account of Estill's Defeat (continued)." *Register of the Kentucky Historical Society* 43, no. 145 (October 1945): 321–41.

———. "A 1792 Offer for the Location of the Capital of Kentucky at Boonesboro." *Register of Kentucky State Historical Society* 31, no. 95 (1933): 174–75.

———. "The Transylvania Colony." *Kentucky Progress Magazine* 6, no. 4 (1934): 186–87.

Drake, Daniel. *Pioneer Life in Kentucky.* Ohio Valley Historical Series no. 6. Cincinnati: Robert Clarke & Co., 1870.

Draper, Lyman Copeland. Manuscripts. Wisconsin Historical Society, Madison.

Dunning, Pam. "Composite Table Cutlery from 1700 to 1930." In *Studies in Material Culture Research*, edited by Karlis Karklins, 32–45. California, PA: Society for Historical Archaeology, 2000.

Durrett, Reuben T., Collection. Perkins Special Collections Research Center, University of Chicago.

Bibliography

Earle, Alice Morse. *Home Life in Colonial Days*. Reprint; Stockbridge, MA: Berkshire Traveller Press, 1974.

Earle, Carville, and Ronald Hoffman. "Staple Crops and Urban Development in the Eighteenth-Century South." *Perspectives in American History* 10 (1976): 7–78.

Edholm, Steven, and Tamara Wilder. "Brief Overview of the Wet-Scrape Braintanning Process." In *Buckskin: The Ancient Art of Braintanning*. Boonville, CA: Paleotechnics, 2001. http://paleotechnics.com/Articles/PDFs/Briefoverview. PDF.

Edwards, Jay D., and Tom Wells. *Historic Louisiana Nails: Aids to the Dating of Old Buildings*. Baton Rouge: Geoscience Publications, Department of Geography and Anthropology, Louisiana State University, 1993.

Egloff, Keith. *Colonial Plantation Hoes of Tidewater Virginia*. Research Report No. 1. Williamsburg: Virginia Research Center for Archaeology, 1980.

Ellis, William E., H. E. Everman, and Richard D. Sears. *Madison County: 200 Years in Retrospect*. Richmond, KY: Madison County Historical Society, 1985.

Enoch, Harry G., ed. *Bound for New Orleans! Original Journal of John Halley of His Trips to New Orleans Performed in the Years 1789 & 1791*. Winchester, KY: privately printed, 2005.

———. *Colonel John Holder: Boonesborough Defender and Kentucky Entrepreneur*. Morley, MO: Acclaim Press, 2009.

Enoch, Harry G., and Anne Crabb. *Women at Fort Boonesborough, 1775–1784*. Richmond, KY: Fort Boonesborough Foundation, 2014.

Eslinger, Ellen. *Citizens of Zion: The Social Origins of Camp Meeting Revivalism*. Knoxville: University of Tennessee Press, 1999.

———. "'Elated by Success and Enriched with Spoils': Wartime Plunder on the Ohio Valley Frontier." Paper presented at the Organization of American Historians annual meeting, April 19, 2012.

———. "Farming on the Kentucky Frontier." *Register of the Kentucky Historical Society* 107, no. 1 (Winter 2009): 3–32.

———. "Migration and Kinship on the Trans-Appalachian Frontier: Strode's Station, Kentucky." *Filson Club History Quarterly* 62, no. 1 (January 1988): 52–66.

———. *Running Mad for Kentucky: Frontier Travel Accounts*. Lexington: University Press of Kentucky, 2004.

Faragher, John Mack. *Daniel Boone: The Life and Legend of an American Pioneer*. New York: Holt, 1992.

Ferguson, Leland. *Historical Archaeology and the Importance of Material Things*. Special Publications 2. Rockville, MD: Society for Historical Archaeology, 1977.

Filson, John. "The Adventures of Daniel Boon." In *The Discovery, Settlement and Present State of Kentucke and an Essay Towards the Topography, and Natural*

Bibliography

History of that Important Country. Wilmington, DE: James Adams, 1784, appendix 1.

Friend, Craig Thompson. *Kentucke's Frontiers.* Bloomington: Indiana University Press, 2010.

Furstenberg, Francois. "The Significance of the Trans-Appalachian Frontier in Atlantic History." *American Historical Review* 113, no. 3 (2008): 647–77.

Gage, Charles E. "Historical Factors Affecting Tobacco Types and Uses and the Evolution of the Auction Market." *Agricultural History* 11, no. 1 (January 1937): 43–57.

General Assembly of Kentucky. "An Act Relating to Establishment of Boonesboro State Park." House Bill No. 156, Frankfort, 1956.

Giuffra, E., J. M. H. Kijas, V. Amarger, O. Carlborg, J. T. Jeon, and L. Andersson. "The Origin of the Domestic Pig, Independent Domestication and Subsequent Introgression." *Genetics* 154, no. 4 (2000). www.genetics.org/content/154/4/1785.

Gray, L. C. "The Market Surplus Problem of Colonial Tobacco." In *Essays on American Colonial History,* 2nd ed., edited by Paul Goodman, 240–59. New York: Holt, Rinehart and Winston, 1972.

Hall, James. *Sketches of History, Life and Manners of the West.* Vol. 1. Philadelphia: Harrison Hall, 1835.

Hammon, Neal O. *John Floyd: The Life and Letters of a Frontier Surveyor.* Louisville, KY: Butler Books, 2013.

———. "Land Tenure in Virginia and Kentucky." Shelbyville, KY: unpublished manuscript, n.d.

———, ed. *My Father, Daniel Boone: The Draper Interviews with Nathan Boone.* Lexington: University Press of Kentucky, 1999.

Hammon, Neal O., and Richard Taylor. *Virginia's Western War, 1775–1786.* Mechanicsburg, PA: Stackpole Books, 2002.

Harrison, Lowell H., and James C. Klotter. *A New History of Kentucky.* Lexington: University Press of Kentucky, 1997.

Hay, Charles, comp. "History of the Pioneer National Monument Association and the Fort Boonesborough State Park Association." Typescript prepared by author. Richmond, KY: n.p., n.d.

Henderson, Archibald. "The Creative Forces in Westward Expansion: Henderson and Boone." *American Historical Review* 20, no. 1 (1914): 86–107.

———. "Richard Henderson and the Occupation of Kentucky, 1775." *Mississippi Valley Historical Review* 1, no. 3 (1914): 341–63.

———. "Richard Henderson, President of the Transylvania Company." *Kentucky Progress Magazine* 6, no. 7 (1935): 356–59.

———. "The Transylvania Company: A Study in Personnel: James Hogg." *Filson Club History Quarterly* 21, no. 1 (1947): 3–21.

Bibliography

———. "The Transylvania Company: A Study in Personnel. 3. The Hart Brothers: Thomas, Nathaniel, and David." *Filson Club History Quarterly* 21, no. 1 (1947): 327–49.

Henderson, A. Gwynn. "Dispelling the Myth: Seventeenth- and Eighteenth-Century Indian Life in Kentucky." *Register of the Kentucky Historical Society* 90, no. 1 (1992): 1–25.

Hening, William Waller. *The Statutes at Large, Being a Collection of All the Laws of Virginia, from the First Session of the Legislature in the Year 1619.* Vols. 9 and 10. Richmond, VA: George Cochran, Printer, 1822.

Hill, Richard H. "Callaway Family Data." *Filson Club History Quarterly* 29 (1955): 331–38.

Hinderaker, Eric. *Elusive Empires: Constructing Colonialism in the Ohio Valley, 1673–1800.* Cambridge: Cambridge University Press, 1997.

Hopkins, James F. *History of the Hemp Industry in Kentucky.* Lexington: University Press of Kentucky, 1980.

Hosterman, John W., and Sam H. Patterson. *Bentonite and Fuller's Earth Resources of the United States.* US Geological Survey Professional Paper 1522. Washington, DC: Government Printing Office, 1992.

Hughes, Sarah S. *Surveyors and Statesmen: Land Measuring in Colonial Virginia.* Richmond: Virginia Surveyors Foundation and Virginia Association of Surveyors, 1979.

Imlay, Gilbert. *A Topographical Description of the Western Territory of North America.* New York: Samuel Campbell, 1793.

Inman, Natalie. "'A Dark and Bloody Ground': American Indian Responses to Expansion during the American Revolution." *Tennessee Historical Quarterly* 70, no. 4 (2011): 258–75.

Jillson, Willard Rouse. "The Transylvania Memorial." *Register of the Kentucky State Historical Society* 33, no. 105 (1935): 368–70.

Johnson, Leland, and Charles E. Parrish. *Engineering the Kentucky River: The Commonwealth's Waterway.* Louisville, KY: US Army Corps of Engineers, Louisville Engineer District, 1999.

Jones, Olive R. "Cylindrical English Wine and Beer Bottles, 1735–1850." In *Studies in Archaeology, Architecture, and History.* Ottawa, ONT: National Historic Parks and Sites Branch, Environment Canada, 1986.

K&V Cultural Resource Management. *Constant's Station: Mitigation of Site 15CK461, Winchester, Clark County, Kentucky.* Report prepared for the Winchester-Clark County Industrial Park Authority, 2012.

Karan, P. P., and Cotton Mather. *Atlas of Kentucky.* Lexington: University Press of Kentucky, 1977.

Kars, Marjoleine. *Breaking Loose Together: The Regulator Rebellion in Pre-*

Bibliography

Revolutionary North Carolina. Chapel Hill: University of North Carolina Press, 2002.

Kellogg, Louise Phelps. "A Kentucky Pioneer Tells Her Story of Early Boonesborough and Harrodsburg." *History Quarterly of the Filson Club* 3 (1928): 223–37.

Kentucky Land Office. *Kentucky Doomsday Book, 1779–1780*. Accessed September 2018. www.sos.ky.gov/admin/land/non-military/settlements_preemptions/Pages/Kentucky-Doomsday-Book.aspx.

"Kentucky's Historical Trees: No. 5—The Tall Sycamores at Boonesboro." *Kentucky Progress Magazine* 3, no. 6 (1931): 28–29.

Kilpatrick, Lewis H. "The Journal of William Calk, Kentucky Pioneer." *Mississippi Valley Historical Review* 7, no. 4 (March 1941): 363–77.

Kubiak, Lavinia H. *Madison County Rediscovered: Selected Historic Architecture*. Frankfort and Richmond: Kentucky Heritage Council and Madison County Historical Society, 1988.

Kulikoff, Alan. "Households and Markets: Toward a New Synthesis of American Agrarian History." *William and Mary Quarterly* 50, no. 2 (April 1993): 342–55.

———. "The Transition to Capitalism in Rural America." *William and Mary Quarterly* 46, no. 1 (January 1989): 120–44.

Kurz, Jim. "Looking for Daniel Boone's Fort." Unpublished manuscript, 1990.

Land Grants and Documents Collection. Special Collections and Archives, Eastern Kentucky University, Richmond.

Lee, Jacob F. "Whether It Really Be Truth or Fiction: Colonel Reuben T. Durrett, the Filson Club, and Historical Memory in Postbellum Kentucky." *Ohio Valley History* 9, no. 4 (Winter 2009): 27–47.

Legislative Petition from Inhabitants of Boonsfort, October 16, 1779. Accession no. 36121, Box 366, Folder 1, Virginia State Archives, Richmond.

Littell, William. *The Statute Law of Kentucky: With Notes, Prælections, and Other Observations on the Public Acts*. 4 vols. Frankfort, KY: William Hunter, 1809–14.

Loren, Diana DiPaolo. *The Archaeology of Clothing and Bodily Adornment in Colonial America*. Gainesville: University Press of Florida, 2010.

Macintire, William J. *The Pioneer Log House in Kentucky*. Frankfort: Kentucky Heritage Council, 1998.

Martin, Ann Smart. "Makers, Buyers, and Users: Consumerism as a Material Culture Framework." *Winterthur Portfolio* 28, nos. 2, 3 (Summer–Autumn 1993): 141–57.

———. "The Role of Pewter as Missing Artifact: Consumer Attitudes toward Tableware in Late Eighteenth-Century Virginia." *Historical Archaeology* 23, no. 2 (1989): 1–27.

McBride, Kimberly A., and W. Stephen McBride. "Archaeological Investigation of

Bibliography

Fort Arbuckle." *Journal of the Greenbrier Historical Society* 6, no. 6 (1998): 15–45.

———. "Archaeological Investigations at Fort Donnelly." *Journal of the Greenbrier Historical Society* 8, no. 2 (2006): 21–36.

———. *Archaeological Investigations at Logan's Fort, Lincoln County, Kentucky.* Research Report no. 3. Lexington: Kentucky Archaeological Survey, 2000.

McBride, W. Stephen, and Kimberly A. McBride. "Methods in the Archaeology of Colonial Frontier Forts: Examples from Virginia and West Virginia." In *Historical Archaeology of Military Sites: Method and Topic,* edited by Clarence R. Geier, Lawrence E. Babits, Douglas D. Scott, and David G. Orr, 123–33. College Station: Texas A&M University Press, 2011.

McKeehan, Wallace L. "Archives: The Regulators and the Battle of Alamance." Sons of Dewitt Colony Texas, 2003. Accessed September 2018. www.tamu.edu/faculty/ccbn/dewitt/mckstmerreg1.htm.

Miller, George L., and Robert Hunter. "How Creamware Got the Blues: The Origins of China Glaze and Pearlware." In *Ceramics in America,* edited by Robert Hunter, 135–61. Milwaukee, WI, and Hanover, NH: Chipstone Foundation and University Press of New England, 2001.

Myers, Harvey, ed. *Decisions of the Court of Appeals of the State of Kentucky from March 1, 1801, to January 18, 1805, Inclusive.* Cincinnati: Robert Clarke & Co., 1869.

Neumann, George C., and Frank J. Kravic. *Collector's Illustrated Encyclopedia of the American Revolution.* Texarkana, TX: Rebel Publishing, 1989.

Noël Hume, Ivor. *A Guide to Artifacts of Colonial America.* New York: Alfred A. Knopf, 1978.

Olsen, Stanley J. "Dating Early Plain Buttons by Their Form." *American Antiquity* 28, no. 4 (1963): 551–54.

O'Malley, Nancy. *Drawing Battle Lines at Fort Boonesborough: The Siege of 1778.* Report prepared for the American Battlefield Protection Program, Lexington, KY, 2012.

———. "Field Investigations at Daniel Boone's Frontier Station, Fayette County, Kentucky." Paper presented at the Society for Historical Archaeological Annual Conference, Mobile, AL, January 2002.

———. "Frontier Defenses and Pioneer Strategies in the Historic Settlement Era." In *The Buzzel about Kentuck: Settling the Promised Land,* edited by Craig Thompson Friend, 57–76. Lexington: University Press of Kentucky, 1998.

———. "Frontier Life at Shawnee Springs: Archaeology and History of Hugh McGary's Pioneer Station, Mercer County, Kentucky." Unpublished manuscript, last modified December 15, 2017. Microsoft Word file.

———. *Searching for Boonesborough.* Archaeological Report 193. Lexington:

Bibliography

Program for Cultural Resource Assessment, Department of Anthropology, University of Kentucky, 1989.

—————. *"Stockading Up"*: *A Study of Pioneer Stations in the Inner Bluegrass Region of Kentucky.* Archaeological Report 127. Lexington: Program for Cultural Resource Assessment, Department of Anthropology, University of Kentucky, 1987.

O'Malley, Nancy, and Karen Hudson. *Cultural Resource Assessment of Boone Station State Park, Fayette County, Kentucky.* Archaeological Report 316. Lexington: Department of Anthropology, University of Kentucky, 1993.

Ousley, C. C. "Kentucky at the Jamestown Ter-Centennial Exposition April 26 to November 30, 1907: A Report from the Kentucky Jamestown Exposition Commission." Kentucky Digital Library. Accessed December 2017. http://kdl.kyvl.org/?commit=search&f%5Bpub_date%5D%5B%5D=1907&q=C.C.+Ousley&search_field=all_fields.

Perkins, Elizabeth A. *Border Life*: *Experience and Memory in the Revolutionary Ohio Valley.* Chapel Hill: University of North Carolina Press, 1998.

—————. "The Consumer Frontier: Household Consumption in Early Kentucky." *Journal of American History* 78, no. 2 (1991): 486–510.

Pioneer and Historical Society of the State of Michigan. *Pioneer Collections.* Lansing, MI: Thorp & Godfrey, State Printers and Binders, 1886.

Pirtle, Alfred. "Frontier Defence." *Register of the Kentucky Historical Society* 19, no. 59 (September 1921): 112–14.

Ranck, George Washington. *Boonesborough*: *Its Founding, Pioneer Struggles, Indian Experiences, Transylvania Days, and Revolutionary Annals.* Louisville, KY: John P. Morton & Co., 1901; reprint, Salem, NH: Ayer Co. Publishers, 1986.

Richter, Daniel K. *Facing East from Indian Country: A Native History of Early America.* Cambridge, MA: Harvard University Press, 2001.

Robertson, James Rood. *Petitions of the Early Inhabitants of Kentucky to the General Assembly of Virginia 1769 to 1792.* Filson Club Publications 27. Louisville, KY: John P. Morton & Co., 1914.

Schwartz, Barry. "The Social Context of Commemoration: A Study in Collective Memory." *Social Forces* 61, no. 2 (December 1982): 374–402.

Shammas, Carole. "How Self-Sufficient Was Early America?" *Journal of Interdisciplinary History* 13, no. 2 (Autumn 1982): 247–72.

Shane, John D. "The Henderson Company Ledger." *Filson Club History Quarterly* 21 (1947): 22–48.

Simon, F. Kevin, and Federal Writers' Project of the Works Progress Administration for the State of Kentucky, eds. *The WPA Guide to Kentucky.* Reprint; Lexington: University Press of Kentucky, 1996.

Bibliography

Sivilich, Daniel M. *Musket Ball and Small Shot Identification: A Guide.* Norman: University of Oklahoma Press, 2016.

Smalley, Andrea L. "'They Steal Our Deer and Land': Contested Hunting Grounds in the Trans-Appalachian West." *Register of the Kentucky Historical Society* 114, nos. 3, 4 (2016): 303–39.

Smith, Kevin E. "Bledsoe Station: Archaeology, History, and the Interpretation of the Middle Tennessee Frontier, 1770–1820." *Tennessee Historical Quarterly* 59, no. 3 (2000): 174–87.

Smith, Leland. "A History of the Tobacco Industry in Kentucky, 1783–1860." Master's thesis, University of Kentucky, Lexington, 1950.

Sosin, Jack M. *The Revolutionary Frontier, 1763–1783.* Albuquerque: University of New Mexico Press, 1974.

Staples, Kathleen A., and Madelyn Shaw. *Clothing through American History.* Santa Barbara, CA: Greenwood, 2013.

Stewart, Richard W., ed. *American Military History.* Vol. 1, *The United States Army and the Forging of a Nation, 1775–1917.* Washington, DC: Center of Military History, 2005.

Taylor, Alan. *American Revolutions: A Continental History, 1750–1804.* New York: Norton, 2016.

Thwaites, Reuben Gold. *Daniel Boone.* New York: D. Appleton, 1913.

Tipton, French. Papers, 1780–1901. Special Collections and Archives, Eastern Kentucky University, Richmond.

Towles, Susan Starling. "The Founding of Fort Boonesborough by the Transylvania Company." *Kentucky Progress Magazine* 6, no. 4 (1934): 181–83.

Trabue, Daniel. "The Journal of Col. Daniel Trabue: Some Account of His Ancestry, Life and Travels in Virginia and the Present State of Kentucky during the Revolutionary Period." In *Colonial Men and Times,* edited by Lillie DuPuy VanCulin, 3–160. Philadelphia: Harper, Innes & Sons, 1916.

Turner, Frederick Jackson. "The Significance of the Frontier in American History." In *The Annual Report of the American Historical Association,* 197–227. Washington, DC: American Historical Association, 1894.

Waller, George M. "George Rogers Clark and the American Revolution in the West." *Indiana Magazine of History* 72, no. 1 (March 1976): 1–20.

Weiss, Kathryn H. *Daniel Bryan, Nephew of Daniel Boone: His Narrative and Other Stories.* Forbestown, CA: privately printed, 2008.

Whitaker, Joe Russell. "The Development of the Tobacco Industry in Kentucky: A Geographical Interpretation." Master's thesis, University of Wisconsin, Madison, 1923.

White, Carolyn L. *American Artifacts of Personal Adornment, 1680–1820: A Guide to Identification and Interpretation.* Lanham, MD: Altamira Press, 2005.

Whittenburg, James P. "Planters, Merchants, and Lawyers: Social Change and the Origins of the North Carolina Regulation." *William and Mary Quarterly* 34, no. 2 (1977): 215–38.

Wildesen, Leslie E. "The Study of Impacts on Archaeological Sites." In *Advances in Archaeological Method and Theory*, vol. 5, edited by M. B. Schiffer, 51–96. New York: Academic Press, 1982.

Wilson, Samuel M. *The First Land Court of Kentucky, 1779–1780*. Lexington, KY: privately printed, 1923.

Witthoft, John. "A History of Gunflints." *Pennsylvania Archaeologist* 36, nos.1, 2 (1966): 12–49.

INDEX

Page numbers in italics refer to illustrations.